Complete Guide to ISO 14000

Richard B. Clements

PRENTICE HALL
Englewood Cliffs, New Jersey 07632

Library of Congress Cataloging in Publication Data

Clements, Richard Barrett
Complete guide to ISO 14000 / Richard Barrett Clements.
p. cm.
Includes index
ISBN 0-13-242975-6 (cloth)
1. ISO 14000 Series Standards. I. Title
TS155.7.C54 1996
658.4'08—dc20 95-51111
CIP

Printed in the United States of America

10 9 8 7 6 5 4 3 2 1

ISBN 0-13-242975-6

PRENTICE HALL
Career & Personal Development
Englewood Cliffs, NJ 07632
A Simon & Schuster Company

On the World Wide Web at http://www.phdirect.com

Prentice Hall International (UK) Limited, *London*
Prentice Hall of Australia Pty. Limited, *Sydney*
Prentice Hall Canada, Inc., *Toronto*
Prentice Hall Hispanoamericana, S.A., *Mexico*
Prentice Hall of India Private Limited, *New Delhi*
Prentice Hall of Japan, Inc., *Tokyo*
Simon & Schuster Asia Pte. Ltd., *Singapore*
Editora Prentice Hall do Brasil, Ltda., *Rio de Janeiro*

To Sarah Lynn

ACKNOWLEDGMENTS

The creation of a book on ISO 14000 is impossible for a single person to complete. I am indebted to the dozens of professionals who took the time to help me locate information and to form interpretations of the standard. This includes people such as Leon Przybylaatul, Gene Irons, and Sandy Bedzis at Underwriters Laboratories, Steve Hickel, James Fava, Joseph Cascio, Rose Tomasello, John Smintec, Amy Zuckerman, Andre M. Everett, Lisa Hamilton, Bill Terry, Mark Marrow, and the dedicated staff at Solution Specialists who endured the endless cataloging of information.

I would also like to acknowledge the organizations that helped me in this project. This includes the Caledonia Township Office, the Kent County Health Department, the Michigan Department of Natural Resources, the Michigan Occupational Safety and Health Department, the Occupational Health and Safety Administration, the Environmental Protection Agency, the Environmental Assistance Center of Michigan, the West Michigan Environmental Action Council, the NIEHS Clearinghouse, Mr. Mark Moys of the European Commission, *The Detroit Free Press*, the American Society for Testing and Materials, the American Society for Quality Control, CEEM Information Services, the Internet, and the National ISO 9000/14000 Support Group.

I also want to thank a piece of technology that saved me from another attack of carpal tunnel syndrome and sped the writing of this book—namely, the Kurzweil Voice system. All the typing and editing of this book was done by voice recognition software. No keyboards were harmed.

ABOUT THE AUTHOR

Richard Barrett Clements is President of Solution Specialists, a firm specializing in management and quality assurance technologies for international competitiveness. He is the author of several books on the subjects of quality, computers, and management. This includes the bestsellers *Handbook of Statistical Methods in Manufacturing* (Prentice Hall), and the audiocassette tape "ISO 9000: Opportunity within Confusion." He is best known for his pioneering work in using modern technology to create interactive user groups of companies sharing competitive experiences.

Mr. Clements is one of the founders of the National ISO 9000/ISO 14000 Support Group. This is a third-party, neutral organization dedicated to providing outreach support to companies seeking ISO 9000 and/or ISO 14000 registration. The Support Group has foreign offices in Dublin, Ireland, and Sao Paulo, Brazil. Numerous local support groups are also affiliated with the National Support Group.

Currently, Mr. Clements is an ISO 9000 assessor registered with the Institute for Quality Assurance in England. He is a nonvoting participant in Technical Committees 176 and 207, which are responsible for the creation and revision of the ISO 9000 and ISO 14000 standards, respectively.

Mr. Clements holds a bachelors degree from Michigan State University and a masters degree from the University of Chicago. He is actively pursuing post-graduate studies. Best known for his "generalist" approach to technology, he has the ability to express complex methods in terms of stories and simple analogies to make the methods easily understood by a wide audience. His writings have twice earned him the Golden Quill award from the American Society for Quality Control.

CONTENTS

Chapter 5

ECO-LABELING–HOW TO LET THE PUBLIC KNOW ABOUT YOUR ENVIRONMENTAL MANAGEMENT SYSTEM–101

Chapter 6

HOW TO IMPLEMENT ISO 14000 USING ISO 9000 AS A GUIDE–119

Chapter 7

EXAMPLES OF IMPLEMENTING ISO 14000 WITH AND WITHOUT ISO 9000–145

Chapter 9

HOW TO PREPARE DOCUMENTATION FOR AN ISO 14000-BASED ENVIRONMENTAL MANAGEMENT SYSTEM–207

PREFACE

In the 1960s, my science teacher asked our class what the word *ecology* meant. After a brief pause, one student suggested that it was "the study of colleges." At the time it brought much laughter. However, for everyone in that class it was the beginning of a widespread consciousness of environmental issues.

Thirty years later, environmental issues affect many aspects of our lives. We face many regulations in our personal and professional lives. If you have worked in a manufacturing company during the previous five years, you will have experienced or heard about ISO 9000. The ISO 9000 revolution has changed the way we look at management systems.

ISO 9000 introduced the concept of a voluntary international standard for a minimal system of management. ISO 14000 will introduce this same concept to the issue of environmental management. In fact, ISO 14000 will share aspects with ISO 9000. As you read this book, you will discover that both ISO 9000 and ISO 14000 can successfully coexist. In addition, both ISO 9000 and ISO 14000 share common goals in safety and health issues.

This book was written with the concept of these two standards representing a continuing evolution in the way a company is operated. It is a book for people both familiar and unfamiliar with ISO 9000 and international standards.

To assist in the writing of this book, I have set up a fictitious manufacturing company. I then approached all governmental and environmental bodies that would normally affect this company's operations. I attempted to collect all regulations related to this particular manufacturing company. Then I took both ISO 9000 and ISO 14000 together to come up with a management system that would affect all parties and prove efficient for internal operations. This proved to be a considerable adventure. The adventure will be used for illustrative purposes throughout the book.

Please read this book with the understanding that environmental issues and regulations can be very fluid. In addition, regulations and concerns can vary considerably between nations and states. Therefore, you will need to stay in touch with your own local situation to fully benefit from this book. Good luck and good reading.

Rick Clements

Alto, Michigan
June 1995

HOW THIS BOOK CAN HELP YOU

Environmental management sits between conventional management practices and the conservative end of environmentalism. The ISO 14000 standard and its related family of guideline standards can provide you with a lot of information on what is expected from a conforming company. The *Complete Guide to ISO 14000* will explain this in more detail and will also guide you through the implementation process.

This book and the standard are all that you should need to design, develop, and maintain a system of environmental management. To accomplish that task, this book:

1. Clearly shows how environmental management can be part of your regular management procedures as they now exist.
2. Demonstrates how a company seeking or holding ISO 9000 registration can easily incorporate environmental management.
3. Illustrates each important step in implementation.
4. Examines the method called life cycle assessment and how to use this technique to plan your environmental management system and to verify the environmental benefits of your product or service.
5. Looks at how to conform to eco-labeling requirements and why these represent a great marketing advantage for your company.
6. Provides detailed instructions on how to prepare documentation for an environmental management system that will also benefit your company through greater efficiency and effectiveness.
7. Details implementation paths for different companies to help any company to conform to ISO 14000.
8. Cites, where possible, actual regulations affecting a company and references for finding helpful assistance from outside organizations.
9. Explains the method of auditing your own company's conformance.
10. Establishes a computer bulletin board service that will allow you to ask questions directly of the author. The BBS can be reached by computer modem at (616) 891-9114. This is a U.S. phone number. The author can be queried at the BBS or via e-mail on the Internet at ISOGROUP@CRIS.COM

As with any major change proposed for a company, I recommend careful planning and project management for successful results.

INTRODUCTION

As of this writing in 1995, the ISO 14000 standards were draft international standards. Worldwide acceptance of the standard is not certain, and many challenges lie ahead for a uniform model of environmental management.

Accepted or not, the concept of an environmental management system, especially one designed to dovetail into ISO 9000, has considerable merit. In this book, we will look closely at ISO 14000 and how to create an environmental management system. Such a system would always enable your company to know it was in compliance with environmental regulations. No longer would you have to fear the outcome of an inspection or an audit.

Instead, your environmental requirements and concerns would be fully incorporated into the daily operation of the company. Policies, procedures, and work instructions would guide each person as to what to do and when to do it to maintain conformance. Active internal audit teams and regular management review against known targets of performance would get your company into regulatory conformance and then keep it there.

In addition, there are several marketing advantages to using ISO 14000. For example, you will discover that some, if not all, of your customers are concerned about the environment. By demonstrating a well-documented environmental management system, you will be able to market your company and its products to a wider variety of customers. As you shall see in this book, you can also make environmental claims about your company's product—claims that can be backed up with reliable data.

Therefore, no matter what the final fate of ISO 14000, the concept of an environmental management system is an idea whose time has come. This book will be equally valuable as either a guide to ISO 14000, an introduction to establishing environmental management systems, or both.

WHAT IS ISO 14000?

ISO 14000 is an attempt to establish an international voluntary standard for environmental management. The International Organization for Standardization sometimes referred to as (ISO) in Geneva, Switzerland, exists for the purpose of establishing voluntary industry standards for international trade. To date, the organization has created thousands of standards. For example, ISO 9000 is a model for a minimal system of management for quality assurance. ISO 9660 dictates how to format CD-ROMs so that a CD purchased in Europe will work in a machine manufactured in Japan using music recorded in the United States.

Not all ISO standards are readily accepted worldwide. Some industries have chosen to write their own standards and ignore the equivalent ISO standard. However, ISO standards get fairly wide usage because more than 90 countries voluntarily participate in the creation of the standards. Subcommittees are formed for a particular topic and interested parties can freely offer suggestions and guidance. A working draft is produced for input by all countries. When a reasonable consensus is reached, a committee draft is issued. The draft standard is discussed, and eventually a vote is taken on whether to accept the final draft as an international standard. Each country gets one vote, and a clear majority is needed.

In 1995, ISO 14000 was in draft international standard form. A vote for acceptance is expected in mid-1996. However, the rules of using international standards are fairly flexible. Several countries have already adopted the draft version of ISO 14000 as their national standard for an environmental management system. This has allowed companies within that country to be assessed and certified as conforming to the standard. Thus, ISO 14000 is already in partial effect. If the draft lingers more than a year in draft form, it can also be considered a de facto standard. The United States adopted ISO 14000 as a national standard in early 1996.

The big question is how far it will go in being accepted or imposed on various industries. This will take a few more years to determine. In the meantime, ISO 14000 is effective as a model for coping with the increasing number of environmental regulations and issues.

HOW TO UNDERSTAND ISO 14000

To understand ISO 14000, you first have to understand what is meant by an environmental management standard. To understand that, you have to look at some definitions to distinguish environmental management from other similar ideas.

ENVIRONMENT VERSUS ECOLOGY

The dictionary defines "environment" as the aggregate of surrounding things, conditions, and influences. In contrast, "ecology" is defined as a branch of biology that studies the relationships between organisms and their environment. Thus, the first important point to note is that environmental management is exactly what it says—the management of the things, conditions, and influences within your company.

ENVIRONMENTAL MANAGEMENT VERSUS ENVIRONMENTALISM

To further distinguish an environmental management system, we need to look at another definition. We have already seen that environmental management, as defined by ISO 14000, is the control of surrounding items and forces. In contrast, "environmentalism" is a political movement with many different philosophies. Environmentalism is the concept of protecting natural resources from the negative effects of humans. It can take any of several forms, such as fighting pollution, micro-managing particular species of animals or plants, opposing changes to areas of land, and so forth.

The important point to remember is that environmental management is not environmentalism. Environmental management can use some of the philosophies of environmentalism, but that is not its main intention. Instead, environmental management is the act of studying the environment of your company and developing systems to control that environment to match the needs of the company, its customers, and regulations.

The environment of the company could be the noise level in the shop area, the amount of water the plant discharges every day, the training that employees receive, the conditions of the land on which the plant is located, the quality of the air near the plant, the amount and type of lighting in each area of the plant, the color of the walls, the type of music played in the office area, or any of the other hundreds of possible things, conditions, or influences within your organization.

WHAT A COMPANY HAS TO DO TO SET UP AN ENVIRONMENTAL MANAGEMENT SYSTEM

Environmental management means that the top managers in your company must consciously think about the type of environment they want to have. This vision of the environment can be defined in a set of measurable goals. Some of these goals the management can set; others will be set by regulation. Then management examines the current situation and plans how they will reach their goals.

Naturally, accomplishing the goals described by the management team requires close coordination of effort and efficient distribution of resources. ISO 14000 gives management a model to use for pursuing the creation of an environmental management system. This book explains this process in enough detail so that your company can proceed immediately with implementation.

The primary route to implementation is not to view ISO 14000 as one more program to put in place in addition to your already growing system of paperwork. Instead, ISO 14000 should pull together and make more efficient and effective your ability to cope with the huge number of regulations and internal needs related to your company's environment. This is accomplished by making conformance to your own goals and the external demands of the world part of your company's normal system of management. Later in this book, we will propose how this is done.

WHICH COMPANIES ARE AFFECTED BY ISO 14000?

No one can predict which companies will ultimately be affected by ISO 14000. However, the exploding use of ISO 9000 is an indication of the possible path of growth for ISO 14000.

ISO 9000 was released to the world in 1987. At first, few companies were affected. Many companies were registering to national standards for management systems of quality assurance, such as BS 5750. However, the European Union regulations started to mention ISO 9000 as a faster way to get easier access to their markets, and when specific industries started asking their suppliers for conformance, the use of ISO 9000 exploded.

In 1990, only a handful of companies in the United States were ISO 9000 registered. But by 1995, more than 6,000 companies were registered, with more than 20,000 in line to be registered. The rapid growth in interest is traced directly to industries requiring the standard. The largest of these were the automotive and defense industries.

The critical questions to ask of ISO 14000 are

1. Will any government require the use of ISO 14000?
2. Will entire industries require the use of ISO 14000?

As we will see in Chapter 2, there are already regulations in force in the European Union to force the use of ISO 14000. Also, there is a growing interest for companies to demonstrate that both they and their products are "green." Meanwhile, the U.S. government will not support the use of ISO 14000 by letting conformance relieve some of the many environmental requirements placed on a company. Under current conditions, therefore, the use of ISO 14000 should be heaviest in Europe. However, if major corporations decide that ISO 14000 makes good sense for the internal efficiency of their suppliers while also promoting an "environmentally friendly" image, the growth of ISO 14000 could be even greater than ISO 9000.

As with ISO 9000, virtually any company can use the ISO 14000 standard. Although the first thought is that manufacturing firms are the primary target, a reading of the guideline standards shows that the developers of this standard have already considered applications for small business and service-based companies.

Chapter 1

A DAY IN THE LIFE OF AN ISO 14000 COMPANY

The term "ISO 14000" refers to a family of international standards. There is no one document that uses the ISO 14000 title. Therefore, when referring to ISO 14000 I am referring to a large family of standards. (See Appendix B for a list of these standards.)

THE GROWING INTEREST IN ENVIRONMENTAL MANAGEMENT SYSTEMS

An environmental management system is a well-documented and structured approach to coping with regulations and customer requirements related to environmental issues. Since the 1960s, there has been a growing interest in environmental issues. This, combined with several high-profile lawsuits, has sensitized both workers and industry. As of 1995, the governments of the United Kingdom, Germany, Norway, and the Netherlands will do business only with suppliers that have environmental management systems. The U.S. Department of Energy is also beginning to require an environmental management system for its suppliers.

Just about any company faces a growing number of environmentally related regulations. With world trade increasing, the environmental concerns of other countries are being passed from international corporations down through their supplier network. More and more companies are being required to provide environmental impact information for their products. Faced with this deluge of requirements, the typical company needs to organize its resources effectively to face this challenge. It is a common charge that too much environmental regulation can actually force companies out of a market or completely out of business. In truth, it is the companies that best plan and prepare for such regulations that survive and prosper.

WHY YOUR COMPANY WILL PROBABLY HAVE TO CONFORM TO ISO 14000

As we shall see, most companies will eventually have to conform to a standard like ISO 14000. Several forces and trends are making this inevitable. This is happening because the direction and types of environmental requirements are growing daily. Therefore, a company that wants to remain competitive will have to address these requirements directly.

The best approach to meeting these requirements is a well-documented environmental management system. Creating an environmental management system takes time and requires that your company pass through several stages. This is called "climbing the EMS ladder." Exhibit 1-1 shows this ladder.

Regulations and customer requirements related to environmental concerns combined with health and safety concerns within your facilities are inventoried. This inventory of environmental issues is brought to your management. In turn, the inventory is evaluated and sorted by priority, creating a list of environmental issues specific to your company. This helps management create your company's environmental policy. Such a policy sets the tone, goals, objectives, and targets your company wishes to achieve. From this policy and your list of environmental issues, you build the environmental management system.

Before looking at how such a system is developed, let's examine what a complete environmental management system looks like in daily operations.

HOW A COMPANY OPERATES WITH ISO 14000 AS PART OF ITS MANAGEMENT STRUCTURE

The introduction discussed what an environmental management system is and what it is not. However, no amount of definition can ever paint a clear picture of an environmental management system. An illustration of one possibility will help you to form a clear picture of such a company.

Although there is no single path to environmental management (because there are many ways to form a conforming management system), we need to look at both generalities. At the same time, we also must be specific in our use of an example. Therefore, we shall look at a fictitious company, named Peak Manufacturing. The company may be fictitious, but it was composed from actual observations of conforming and nonconforming companies.

THE COMPANY

John Fuller stepped back from the machine he was repairing. It was 5:30 A.M. and in 30 minutes the first-shift workers would arrive and be ready to use this machine. Taped to the cover of John's tool box was a 10-year-old photograph of John and his wife on their honeymoon. John liked to look at this photograph whenever the world seemed overwhelming.

Exhibit 1-1: The Ladder of Environmental Management System Development

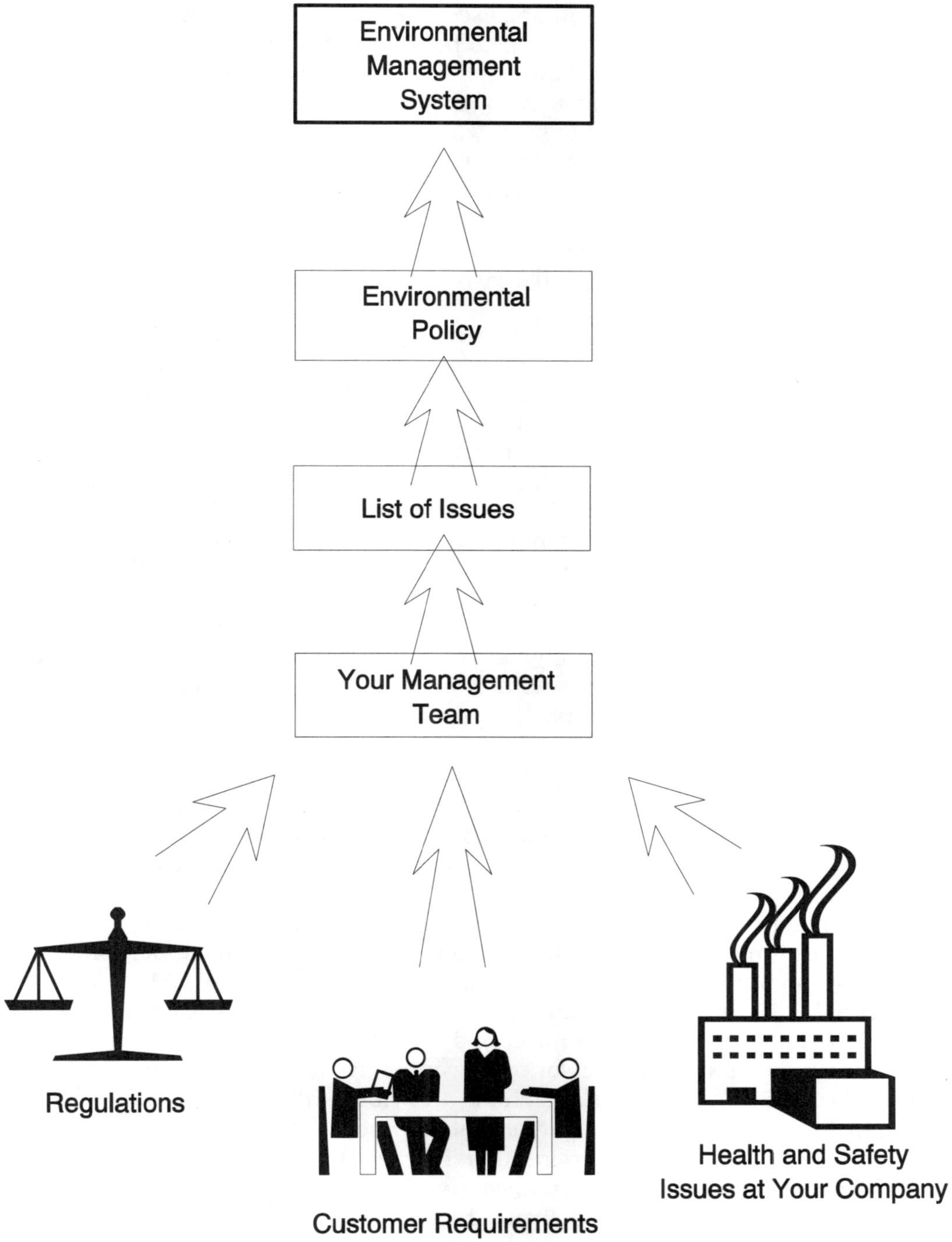

Right now things were fairly overwhelming. John had just attempted to remove a hydraulic hose. Unfortunately, John's attempt to shut off the hydraulic flow had failed. When the hose was removed, it sprayed John, the machine, and the surrounding area with hydraulic oil. The excess oil was now heading for a nearby drain. Luckily, John had the common sense to pour kitty litter in front of the moving fluid.

Many things now required John's attention. He needed to pick the emergency he would handle first. The moment of reflection looking at the picture of his wife calmed him down. He decided to start with picking up the fluid from the floor. More kitty litter was applied. While the fluid was being absorbed, John cleaned his glasses and began looking over the maintenance procedure again.

Something was wrong. John had closed all the valves the instructions had indicated. Still, the fluid had leaked out. So John spread the hydraulic system blueprint out in front of him and began to trace the problem. He now had only 20 minutes to complete the repair.

It took only a moment to see the problem. The maintenance instructions that had been supplied by the machine manufacturer were incorrect. Back pressure was possible if the next valve was not closed. The instructions had failed to mention this. John closed the valve and then removed the hose. Very little fluid came out. At this point, John was able to replace the o-rings and reattach the hose.

Now the valves could be opened and the hydraulic pressure tested. The pressure was fine and the leak that John had been trying to repair was now fixed. John cleaned off the hydraulic fluid from the machine. Then he cleaned up the fluid spill. The saturated kitty litter was placed in a special barrel for waste that would need special handling for disposal.

John completed an incident report. On this report he reported the error in the machine manufacturer's instructions. He also wrote onto the instructions the correct valve to shut down. He showed it to his supervisor, who in turn signed the correction and noted the date. John then packed up his tools and went looking for a clean uniform.

It was now 6:00 A.M.

Jane Thompson pulled her 1988 Ford into the parking lot of Peak Manufacturing. She was the machine operator for the machine John Fuller had just repaired. It was Monday morning. The sun had yet to rise. Her fellow workers were already walking into the plant.

Jane entered the plant and began her day as she always did. First she got a cup of coffee. Then she opened the maintenance log for her machine. She noted that preventive maintenance had taken place over the weekend. This included the annoying hydraulic leak she had recorded the previous week. That meant that she could look forward to a week with little downtime.

Jane pulled out the paperwork she would have to maintain during the first production run. She started the machine and noted all current settings. Then she brought forward the first bin of material to process. The shop floor traveler noted that scrap pieces of the parts were to be marked, logged, and then placed in a specially marked container. Jane placed the first set of parts in the machine and pressed the safety buttons to activate the machine.

It was now 6:15 A.M.

Alice Kroon, the industrial nurse, was just arriving for her first-shift job. She really had two primary roles within Peak Manufacturing. The first role was nurse to the work force. For this she needed to patch cuts, bruises, and other small injuries. Her second role was safety coordinator for the plant. For that task, she had to educate employees on how to avoid accidents. Occasionally, she also had to audit the safety procedures used at Peak Manufacturing.

Alice began her day by rotating the numbers on the plant sign that showed how many workdays since the last serious accident. Alice now rotated the number to 362.

At 7:00 A.M., Karen Gelling arrived an hour early for her job as regulatory conformance coordinator. A major part of that job was tracking and updating environmental regulations. This aspect of her job was the reason she had to come to work so early in the morning. Regulations, especially those related to the environment, were constantly changing. Therefore, Karen constantly had to monitor these changes and keep management informed.

As Karen started up her computer, she reached for the CD-ROM that had arrived in the mail on Friday. This was inserted into her computer's drive. The disk contained the most recent state regulation updates. She began to search through the list of changes.

The number of copies of a water discharge permit to file with the state had just been decreased. The Treasury Department no longer needed a copy. Karen noted this in her work instructions for water discharge permits. Then she noted the change on her weekly report about regulation changes. On this report, she also commented on what she had done to make sure this change was in effect at Peak Manufacturing.

Next she noticed that the Environmental Protection Agency (EPA) was going to be holding hearings in nearby Grand Rapids, Michigan, on proposed changes to the Clean Water Act. She knew that her manager was keenly interested in this topic. So she sent him an e-mail message.

At 8:00 A.M., the bulk of the professional work force entered the building. As was usual for a Monday morning, the department heads met with the president of Peak Manufacturing. The purpose of that meeting was to review the performance of the company during the previous week and to plan the activities for the new week.

Many topics were discussed. For example, the material review board had met the previous Friday. The scrap rate for several parts was becoming too high. The material review board had decided that some solutions to prevent these problems would have to be implemented by upper management. That meant that the procedures used in the manufacturing area would have to be modified. Such modifications require top-level approval. Ben Wright, plant manager, had been persuaded to push these changes through top management.

Ben confronted senior management on this issue. There was lively discussion about this topic. The engineering manager felt that the fault lay with quality control measures. The quality control manager felt this was unfair. Luckily, the president of the company was able to reach a common ground. Within an hour, the management committee had reached agreement. A brief action plan was developed, with specific people assigned particular tasks.

While Ben Wright was making his case, his assistant—the production supervisor—was beginning a bad day. John Little had been production supervisor for more than seven years. He had seen bad days before. This one was no exception. Two of the seven plastic injection machines were down. Both machines were producing parts that the customer had wanted three days ago.

Machine Maintenance had put every man they had on the job. To fix the first machine, the maintenance people would have to use a special solvent to clean out some of the machine's parts. They first cleared the machine operators from the area. Then they opened several windows near the machine. Next, they donned protective breathing apparatus.

Another group of maintenance people were busy on the second machine. All its components were working fine. Unfortunately, it was no longer producing parts to specification. A large pile of scrap parts was accumulating next to the machine. A worried looking production crew leader was watching the pile grow.

Tara Glinter, industrial engineer, was sitting in a meeting room on the other side of the plant at this time. In the meeting with her were several other engineers, a sales representative, and a supervisor of quality assurance. This group had met to discuss the newest request for a quote.

The request had several difficult requirements. Foremost was a request to use a new Teflon composite plastic resin. The company had never used such a material before. Most of the engineers were worried about the company's ability to meet the requirements of this request.

Tara and the quality assurance person were arguing in favor of initial production capability tests. They thought these tests would establish the operational characteristics of the new material. In particular, they wanted to conduct a designed experiment. In that way, they would be able to establish sources of variation, thereby enabling the engineers to design a product of low variation yet keep it highly profitable.

At 9:00 A.M., a group of employees entered the small training room to attend a workers' right-to-know seminar. Jan Stephen from the Michigan Department of Labor would be their instructor. She began by handing out small informational booklets. Attached to each booklet was a small card with a familiar looking diamond pattern.

Shortly after this, Fred Sears, building attendant, lowered himself into the service tunnels below the manufacturing plant. Several yards down the tight-fitting tunnel, Fred found what he was looking for. On a small access panel, there were several meters. Fred shown his flashlight onto two of the dials in particular. He noted their readings in his water discharge log.

Around 10:00 A.M., a college student working as a material handler twisted his way through stacks of received goods. He recovered a small hand cart from behind one pile. Quickly, he loaded the small cart with recyclable palettes and transported them to a waiting truck. Once aboard, he signed some paperwork and went on break.

Meanwhile, not far away was Ed Healy. Ed picked up a molded part and tried to place it in a measurement fixture. It would not fit. He pulled the part out and looked at it again. This time he tried to use a bit more pressure to insert the part. It was no use. The part was the wrong size.

Ed reached for his work instructions for this particular job. He looked up the procedure for designating a scrap piece. He discovered that he had to put a red mark on the affected part. Then he needed to note on the back of his control chart for this process what had been observed. He also needed to notify the quality assurance inspector for his department.

Jill Thompson slid into her car and pulled out of the Peak Manufacturing parking lot. She had a morning appointment with Mark Van Plueg of Caledonia Township. Mark was the township planner. Jill was meeting with Mark to discuss the zoning issues that would be involved in the building of an extension to the warehouse area at Peak Manufacturing.

Mark had several concerns. First, there was the problem of additional water usage. The wells that supplied that area of the township were already being taxed to their maximum usage. Second, the planning commission had yet to vote on the new use proposal. Third, Mark feared that the neighbors would object to this new project. A similar project near Peak Manufacturing had been vigorously opposed by the nearby condominium owners. They felt that this type of development took away from the value of their property.

Jill was trying to set up a meeting with the owners. She too was afraid of opposition. And feelings in the neighborhood would go against her company's policy of being a friendly neighbor in the community. She and Mark were going to have several such meetings before this issue was resolved.

Back at the plant, the plant manager had left the management committee meeting. As he walked out onto the factory floor, he saw red lights flashing on top of two of his most important machines. His pace quickened. Before he could reach the first machine, he saw a worker coming down the aisle in the opposite direction.

"Hey, you! This is a safety glasses area!" he shouted. The startled worker quickly grabbed a pair of safety glasses from his back pocket. He put them on and quickly headed in another direction.

When the plant manager reached the first troubled machine, he reached for the process log. He read it quickly and found that the machine was running fine on Saturday. However, when the first run was attempted this morning, all the parts were defective.

"Fred," he shouted to the plant supervisor, "what's the story?"

"We don't know. We've tried everything listed from the reaction plan with no success. We have some ideas, but it will take time to find the answer," responded Fred.

"We don't have time," replied the plant manager.

In another part of the plant, a purchasing manager was attempting to complete an order for new plastic resin. As he worked on the purchase order, he was also using a checklist. The checklist detailed all the items that must be accounted for on any purchase order. One of the items involved a check on whether environmental regulations were involved.

He called Karen and asked her to check into this. She asked whether there was a particular concern. He indicated that while being molded, this particular resin would give off fumes. She replied that both the Clean Air Act and indoor air quality regulations would have to be reviewed. She would get back to him on this. The purchase order would have to be put on hold until this information was available.

While this conversation was taking place, the warehouse manager was making his weekly check of the rat traps and poisons placed around the warehouse to control rodents. If too many rodents got into the warehouse, the corregate and pallets could suffer. Halfway through his inspection tour, the warehouse manager stopped to get a drink of water from a drinking fountain.

By now, lunchtime was approaching. The first-shift machine operators filed into the lunchroom. Many elected to buy the day's lunch of cheeseburgers, fries, and salad. The contracted food service employees had already finished filling the food bins and were now collecting money from the workers.

The preventive maintenance people were still at the two down machines looking through past histories and trying to think of something new to try. Little did they know they were only minutes away from an answer for the first machine.

At noon, the office people began to wander into the lunchroom. Sarah Perkins from sales was there with a prospective customer. They were not there to eat but to tour the facility. The visitor had been shown the engineering area, the order-processing area, and the lunchroom with its employees. They were on their way to the production plant.

As they entered the production area, both Sarah and her visitor put on their eye protection. The visitor asked for and got ear plugs. Although Sarah had gotten used to the noise around the machinery, the visitor noticed its high level. As they proceeded out into the production area, the visitor paused to note the company quality policy hanging on the wall. He would see it several more times on this tour. He would also see the production plant productivity board. This bulletin board of charts was particularly impressive to the visitor. It had everything he was looking for and a few extra pieces of information, including the company's environmental policy.

It also had charts showing the level of quality being achieved in the plant. The plant-wide scrap rate was noted. Also noted were the most common reported defects of the last 30 days. Next to this was the number of inventory turns and the accuracy of inventory placement. Finally, a list of environmental targets was shown along with current performance against those targets. Framed in the center of the board was the ISO 9001 certificate the company had earned the previous year. The visitor took several notes.

After lunch, the maintenance people reported that the first machine was back in service. The operators quickly started production. The first several pieces produced by the machine were checked carefully. The statistical process control (SPC) charts for the machine showed statistical control.

Industrial engineer Todd Robinson settled down to a long afternoon of observing the new assembly procedure for an automotive part. Seventeen pieces of material had to be placed together accurately to create the final component. As the afternoon dragged on, Todd noted that the assembly people were having a hard time identifying the correct orientation of a key piece.

Todd put down his notepad and stopwatch and stepped up to the assembly table. He also had trouble making the pieces line up. He paused and thought about the problem for a moment. Looking around, he noticed that the placement of the lights threw shadows over the parts when employees' hands were inserting pieces. A second set of lights at a lower level was the answer. He noted this in his report.

Edna Brown swept up the plastic chips that had formed around her workstation from all the part trimming she had done during the first shift. These were deposited into a special bucket for use in regrinding and recycling the plastic. Unfortunately, dirt also swept up got into the bucket. Tomorrow, a machine operator would curse as a sudden rash of visual defects appeared in his newly molded parts.

The internal audit team was performing the scheduled check of record keeping in the plant. During this afternoon they were checking the records stored in the quality assurance area. The audit team leader asked for the corrective action log. The audit team scanned the list and noted that all action items older than 30 days were signed and closed. They noted this on their audit sheets. At that same moment, far away, an older man sitting at a desk at the Department of Natural Resources in Lansing, Michigan, was signing the approval for an air discharge permit for the company.

Back at Peak Manufacturing, company truck driver Ed Healy pulled out of the parking lot with a two-and-a-half-ton truck filled with corregate and paper trash from the front office. It was Monday and time to take this used material to its proper destinations.

The first stop was a corregate manufacturing plant. They would buy the old corregate and grind it up to make new packaging compounds. The paper waste would be hauled down to the waste energy plant in downtown Grand Rapids. Here the paper was dumped into a hopper. Ed had to get the paper weighed and then sign some forms. The amount of paper would be charged back to the company as trash removal. The energy created by the burning of the material would be converted to electricity for the downtown area.

Tomorrow, financial clerk Ellen Helen would collect the slips from Ed and note these into accounts payable and receivable. Financial manager Jordan Johnson would collect these figures to calculate the savings and costs for recycling programs. They would be compared to the cost of the collection and hauling. They would also be compared against the cost of alternatives.

Meanwhile, the company president was heading home to take a shower and dress for a dinner with the Michigan Environmental Council chairman that evening. The president was concerned about the perception of his company in the community. He lived here and had raised his children in this community.

The topic of discussion over dinner would be how the company could better conform to the environmental expectations of the community. This request had caught the chairman of the council off guard. The chairman had his staff draw up a list of expectations for any company asking this question. The chairman would still be worried about the fact that in 15 years of operation, this was the first time a company had approached the council with such a request.

The second shift was now starting up. Many operators read through the process logs for their machine. Others were studying the work orders of the day and the shop floor travelers attached to raw materials awaiting processing.

Roy Robson had been an engineer for over 20 years. Before him sat a large collection of paperwork. These papers represented days of work on the product life cycle of the company's newest product. He had traced the environmental impact of each component of the new product from the point of customer use back to the use of raw materials.

His study indicated that there were several points in the life cycle of the product where the company could save money and also assure a "green" product. He felt that the company could benefit from the adoption of his suggestions. However, Roy was not too confident in his ability to make a presentation to management. This troubled him.

Diane Eaton had been in engineering for over a year now. Earlier that day, she had finally been able to get through to the Environmental Protection Agency to ask about the eco-labeling required for their new line of products in Europe. The agency told her to consult the Department of Commerce.

Now Diane was on the phone with a representative of the U.S. European Trade Office. This person told her that eco-labeling was not needed for their type of product. This was proving to be the breaking point for Diane. Just a few minutes earlier, the European Union's Trade Office had just sent her a fax saying that an eco-label *was* required.

On her desk was the draft for the recycled content label for the new product. It had the markings and wording needed for the voluntary system of eco-labeling used in the United States. Diane's problem was figuring out what the European Union would like to see on the product. Unfortunately, the U.S. and European agencies couldn't agree on this point.

In frustration, Diane hung up the phone and typed out a fax for the British Standards Institute. "Please send me everything you have on eco-labeling," was the basic message. Glancing at her watch, she realized that the London community was done with work for the day. She scheduled the fax to transmit after midnight to catch the beginning of the workday in England.

At 5:00 P.M., it was as if someone had blown a whistle. Most of the office employees got up from their desks and headed for the parking lot. Back in his office, the purchasing manager was looking at one last purchase order awaiting his signature. This one was for a hazardous chemical used to clean machine parts. Even though it was only an order for ten gallons, several regulations applied. These involved the employees' right to know, community emergency plans in case of a spill, and handling restrictions applied to transportation of the product. "What a hassle," thought the manager as he signed the paper. Then he turned to his computer and tapped out several e-mail messages for the warehouse, engineering, maintenance, and laboratory people who would be involved in the receipt and use of this chemical. The messages were reminders that the material was coming and what the expectations were for each person involved.

The e-mail went first to the LAN server. Here it was stored on an array of hard disks before being sent to the proper nodes. Later that night, the second-shift LAN manager would make a backup of the messages that would be stored in a nearby bank vault. Three months from now, copies of those messages would make a major contribution to the defense of the company in a court of law holding a hearing on the potential liability suit filed by an injured employee.

At 7:00 P.M. that evening, the local planning commission held its meeting. Several business items were discussed first. Finally, Jill Thompson had her chance to speak. She had worked carefully on her presentation. She explained why the company needed the proposed expansion. She talked about the impact on the neighborhood, traffic, and the economy of Caledonia.

The board then opened the discussion to the general public. Several people from the community wished to speak. Some voiced concerns about water runoff from the new parking lot. Some voiced concerns over the access road attached to 68th Street. A few spoke up for the company. They pointed out that the company had approached all the neighbors and asked for their feedback early in this process. Few companies had ever done this before in their community.

The board called a close to comments after 45 minutes of discussion. Then the board members began to discuss the proposed expansion publicly. It was clear that not all board members were convinced that the expansion would be detrimental to the community. However, many could see the reasons for concerns from some community members.

After much discussion, the board took a vote. The vote was 5 to 4 in favor of approving the expansion. Jill felt relief. However, she knew that this was only the first victory in a long battle. Now the recommendation of the planning commission would be forwarded to the township board. They had the power to overrule the decision of the planning board. At the next township board meeting, the issue would be discussed again. Therefore, Jill had another presentation to prepare. At least this time she would have the planning board's approval to back up her case.

Back at the plant, the second shift was beginning to wind down. Soon the third shift would come on duty. The third shift was composed mainly of maintenance people. Their job was to clean up the shop and do preventive maintenance on the machines. They would also read through the process logs and reaction logs of the previous day. While they worked, most of the other employees slept.

WHY ENVIRONMENTAL CONCERNS ARE MIXED IN WITH MANY NORMAL DAILY OPERATIONS WITHIN ANY COMPANY

Let's look back on our example story and discuss where environmental concerns occur. At the beginning of the story, John Fuller had worked to correct a problem on a machine. The hose had fallen off and sprayed oil. The environmental impact of that accident is fairly obvious. The oil spray in the air was a breathing hazard. The oil running toward the water drain presented another hazard—the pollution of the water table.

Less obvious were other environmental factors. One was a method for picking up the spilled oil. This had to be done correctly if further environmental damage was to be prevented. For example, if the oil had been picked up using rags that were thrown into a normal trash can, the oil would have found its way into a landfill.

Another less obvious part of the environmental management system was John's use of an incident report to indicate that the instructions for this machine were flawed. This information would find its way first to industrial engineering, who would investigate this with the manufacturer. Also, the management would see the report and might take additional actions. This would help prevent the problem from occurring again, thus preventing a future environmental problem.

The machine operator, Jane, used a setup sheet for starting her production run. Part of those instructions indicated that scrap material had to be clearly marked and documented. Obviously, tracking and measuring scrap rates was critical to profitability and also for evaluating the environmental effect of wasted material. Less obvious were the dual safety buttons that Jane pressed. These were part of the safety system on the machine. By providing a safe working environment, the company was being effective and efficient.

The health and safety of the employees represents the quality of work life in the plant. The issues of health, safety, and work life represent the working environment of the company—that means these same issues can be seen as environmental in nature. Therefore, they too come under control of the environmental management system.

We could see this in the activities of the company nurse. She tracked injuries experience by the work force. She also provided safety and health information. And she also conducted regular safety procedure audits. As we saw at Peak Manufacturing, they had 362 days without a serious accident. We can assume that this was the result of a proactive management system that addressed each environmental concern, such as worker safety.

The obvious indication of an environmental system being in place should have been the job of Karen Gelling. She was in charge of tracking environmental regulations. Karen had to draw from several resources to keep track of current regulations. Such regulations were both obvious and subtle. Rules from local, county, state, and national governmental bodies were being issued constantly. In addition, environmental regulations were occasionally buried within other rules. For example, the environmental impact of the new parking lot would be part of the township's zoning code.

Less subtle was the communication between Karen and management. An environmental management system requires clear communication between departments. The discovery of a new regulation or requirement that would affect other people within the company has to be reported. Therefore, sending e-mail to other managers represents a key component of the environmental management system.

Management of any company would be the key players in an environmental management system. Peak Manufacturing is no exception. Early on that Monday morning, the management team would need to discuss common concerns about the company and its profitability. As you shall see later in this book, profitability is closely tied to environmental management.

The scrap rate at the company was too high. Correcting this problem would result in more efficient use of resources—in this case, expensive resources. Plus, throwing away scrap parts represents a negative environmental impact. Therefore, correcting an environmental problem can also result in a more efficient company.

At this point, notice the actions of the management team in this example; especially, the part where the president is able to reach a consensus on a critical issue. The ability of management to work successfully as a team is critical to the success of an environmental management system.

Another indication that an environmental management system was in place was the use by the preventive maintenance people of a solvent and the providing for adequate ventilation. Such a cautionary step indicates a concern for the air quality within the plant. Air pollution is not always an external problem. Several studies have determined that the air within a building has a lower quality than the air outside the building.

Less obvious was the rush to bring the two broken machines back on line. While these machines are down, they are not producing quality parts, which has a negative economic impact on the company. The subtle environmental effect is the creation of a pile of scrap parts while the machines are being tested and the electrical energy used unproductively.

The industrial engineer, Tara Glinter, represents another aspect of an environmental management system; specifically, where an environmental system is connected to the quality system. In this case, she and other department representatives were discussing a request for a quote. As part of an ISO 9000 system, such a quote must go through a contract review. Part of that review is to ensure that the company can make the parts to customer specifications.

The request by the customer for the company to use a new form of plastic meant that the company needed to evaluate its ability to use the new material. The use of a designed experiment would establish both capabilities and sources of variation. This would allow the company to create both a design and a setup sheet that would maximize the material's use. A simple capability study would not give this ability. Therefore, the extra effort would result in more information. This information can be converted into a more efficient manufacturing process by giving data on what to expect during processing. Thus, a company can control cost, quality, and environmental issues at the same time without putting these issues into conflict. As we shall see later, combining different concerns within a company into a single management approach will save money, increase quality, and promote a better environmental response.

When most people hear the term "environmental management system" they first think about common and widely known regulations such as the right-to-know law or Clean Air Act. In fact, many managers believe that an environmental management system focuses only on the state and federal regulations with their related paperwork. Actually, a well-run environmental management system will focus on regulations, customer requirements, and common sense for the issues it will address. Also, such a system well be integrated into other aspects of the company's existing management structure.

In our particular example, the company is located in the state of Michigan. Thus, there is a Michigan right-to-know law in effect. This requires the use of visible charts in the work areas and the need to train many members of the work force on the issue of hazardous chemicals. In Michigan, the law requires a communication program designed to safeguard the handling of hazardous chemicals through the labeling of containers, availability of Material Safety Data Sheets, and proper training to use these resources. The law is part of the Michigan Occupational Safety and Health Act. It is also part of the Federal Hazard Communication Standard. This federal regulation is fully adopted by the Michigan law.

Peak Manufacturing is obviously training its workers to conform to this regulation. Having a person from the Michigan Department of Labor as an instructor in the training program adds credibility to the system.

The building attendant going down into the service tunnels to read some water meters represents just one measurement being taken as part of the environmental management system. Top management at the company should have set targets on water discharge as part of their business plan. These targets should be based on amounts allowed under a discharge permit registered with the state and possibly even the county. The taking of a reading of the water meter represents a simple task, yet it is a critical component of an environmental management system.

Recycling is often seen as an environmental process. This is not entirely true. When the young college student moved some recycled pallets to a waiting truck, he was completing just one cycle of the life of the pallets. By sending the pallets back to the supplier, the company is actually saving money. The pallets will be used repeatedly, eliminating the need to purchase or assemble new pallets for future manufacturing needs. At the same time, critical timber resources are conserved.

Another subtle sign of an environmental management system being in place was the use of a control chart for a process. In our example, the machine operator named Ed had to note the cause of a part out of tolerance on his control chart. This information will identify special causes of variation in the process. By obtaining statistical control of the process, a company will avoid scrap, waste, and the extra cost of manufacturing that comes from getting rid of scrap and constantly correcting the process. This has both economic and environmental benefits. Later, we will see how this is achieved by combining a company's environmental management system into a management culture focused on total quality management.

Jill's meeting with the township planner and the meeting that evening with the planning board represent another key aspect of an environmental management system. Mainly, the interaction between a company and its neighborhood. This includes many stakeholders of the environment. For example, the people that work at the plant have a stake in any environmental impacts. Also, the local, county, state, and federal governments have an interest in the environmental issues related to the company's operation. The owners and managers of the company are also concerned about these issues. Thus, any environmental management system has to take into account the many occupants and concerned parties of the environment controlled by the company.

At one point in our example a worker was confronted because he was not wearing his safety glasses. As mentioned before, safety in the workplace is an environmental concern as much as it is a concern about liability.

We also saw the plant manager applying pressure on the preventive maintenance people to get down machines back on line. This represents one of the major problems encountered with an environmental management system. Namely, you must balance environmental concerns against the requirements of running a profitable company. It is tempting to disregard an environmental concern when time or money seem to be a more pressing issue. As we shall see, discipline is a key characteristic you must require of your managers and workers.

At this point in our example a purchasing manager was concerned about fumes that could be given off during the molding of a particular resin. He knew enough to be worried about the Clean Air Act. However, he was not certain. Therefore, he contacted the environmental regulation expert on site. That person, in turn, would have to look for any regulations that may apply. Less subtle would be a discussion of the effects of the fumes on the work force. Again, the interior environment of the factory is also a concern of an environmental management system.

One unusual aspect of an environmental management system is the control of pests within the company. Problems such as mice, rats, insects, and other biological threats have to be dealt with while maintaining conformance to regulations and internal procedures. For example, it is easy to place large quantities of poison in a warehouse to eradicate rats. However, other problems could be created.

First, there is no guarantee that the poison will kill all rats. Instead, a company may find that they have created a new race of rats resistant to the poison they are using. The eradication program then will become less effective over time. Second, the use, disposal, and possible loss of the poison could create contamination hazards. So an environmental management system must address these types of problems. Also, the county had regulations that apply to the control of rodents.

Less obvious was the warehouse manager stopping to get a drink of water. Although water quality is sometimes taken for granted, every country in the world has had some problems with its water quality. An environmental management system must also address this issue where it was a priority. For example, a factory built using a new water system could not assume the quality of the water is assured by the local water utility. Initial tests of the water would have to be conducted. These would be followed with regular testing.

In Kent County, it is a regulatory concern when a company provides food services for the employees. The environmental health division of the county health department is responsible for regulating such activity. An environmental management system must also be concerned with employee health.

The overall appearance of a company involves housekeeping, quality of the workplace, and safety considerations. These are the factors that the potential new customer visiting the example client will be looking for. A good examiner of a new client company will notice the overall appearance and housekeeping going on within the company. A safe and tidy company is usually a reflection of a management system concerned with efficiency and effectiveness. It can also be the byproduct of an environmental management system. In this example, the visitor noticed the high noise level. Ambient noise is part of a company's environment.

Another industrial engineer, Todd, spent some time trying to solve a problem with assembly. He had noticed that the lighting conditions were inadequate. Like the noise level in a factory, lighting is also part of your environment. Therefore, noise and light levels are another concern of an environmental management system.

The case of the machine operator sweeping up pieces of plastic around her machine is another example of recycling materials. Although this is a good example of conserving resources, it will turn out to be a major cause of problems tomorrow in the molding process. Contamination will make the plastic that is reused unacceptable. Therefore, this is an example of an environmental and quality problem that will have to be addressed by an environmental management system.

Internal auditing is a requirement not only for a management system, but also for an environmental management system. The example uses an examination of the corrective action log as an audit item. As we shall see later, this represents several aspects of an environmental management system. It includes keeping records, performing corrective actions, following procedures, and preventing recurrence of the problems.

Also highlighted was the issuance of an air discharge permit. This would represent a normal activity for most manufacturing companies. For the example company, the state of Michigan issued such a permit.

Another highlight was the recycling of office scrap paper and corrugate. These are common practices in many businesses today. Sometimes, as in the case of this example, the scrap is burned to create energy. Sometimes the energy is created on site; sometimes the material creates energy for the community. Some companies can generate income from the recycling effort. In any case, the recycling process frequently reduces the overall cost to the community. However, we shall also see that some popular environmental programs are not always in your best interest.

The brief comment on the surprise expressed by a local environmental action group when the president of this example company had asked for assistance is taken from real life. Currently, it is unusual for a company to seek feedback from public environmental groups. Under ISO 14000, this may change. An aggressive company would seek out the opinions of any group concerned about the environment in which the company operates. Later in this book, we will see how this issue affected the drafting of the international environmental standard.

The life cycle of a product is a critical concept to be aware of when setting up an environmental management system. The life cycle of a product involves the environmental issues affected by the product from cradle to grave. It can also involve second and even third life spans for the product. For example, your product may be used after its original purpose has been exhausted for a purpose never conceived of during its original design. We shall also look at this issue in later chapters.

The experience of the new engineer trying to obtain information on eco-labeling represents one of the factors that led to the creation of an international environmental standard. Namely, the fact that nations and corporations around the world are beginning to make environmental requirements that reach outside the target company. In this example, the requirements for a European company affect the actions taken at Peak Manufacturing.

However, the new engineer was also experiencing a common problem with multiple regulations and requirements for the same topic. What she discovered was that customers and regulators often cannot agree with each other's interpretations. This can lead to confusion. And, any good environmental management system should be able to account for such possibilities. This is an issue addressed later.

Another sensitive point brought up in the example is the multiple regulations and requirements that apply to a single item. In this example, that item was a small container of hazardous chemicals. Companies will discover that conformance to regulations and requirements sometimes outweigh the value of the task to be completed. Therefore, a good environmental management system will have flexibility built in, even when the regulatory environment has none.

Still another sensitive point for companies is the issue of maintaining a paper trail that could be used against the company. This is a problem for a company that will not or does not conform to regulations and requirements. The documentation they create for their environmental management system may ultimately work against them. Therefore, a company cannot begin an environmental management system without serious commitment by management to support conformance to all requirements and regulations.

As a side note, our example specifically identified electronic documentation being kept. When this is the case, then a system of backup is critically important. This is another point we shall make several times in this book.

Finally, the example ended with a third shift dedicated to preventive maintenance. Part of their regular duties is to keep the machinery working as intended. That would include anything about the equipment that might pose an environmental threat.

WHAT WAS MISSING FROM THIS STORY?

To many, this story seems to be missing several elements. Where are the cans for collecting funds to save the whales? Why aren't the employees car-pooling? Where are the solar panels for collecting extra electric energy? Where is the compost pile for the garbage? Why didn't the parking lot extension require an environmental impact statement?

These questions represent environmental concerns. Although these could be part of an environmental management system, they are not requirements. Instead, your company has to address the immediate environmental concerns of your company. You will quickly discover that many of these "environmental" issues are really issues about productivity, quality, health, and safety. The environmental management system a company establishes will have to meet several requirements. However, these requirements are common to a management system, and if read by themselves it would not be obvious that the system being designed was for environmental issues.

Therefore, you must remember this one important point: This book addresses the issue of establishing an *environmental management system.* As we shall see, even without ISO 14000 there is growing pressure for companies to form some sort of system to cope with increasing numbers of regulations and customer requirements that are related to environmental concerns. In this book we will look at environmental management systems as an extension of a company's already ongoing pursuits of higher quality and lower prices. We shall also look at the use of environmental management as a marketing tool. Although this seems selfish, in reality it makes no sense to develop an environmental management system without regard to these concerns.

SUMMARY-REVIEW OF ENVIRONMENTAL CONCERNS

From the previous discussion, we have seen that there can be many sources of concern about the environment your company controls. And, as we shall see in later chapters, one of the first steps management must take is to survey their particular concerns within their own company. Some possible environmental factors to monitor, track, and manipulate could be the following:

1. *Safe handling of chemicals.* Many state, local, and federal laws apply to the shipping and handling of chemicals and other similar materials. This implies that the company should have proper procedures concerning the shipping and handling of such items. A company could track the number of accidents related to such shipping and handling. It could also audit the performance of the shipping and handling procedures.

2. *Safe disposal of chemicals and other hazardous materials.* An even more sensitive issue is the disposal of chemicals and other hazardous materials. This will involve regulations and permits. In addition, a company will find that there is an ever decreasing number of options for proper disposal. Therefore, a company has to plan ahead for proper disposal.

3. *Noise and lighting.* Both noise and lighting levels within a company are environmental concerns. These can be accurately measured, but determining the proper level of each can prove tricky. Local, state, and federal guidelines typically have to be consulted.

4. *Quality of work life.* Related to noise and light issues is the topic of the quality of work life. This involves everything from noise and light to indoor air quality to housekeeping to management style. Any company should think about the quality of work life as part of the planning process in establishing an environmental management system.

5. *Discharge of polluted air.* Air pollution can involve the discharge of pollutants by an airborne method both internal and external to your plant. Therefore, a company has two issues to consider. First, the obtaining of discharge permits for air pollutants external to the plant. Second, the level of air quality within the plant. Both of these can be measured.

6. *Water discharge and waterborne pollutants.* Similar to the issue of air pollution is the issue of water pollution. This too can be easily measured. However, a related issue is the amount of total water discharge into the environment. Many communities have only limited capabilities to absorb large quantities of discharged water. Therefore, your company has to plan accordingly.

7. *Environmental impacts on the neighborhood.* Everything from the type of lighting on the outside of your building to the impact of your company on local flora and fauna might be held accountable. For example, a recent movement is trying to reduce the level of light escaping upward from lights on streets and buildings. This movement is actually trying to keep night skies dark for astronomy. More familiar to most companies is the occasional requirement for an environmental impact statement.

8. *Recycling activities.* Recycling is not only a recent fad but a long-term trend for industry. The cost and availability of some materials has forced most companies into recycling. Some products pose a risk if they end up in landfills. Therefore, producers of such products must plan and implement product recycling programs.

9. *Packaging.* New regulations have allowed companies to advertise the environmentally friendly nature of their products. Other requirements address the content and nature of the packaging used. Eco-labeling is just one example of new packaging requirements that have to be considered within your environmental management system.

10. *Product life cycle.* As mentioned previously, the life cycle of your products becomes a critical concern of your environmental management system. This involves tracking the environmental concerns of the product from cradle to grave. We shall address this issue in Chapter 4.

11. *Conservation of resources.* Often confused with environmentalism is the conservation movement. It should be noted that proper engineering is actually a form of conservation. A good engineer designs a product to obtain maximum impact and application from a minimum of resources. As we shall see, this will be a common theme within this book.

When developing your environmental management system, such concerns as those listed here and any other concerns discovered by your management have to be addressed. You will need to first survey the environmental concern of your company. Then you will need to develop a system to track each of these concerns. Therefore, you will also need to develop goals and targets for each concern. This, in turn, implies that you will have to develop a method of measuring each concern using discrete numbers.

FORCES THAT REQUIRE YOUR COMPANY TO DEVELOP AN ENVIRONMENTAL MANAGEMENT SYSTEM

We have seen from the previous discussion that there are many concerns that management must address when the issue is the environment. We have also seen that the environment encompasses the immediate surroundings as well as the interior of a company. It also involves the environmental impact of the product the company produces. Therefore, there must be many forces at work to develop such a wide spectrum of concerns.

Let us take a moment to examine these forces in general.

1. *External forces.* There are three basic external sources of concern about the environment. The first is regulation. Local, state, and federal regulations related to the environment are quite common. However, a new source of external requirements is the international community. The introduction of treaties such as GATT and NAFTA have opened up international trading.

In a world of free trade between nations, there is a need for common standards to be applied. ISO 14000 is just one example of an international standard. Another international standard is ISO 9000. It is a voluntary standard for a management system of quality assurance. In the few years since it was introduced, ISO 9000 has been widely accepted and required of various companies. Today, over 60,000 companies are registered to this standard. It is entirely possible that ISO 14000 will follow a similar path.

Customer requirements are the second source of concerns. Many corporations are finding that they must conform to environmental regulations that also have to be applied to their suppliers. Sometimes they also find that nonregulatory pressures or an outward concern for the environment are driving them to place environmental concerns within their purchasing agreements. Most common of all are the environmental issues placed within purchasing agreements with a governmental unit. When your company does business with these corporations or governments, it inherits a list of environmental concerns that have to be addressed.

The third source of concerns comes from the community at large. Today, most communities are sensitive to several environmental issues, such as pollution, recycling, noise, and related problems. There may exist in the community several environmental concerns related to the conduct of your company. A modern manufacturing management team has to be sensitive to these issues as well.

2. *Internal forces.* The sensitivity of the general public to environmental issues also applies to your employees. They too are sensitive to environmental concerns. In addition, regulations apply to the work force concerning environmental-related issues. We have already looked at the right-to-know laws. There are also many regulations that apply to worker health and safety. All these sources must be addressed as part of your environmental management system.

Another source of internal concern are the engineering and plant operations. The need to maximize the use of floor space and the need to develop a product that is environmentally sound create more internal concerns. These also have to be addressed within your environmental management system.

3. *Marketing opportunities.* Because the community at large has environmental concerns, careful and deliberate control of environmental concerns within your system of management can create many marketing opportunities. In addition, laws are allowing these opportunities to be better exploited.

For example, it is now possible to advertise the recycled content of your product and its packaging. This has been shown to be a marketing advantage. If your company can demonstrate an effective environmental management system, it should gain some marketing advantage to sell products or services to corporations.

Opportunities such as these are very desirable to most management teams and can lead to additional concerns about environmental issues. Thus, the need for a management system that addresses these concerns becomes more obvious.

4. *Need for continuous improvement.* Because most companies today find that they must reduce costs and improve quality, they have implemented systems of continuous improvement. Others have adopted such systems because customers have required continuous improvement. Either way, environmental concerns can be seen as part of a system of continuous improvement.

Environmental concerns can almost be seen as design inputs for both the product and your manufacturing systems. Therefore, not only should you meet the target for environmental conformance, but by striving to exceed these targets you demonstrate commitment to environmental concerns and an effective management system.

THE NEED FOR A UNIFIED SYSTEM OF MANAGEMENT FOR ENVIRONMENTAL CONCERNS

Now that we have examined the sources of environmental concerns and the sheer volume of regulations related to environmental issues, it should be obvious that the most effective path for any company is to develop a management system for environmental concerns. Even without considering ISO 14000, there exists a great number of reasons to develop an environmental management system.

An environmental management system will help your management team to cope with all local, state, federal, and international requirements. It will also help your company to cope with internal concerns about the environment. It will assist your company in appraising the concerns of workers and neighbors. As a bonus, it will open doors to the opportunity of marketing the environmental effectiveness of your company.

The following chapters in this book will discuss these points in detail. A common theme of the book is how to achieve these objectives at low cost with minimal additional personnel. Also, the book shall examine how to make such a management system profitable for the company. Part of that will come from avoiding fines related to nonconformance to regulations and customer requirements. Most of the profitability will be obtained through conservation of resources and effective use of engineering techniques. Part of that will be the rapid use of corrective actions and the liberal use of preventive actions.

THE LIBRARY OF REGULATION

To illustrate further the need for a unified system to cope with environmental issues, you need only to begin to form a library of regulations. In our case, our fictitious company applied to several governmental bodies for copies of regulations that would apply to a small manufacturer. When we had finished collecting the required regulations, we found that we had over four linear feet of printed material.

As you can imagine, this represents an overwhelming task even for a small team of technicians to track and maintain. Conforming to all the pertinent regulations requires a coordinated and disciplined approach by management. Otherwise, you will find that your company spends all of its time preparing for compliance audits and inspections. In other words, there is a constant chase to quickly achieve conformance levels for the type of upcoming inspection.

A uniform management system would allow your company to set specific targets to be achieved to meet both regulations and customer requirements. Then, in turn, all key people at your company would have assigned and coordinated tasks. Therefore, your company first seeks to conform to all requirements and then to maintain those levels. Eventually, the company also seeks continuous improvement where it makes economic sense. This makes your company constantly prepared for inspection and audits by outside agencies or customers.

In effect, everyone at your company becomes an environmental manager. Not everyone will think of themselves as an environmental manager, but they will be aware that their job has some environmental responsibility. The same way that people working at a company registered to ISO 9000 are aware that their job has a direct effect on the final quality of their product.

TIES TO OTHER FORMS OF MANAGEMENT SYSTEMS

Speaking of ISO 9000, this other voluntary international standard for a management system for quality assurance is one of the most rapidly growing models for a system of management. It does not have to be seen as being in conflict with ISO 14000. Instead, as we shall see in the next chapter, ISO 14000 is actually a close cousin to ISO 9000. Therefore, you should be able to develop one management system to cover all standards.

It should also be noted that ISO 9000 has expanded its realm of concerns to the issues of health and safety. It is expected that with the 1999 revisions to the ISO 9000 family of standards, this connection will be expanded further. Likewise, ISO 14000 also has some concern for health and safety issues. Thus, any gap that may exist between these two standards should continue to close.

Another popular management model is called total quality management, or TQM. There are several models for total quality management. One is found in applying ISO 9004-1, "Quality Management and Quality System Elements Guidelines." Another can be found in the criteria for the Malcolm Baldrige Quality Award. Still other models exist. ISO 14000 can easily be adopted into these types of management systems.

This is possible because the models for TQM also encourage the use of requirements that are also found in the ISO 14000 standard. For example, corrective actions, preventive actions, continuous improvement, and benchmarking against outside performance measurements are common to these two systems.

Management systems based mostly on the idea of reengineering the corporation or seeking to turn around the profitability of the company are also mutually compatible with ISO 14000. Greater efficiency and effectiveness within a company is highly dependent upon a well-structured and disciplined management system. In addition, such companies would be seeking better use of existing resources and looking for methods for improving their competitive position. As we shall see, ISO 14000 can give your company both.

BENEFITS OF AN ENVIRONMENTAL MANAGEMENT SYSTEM

There are benefits from creating any form of a structured, disciplined, and well-documented management system. What follows is a brief discussion of the most common benefits that can be achieved by an environmental management system.

1. *Conformance to regulations.* The greatest benefit of having an environmental management system comes from being constantly prepared for inspection and audit. Outside regulatory agencies can and will examine your current levels of conformance. This may take the form of an audit of your site or records. It could take the form of sampling the air or water near your company. It could involve the random inspection of materials being shipped from your plant or from your suppliers. It could also come in the form of the random sampling of your product in the field.

It is easy to see that an examination of your environmental conformance against regulations could come at any time. Therefore, the best strategy for a company would be to have continuous conformance. The best way to assure continuous conformance would be a continuous system of managing environmental issues. ISO 14000 is a model for such a system.

By requiring specific people within your company to achieve particular tasks and to maintain environmentally related systems, you can assure continuous conformance, especially if you pay close attention to the concept of feedback to management. This involves internally auditing your environmental management system for its conformance and effectiveness. The results of this type of audit is given to management so that they can take corrective action and design ever more efficient procedures and work instructions.

2. *Conformance to customer requirements.* Also of great importance is the benefit of meeting customer requirements. Many companies today are familiar with the need to meet the quality requirements issued by customers. To adjust to an environmental management system, the existing system of coping with other customer requirements is expanded to account for environmental requirements. Those requirements can come from customers, regulators, community pressure, or internal needs.

In other words, customers are seen as the next person in the process of developing and manufacturing your product. Customers are also seen as people who have a stake in the environment that your company can control. This would include regulators and community groups. Also, the final user of your product is seen as a customer. This includes the people who buy your product and the people who eventually will have to dispose of your product.

By conforming to the requirements of these multiple customers, your company should reap the benefits of satisfied customers. It has been shown that meeting quality requirements of customers is very competitive for a company. Now it is beginning to look strongly as if meeting the environmental requirements of your customers can also have a great economic benefit.

The economic benefits can be both external and internal to your company. An example of an internal benefit would be the careful recycling of scrap plastic resin. By calculating the amount of reground plastic that can be placed in virgin material without upsetting the quality characteristics of your product, you can save considerable amounts of money.

An example of an external benefit would be the design of your product for easy recycling or disposal. Take the case of a plastic part that uses a formulation of plastic resin that can be remelted and used for other applications. This is currently being done with the plastic used to make toner cartridges for copy machines. The company that makes the cartridge offers to recycle it for free. The customer benefits because it does not have to dispose of the cartridge. The community benefits because the cartridge does not end up in a landfill. The company benefits because it doesn't have to buy additional plastic to make new cartridges and its marketing image is enhanced.

3. *Greater marketability for your company.* Continuing with the marketing theme, a company with an established environmental management system—especially one registered to a recognized international standard—has a marketing advantage. Currently, many companies are trying to portray themselves as being "green." A company that is able to demonstrate its commitment to the environment, especially one that can show a seal of registration, will appeal to environmentally conscious customers.

These customers might be larger corporations also looking for ways to enhance their environmental image. Such a corporation would be highly interested in working with a supplier that has an established environmental management system. The end users of your product might be conscious of looking for a company that shows concern for the environment. An example of this is the popularity of using recycled paper as part of your packaging. The process of recycling paper is seen as environmentally friendly and good for the future of trees.

However, a customer will not be aware of your environmental management system unless you take the effort to make your system known. That means you should look into eco-labels, seals of certification, and other obvious ways to highlight your company's environmental commitment. I will discuss these points throughout this book.

4. *Better use of resources.* A good environmental management system will also be a good system of conservation; specifically, the conservation of resources. These resources can be the raw materials that you process, the people who you employ, the money that you need to operate, the time it takes to produce your product, or the surrounding environment of your company. Each of these resources represents a large array of possibilities.

By carefully surveying the resources that your company uses, especially those resources that keep your company competitive, your management team can plan for conservation efforts that will yield the greatest economic benefits. Thus, your environmental management system can actually become a profit center.

5. *Reduction in the cost of operation.* Highlighting just one of the possibilities discussed under item 4 is the cost of operating your company. A careful examination of those costs will uncover several things that could be considered environmentally related, such as the cost of complying with environmental regulations. If you establish an effective environmental management system, those costs should be minimized.

Another example would be the implementation of a just-in-time system of production. Such a system would minimize the amount of material being held in process. It would also reduce the time that any one component of raw material stayed in storage. By minimizing storage time, you also minimize the probability of spillage or other environmental threats. More efficient operations can therefore have positive environmental outcomes.

6. *Better communications among departments.* As we shall see, a good management system relies on written policies, procedures, and work instructions. This includes lists of goals, targets, and objectives each person, department, and site is expected to achieve. When such a management system is well documented, the people working within such a system can readily refer to instructions and other guidance. This results in better communication between the management and the rank and file.

Another benefit of a well-documented management system, especially one where top management is constantly evaluating the effectiveness of the system, is better communication among departments. Take the example of contract review. When a customer submits a contract to your company, several departments must evaluate your company's ability to meet the stated and unstated requirements. This includes the customer's environmental requirements and any regulatory mandates that could apply. Engineering needs to freely communicate with purchasing, quality assurance, legal, and other such departments. If this process is carefully described by a procedure and supported with easy-to-use forms or electronic mail, greater efficiency is almost inevitable.

7. *Higher quality.* An interesting byproduct of concern about environmental issues affecting your company is the opportunity to achieve higher qualities within your services or product. For example, the manufacturer of a chemical compound that is used as a household detergent may want to develop a formulation that minimizes the amount of phosphate in the mixture. By developing such a formula the company is minimizing the impact on the environment from the use of the product. At the same time, this new formula may prove easier to manufacture, package, and transport. More likely, the chemicals used to make up for the performance achieved by the phosphate may actually make the product more stable or less expensive. Thus, the overall quality of the product is increased.

This type of activity, in which both the environmental effect and the quality of the product are improved at the same time, is now becoming a common practice in industry. The widespread use of designed experiments is just one example. Quality function deployment is another example. For both of these methods teams of professionals study the product and establish a list of desirable characteristics. Then through statistical methods they establish relationships and sources of variation. This results in mathematics models of the product's design. When you have a predictable model of your product's characteristics, you can manipulate these to accomplish several outcomes simultaneously.

8. *Makes each manager's job easier.* One of the greatest problems facing a manager today is the need for constant "firefighting." In other words, today's manager is expected to fill several roles at the same time. A manager is expected to train and develop his or her people, plan and organize the unit's activities, increase levels of quality, audit the unit's performance, in addition to several other tasks. If you add to this the need to be conscious of environmental concerns, the manager's job becomes overwhelming.

A well-developed system of environmental management will actually be part of a well-written system of general management. Goals and objectives along with written procedures and work instructions will be available. This gives the manager the ability to plan, coordinate, monitor, and constantly improve several processes at the same time. This is possible because you can combine concerns about the environment, health, safety, training, quality, and the like into each procedure. By addressing all concerns when procedures and work instructions are developed, you make the task of conforming much easier. Even more important, you make the understanding of what has to be accomplished much more clear.

Armed with written procedures and work instructions plus a list of goals and objectives, a manager can train his or her people much more quickly and give them more authority to make independent decisions. This reduces much of the firefighting that most managers experience. Take the example of creating reaction plans for the workers. When a simple problem is encountered, the worker is already equipped with a list of actions to take before notifying a supervisor. Most simple problems are solved by the person at the process and a supervisor or manager need not be directly involved.

9. *Higher levels of safety.* As we have indicated before, safety is part of the environment that your company controls. Increasing the level of safety within your plant is one of the major goals of most environmental management systems. Proper procedures for handling hazardous chemicals is just one example in which safety and an environmental concern meet. Proper handling results in no spills of an environmentally damaging material. It also results in no injury to the person handling the material. Thus one procedure for the environmental system results in two benefits.

10. *Improved community image.* With an established environmental management system, your company will be more visible in the community as a company concerned about the environment. Take the example of Herman Miller, Inc., of Zeeland, Michigan. Its county is under strict air quality monitoring for ozone. When ozone levels set by the federal government are exceeded, an ozone alert goes into effect. This means that people should avoid driving their cars and filling their gas tanks. To assist in this effort, it is the policy of Herman Miller to give out ice cream and soda for free on hot days. Hot days are the most likely to create excessive ozone. The free food keeps employees in the plant during the day and discourages them from driving to lunch. This is frequently featured on the local news, creating a positive image for the corporation.

11. *Consistency of policies.* Because an environmental management system requires the writing and strict following of those written policies, the overall management system improves in its consistency of policies. This is especially true for companies that take the time to coordinate their health, safety, quality, financial, and environmental management policies. This is discussed later in the book.

12. *Improved management confidence.* A modern environmental management system requires making decisions based on facts. In addition, it also requires operation under controlled conditions. These controlled conditions are first planned and then implemented by a management team. Because the management team needs to establish this system and then coordinate its dissemination to all employees, managers have greater confidence. This confidence comes from a complete understanding of the goals the company is promoting.

13. *Organization and personal satisfaction.* As we shall see in the next chapter, most people today are concerned about the environment. Therefore, to be an active part of a planned and well-managed environmental system at work leads to greater personal satisfaction. Because people are being given ownership of the responsibilities related to environmental conformance, there is also a greater level of satisfaction for the organization.

14. *Improved performance related to customer needs.* An effective environmental management system requires the ability to first establish and define customer requirements related to the environment. Then those needs have to be met during production, installation, and servicing of your product. If a need is not met, then you are required to have a preestablished corrective action system. Through the use of written work instructions and standard operating procedures, you will find that your company can respond much faster and more effectively to customer needs.

15. *Consistency of supplier relationships.* Another aspect of a complete environmental management system is the passing of environmental goals onto your suppliers. After all, it is suppliers that will ship in raw materials, hazardous substances, controlled goods, and other such materials. It is also an outside supplier that will probably provide a company with environmental auditing reports. By establishing a fixed set of supplier requirements and communicating these to the appropriate supply companies, a company will promote consistency in more relationships with suppliers.

16. *Demonstrating capability.* The central objective of ISO 14000 is the same as for most international and national standards—to demonstrate your company's ability to meet a stated model. In this case, the model is an environmental management system. By obtaining registration to this standard, your company has demonstrated that it has a written, established, and well-maintained system of management. Within the system is also a demonstration of your ability to meet external and internal environmental requirements. Such a demonstration can be used for other purposes, such as marketing, public relations, and community affairs.

17. *Increasing access to capital.* By having an established and documented management system for environmental protection, you can reassure the concerns of current and potential investors. This would include obtaining capital from banks and other sources.

18. *Limitation of liability.* Environmental lawsuits are now fairly common. An effective system of environmental management means that your intentions and your efforts to meet environmental targets and the requirements of regulations are well documented. Therefore, a company will have an excellent source of documentation for developing a defensive argument in court. If information is well documented, a company may have enough evidence of its attempt at compliance to avoid the court case altogether. However, it should be noted that the same documentation can be used against a company in a court of law. Therefore, the need for top management to continuously monitor and improve the environmental management system becomes even more obvious.

19. *Securing insurance, permits, and other authorizations.* Because the environmental management system is well documented, a company will be able to explain and demonstrate its current environmental goals and policies to insurance representatives and government officials. This increased ability to communicate should facilitate quicker action in obtaining needed insurance, permits, and other forms of authorization.

20. *Technology transfer.* While developing an environmental management system, a company may also be developing technologies that can be used by other companies in their quest for environmental conformance. Therefore, it is developing a marketable service or possibly a new product that can be marketed. Also, by having a well-documented system, a company may have the information needed to apply for grants or for participation in a technology transfer program. Either way, the company can benefit.

SUMMARY

The purpose of this chapter was to introduce you to the look and feel of an environmental management system. We looked at a day in the life of a company using such a system. Each company that decides to implement an environmental management system will find that the system its designs may not entirely resemble this example. However, each company will pursue the same benefits that have been outlined. If additional benefits are discovered or desired by your company, then by all means pursue those goals as well.

The reader should note that in 1999 the ISO 9000 standard will be revised. Other current plans for the new family of standards for ISO 9000 will expand to include management methods for the issues of quality, health, safety, finance, and the environment. It will also encourage the use of total product life-cycle planning—a concept discussed in later chapters. Thus, conforming to ISO 14000 will prepare your company partially for the new ISO 9000 standard.

Chapter 2

BIRTH OF AN INTERNATIONAL ENVIRONMENTAL MANAGEMENT STANDARD

The birth of ISO 14000 was not a linear event. That is, there was no series of identifiable events that led directly to its development. Instead, it was really born of an environment that existed by the 1990s. In fact, so many factors played a part in it coming to existence that it would be a subject for a book of its own.

In the end, an international environmental management standard was the result of demand from industry. Why industry had such a need for such a standard can be seen as the result of several conditions existing at the same time. These conditions led to a need for a coordinated approach to dealing with the environment.

BACKGROUND

Let us begin by examining the first set of conditions, namely, regulations. In the United States, legislation related to the environment has been enacted over the past 100 years. Many people believe that environmental laws are a recent fad. This is not true. The only thing that is recent and popular is the widespread interest in the environment.

The widespread interest in issues such as pollution, ecology, and the environment suddenly emerged near the end of the 1960s. This was the rebirth of a movement that has existed under several names since the 1800s. At first, it was called conservationism. People took an interest in the bountiful resources discovered as the United States grew westward.

This movement resulted in many new ways to look at natural resources. In the laws, one of its effects would be the system of national parks to preserve large sections of land and its related wildlife. From this point on, the number of laws related to protecting the environment would continue to grow. When the environmental movement of the 1960s emerged, it would touch off a large increase in the number of laws created to protect environmental resources. (Exhibit 2-1).

Exhibit 2-1: The Growing Number of Environmental Regulations During the Twentieth Century

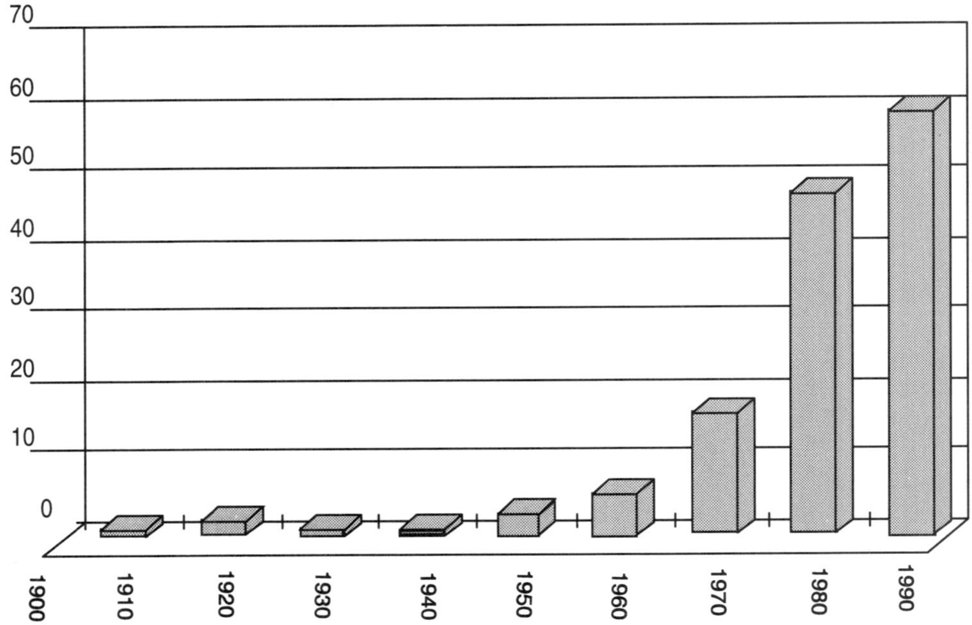

In the United States, the first environmental law was enacted in 1899. It was called the Rivers and Harbors Appropriation Act of 1899, also known as the Refuse Act of 1899. In 1910, the Insecticides Act was passed. The Public Health Service Act was enacted in 1912. It is interesting to note that in 1924, the Oil Pollution Act was passed.

We can see that issues that we confront today are not new. Instead, they have been long-running concerns. For example, the first Air Pollution Control Act was enacted in 1955. The real change comes from seeing that the number and scope of such laws increased dramatically during and after the 1960s.

The result is that most businesses now find that they face a bewildering array of regulations related to the environment. Just listing all the environmental regulations in the United States would create a book of great magnitude. In fact, there are so many regulations a company can only cope by adopting a systematic approach to these regulations.

INTERNATIONAL ENVIRONMENTALISM

In the last chapter, I pointed out that environmentalism is different from an environmental management system. However, the rise of the environmental movement is one of the prime conditions that led to the development of an international standard for environmental management systems.

The unique characteristic of the environmental movement was that it took hold almost worldwide. Both communist and capitalist countries experienced the rising political power of people interested in the environment. Even many of the developing nations took part.

In Europe, the most pronounced indication of the international effect of environmentalism was the birth of the Green Party. Soon many countries had a "green" political party whose purpose was to promote legislation to protect the general natural environment. Their political power was to rise during the 1980s. This placed greater pressure on governments to respond to a general concern about the loss of natural resources, pollution, population, and the impact of having a highly industrialized society.

The birth of the green parties worldwide can be traced to the 1983 success of the German Green Party in national elections. Because even small political parties in Europe can directly influence government policy, this election result proved to be significant. When the elections for a European Parliament were held in June 1989, the Green Party in Britain won 14.9 percent of the vote. That would prove to be the best result ever recorded for a Green Party at a national level.

By 1990, the popularity of the green parties began to evaporate. The German Green Party was unable to get over 5 percent of the vote. The recession of 1990 would take a considerable toll on green parties worldwide. However, by that point they had already had a considerable influence on national policies.

The first effect was to create an environment of green consumerism. The end-users of industrial products were now educated and sensitive to the environmental impact of products. For example, people are now reluctant to let a company known to be a deliberate polluter locate in their community. Local zoning boards now look closely at the issue of environmental impact.

A second effect was the installation of an environmental bureaucracy. Bureaucracies tend to get in the habit of enacting more regulations. This means that a company today can expect even more regulations related to the environment.

The third effect is to muddy the philosophical waters on what it means to protect an environment. Because of the long-running debate between society and industry on the issues related to pollution, people now see that when you want growth and development of your standard of living, pollution is inevitable. The problem today is to strike a balance between the need for growth and the desire for minimum environmental impact.

Companies now find that the regulations they have to deal with are just a reflection of concerns from the community at large. That means that most companies also have to think about their relationship with the community concerning environmental issues. Therefore, once again, a coordinated system of management seems to be the logical tactic to adopt.

National governments too find that they must walk a fine line of keeping environmentalists happy at the same time that they need to promote economic growth. There is a need for international cooperation and a systematic approach to coping with issues of environmentalism and economic growth.

INTERNATIONAL TRADE

Treaties such as NAFTA, GATT, and the European Union represent a recent movement toward worldwide free trade. However, the goal of free trade is not an easy one to accomplish—especially when dealing between national governments.

Take the example of the European Union. It began as the Common Market of Europe. Through many difficult years of negotiation and cooperation, it led to the European Community. The European Community created a need for standards that could be used by many nations. In other words, international standards are a critical component of world trade. With the change from being the European Community to being the European Union, the demand for such standards has increased. The number of participating countries has also increased.

International standards allow a company in one country to communicate its needs to companies in other countries. For example, ISO 9000 is a standard for the model of a management system for quality assurance. It was created by the International Organization for Standardization in Geneva, Switzerland. This organization coordinates the creation of voluntary standards for international use. It is not the only organization performing this task, but it has played a major role in helping foster the growth and development of the European Union.

At the same time, the United Nations has also pursued environmental concerns among nations. For example, in 1972 there was the Stockholm Conference on the Human Environment. This led to a series of discussions on the international effect of pollution and the variety of opinions on how to protect the environment. All of this culminated in the 1992 UN Conference on Environment and Development (UNCED) held in Brazil.

This conference brought together major leaders from around the world to sign a series of declarations. The major theme that would evolve was the concept of "sustainable development" while maintaining environmental friendliness. Each country then promised to develop policies to support this idea.

European countries were already pursuing a similar course. One title of such EC regulations was *The Eco Management and Audit Scheme Regulation,* (EMAS) which is known as the "Eco audit." It is voluntary for industry and services but compulsory for the governments of the 12 member states to set up national organizations for its administration and certification.

The simple explanation of the regulation is that if you implement an environmental management system, you will automatically qualify for accreditation to the requirements of the Eco audit. Achievement of the Eco audit allows the display of a prestigious logo and listing in an EC-wide published honors list. For the first time, industry could demonstrate that it is truly facilitative toward the community and aggressively market that claim. Therefore, international pressures were brought to bear on companies wishing to conduct worldwide trade to conform to a regional or even international model of environmental conformance.

THE COMBINED EFFECT

Taking the pressures from the business community, national governments, the local community, regulations, environmentalists, and customers, a condition was created whereby a company needed a systematic approach to meeting all these needs. In addition, the political realities of world trade forced the solution to take the form of an international standard.

Unfortunately, by the time the need for an international standard was realized, there were already many national standards for environmental management systems. It was hoped that one of these national standards could be quickly adopted as the international standard.

Take the case of British Standard 5750, a model for a management system of quality assurance. The European Community Treaty meant that companies working within the Community needed a standard for supplier quality assurance. The International Organization for Standardization used BS 5750 to create ISO 9000. Not only were the requirements of the British standard adopted, but so was the system of third-party registration.

When the need for an international standard was realized, people looked toward another British standard—BS 7750. This was a standard for a system of environmental management within a company. As it turned out, the hopes of adopting this British standard as a new international standard were not to be fulfilled.

BRITISH STANDARD 7750

BS 7750 was published on April 6, 1992, under the title Environmental Management Systems. BS 7750 is a standard that was developed by the British Standards Institute (BSI) as a response to the need for a uniform system of environmental management. It gives any organization a model for developing a management system that addresses all environmental questions. The environment is seen as both natural and man-made. In other words, "environment" as the dictionary definition, not the political definition.

The elements in BS 7750 that can be virtually copied and adapted from ISO 9000 are

Commitment and policy
Organization and personnel
Records and control of documentation
Audits and reviews
Contract review or customer brief
Procurement
Handling and storage
Packaging and delivery
Servicing
Design control
Operation or process controls or procedures
Inspection and testing
Control of measurement and testing equipment
Control of nonconforming product
Statistical sampling

Throughout, the standard reference is made to the similarities between dealing with a customer and satisfying the demands of the environment. Comparisons are made between drawing up a specification in discussions with a customer and deciding what measures are needed to satisfy the demands of a clean environment. The very legislation or regulations can be seen as parts of the specification.

At the time of its release, BS 7750 was the first national standard for environmental management systems in the European Union. It was thought at that time that this standard would be adopted as ISO 14000. Such logic was reasonable. After all, BS 5750—the standard for quality management systems—was adopted almost intact to make ISO 9000.

BS 7750 did not become ISO 14000. The standard was written specifically to comply with the Community Eco-Management Scheme that went into effect in 1994. Although BS 7750 met the eco-management and eco-audit requirements in the European Union, it was seen as too limiting for companies in countries outside Europe. Therefore, as ISO 14000 was developed, the standard was made more flexible and acceptable to the world community.

BS 7750 did have a major influence on ISO 14000, however, so we should take a moment to examine it in detail to see how ISO 14000 was modeled after the intent of this standard.

INSIDE BS 7750

BS 7750 introduces the idea of forming a single management system to handle all environmental concerns. This is both effective and much more efficient in terms of costs. BS 7750 shares many characteristics with ISO 9000. Let's look at one particular example, paragraph 4.3.3, "Management Representative."

> *The organization shall appoint a management representative who, irrespective of other responsibilities, shall have defined authority and responsibility for ensuring that the requirements of this standard are implemented and maintained.*

This is *identical* to paragraph 4.1.2.3 in ISO 9001. All that has changed is the word "organization" for "supplier." And this is not the only place where this occurs. Several of the environmental requirements are drawn straight from BS 5750, or as we know it, ISO 9001.

The key to implementing BS 7750 is to develop a system of prevention. In other words, it is much cheaper to prevent an environmental problem than it is to pay for its effects. Any company that has faced an EPA fine and a collection of civil suits can testify to this. It also demands that the company create a library of environmental issues. These issues are drawn from regulations and customer requirements. For example, the Clean Water Act deals with the pollution of water by industry. For your particular company, you would look at the specific issues dealing with water pollution from your site. This may be the need to install a filtration system on your main discharge pipe. Your environmental policies do not have to address the entire issue of water pollution—just those aspects that directly affect your company.

At the same time, the relationships between environmental management and occupational health and safety cannot be ignored. In fact, the auditing, training, and record keeping will most likely be shared between these two systems. A company should be able to build its environmental management system out of the existing health and safety system it now has. In addition, the activities of quality assurance and overall operations management will also be closely involved. So, a company should take some time to look at how it can develop its environmental system from existing components of its current management system. In other words, how can environmental concerns be incorporated into the daily management of the company?

IMPLICATIONS OF BS 7750

The main thrust of BS 7750 was that every industry has some responsibility to protect and, if possible, improve the environment. This theme was carried over into ISO 14000. However, ISO 14000 makes it quite clear that the company must balance its responsibility for the environment with its desire for sustainable growth.

Surprisingly, Dr. Taguchi's theory of quality suddenly comes into play with the new ISO 14000 environmental management standard. As you may remember, Taguchi said that quality was measured as the loss society experienced after a product was shipped. In other words, maximum quality represents minimum loss to society. This can easily be applied to the environmental question. Minimizing environmental impact and the use of resources equals both good environmental management and quality, according to Dr. Taguchi's theory. Just like BS 7750 and ISO 9000, the world of quality assurance and environmental control are brought together.

A company may find that capturing the heat in its plant and using it to heat the offices is both environmentally sound and profitable. The same would be true of recycling corrogate, oils, and water. Then there is the issue of making a "green" product that can be used as a marketing tool. Recycling scrap plastic into secondary products is another possible example.

A company begins with an internal review of its environment and its related requirements. A company-wide policy is written and personnel assigned specific tasks. These people draw up the objectives and targets of the environmental management system. Documented procedures and work instructions are generated to support the system. Records are kept. Audits are periodically performed and corrective actions taken to continuously improve the system.

Take the case of Canon and Hewlett Packard. Toner cartridges for their printers and copy machines are environmental marketing nightmares if they end up in landfills. Therefore, they have started clean earth programs where customers recycle the cartridges. With each new cartridge, customers get a shipping receipt that lets them send back the old cartridge to the factory at no charge. This represents a well-developed policy on a particular environmental impact and a set of written procedures. The system is not for the whole company, but you can quickly see the marketing and political advantage of this preventive position.

The internal benefits can be substantial as well. The one thing that gets company owners really upset these days is to imply that another environmental requirement is coming. They already have to cope with right-to-know, discharge permits, recycling ordinances, emergency procedures, noise restrictions, and dozens of other regulations. Because the regulations are not likely to go away, the most economical approach is to cope with the myriad requirements with a single system. Then common planning, reviews, improvements, and training can take place. This saves time, money, and personnel.

BS 7750 can be obtained from:

British Standards Institute
Linford Wood
Milton Keynes MK14 6LE
United Kingdom
441 908 220022 (Phone)
441 908 320856 (Fax)

Global Engineering
2805 McGaw Avenue
P.O. Box 19539
Irvine, CA 92714
(800) 854-7179 (Phone)
(714) 261-7892 (Fax)

FROM BS 7750 TO ISO 14000

The hopes that BS 7750 would be quickly adopted as an international standard were quickly dashed. The first objection came from other governments that already had national standards on environmental management. They did not want the British to dominate the international standard.

The second and most tricky objection came from the United States. Here, environmental concerns are more a matter of litigation than they are of political pressure. Businesses in the U.S. have found themselves sued, picketed, boycotted, and regulated. All of these events have tended to lead to court cases against both the company and the protesters.

In other countries, the pressure for conformance is more political. Companies within the U.S. are faced with growing concerns about liability over environmental issues. Any environmental damage may result in a civil suit with large damage payments. Therefore, the prospect of a standard such as BS 7750 was not welcomed—especially the part about working with the community to establish the levels of environmental commitment for a company.

In its original form, the British standard would have opened the door for environmental activists literally to run a company's management goals. This might also create goals that would make the company uncompetitive. Also, the British standard would have left a large paper trail that could be used against the company in a court of law.

At the same time, many international corporations realized that they should have participated more in the development of ISO 9000. The ISO 9000 standard caught most of the world by surprise. Many corporations discovered that to participate in international trade, this standard was critical. In addition, the standard was developed by seeking feedback from potential users. If major corporations had participated in the development of this voluntary standard, it would have been more friendly to their concerns.

Thus, when it was proposed that ISO 14000 be developed in the early 1990s, many corporations and governments realized that they should play an active role. The result was that BS 7750 was used only as a model for the final standard. The trick was to negotiate a standard that would be useful to industry around the world and not look like additional regulation or paperwork to the Americans.

THE CREATION OF ISO 14000–TECHNICAL COMMITTEE 207

In the early 1990s, industrial demand for an international standard for environmental management systems moved the International Organization for Standardization to create a technical committee. The role of a technical committee is to bring together representatives from many countries to reach a consensus on a voluntary standard that can be used by all participating countries.

In the case of the creation of an international voluntary standard for environmental management systems, the committee that was established was called Technical Committee 207, or TC 207. This technical committee then divides itself into subcommittees and working groups. Each of these groups works on specialized topics.

The scope of activity for TC 207 is to standardize the field of environmental management tools and systems. However, this scope is limited. For example, TC 207 is excluded from the following:

- Working on test methods for pollutants (the task of TC 146—Air Quality, TC 147—Water Quality, TC 190—Soil Quality, and TC 43—Acoustics)
- Setting limiting values on pollutants for effluents
- Setting environmental performance levels
- Standardization of products

At the same time, TC 207 is working in a cooperative effort with TC 176, the committee that works on developing and revising the ISO 9000 family of standards. This is done partly because ISO 9000 and ISO 14000 will have similar registration schemes. Also, these two standards will use ISO 10011 as a common guideline for audit procedures. ISO 10011 is the standard for auditing a management system.

The internal structure of TC 207 is as follows:

- A chairman's advisory group currently led by the Canadians oversees all operations of TC 207; under them is working group 1, which is responsible for the environmental aspect in product standards. After that comes:
- Subcommittee 1 is responsible for the development of the standard for environmental management systems:

  Working group 1 in this subcommittee works on specifications for environmental management systems.

  Working group 2 is responsible for general guidelines for environmental management systems.
- Subcommittee 2 is developing the standard for environmental auditing and related environmental investigations:

  Working group 1 is developing the general principles for this topic.

  Working group 2 is creating audit procedures.

  Working group 3 is responsible for qualification criteria for environmental auditors.

  Working group 4 is looking at environmental site assessment.
- Subcommittee 3 is developing a standard for environmental labeling:

  Working group 1 addresses guiding principles for environmental labeling practitioner programs and systems.

Working group 2 looks at type II (self-declarations) environmental labeling.

Working group 3 addresses basic principles of all environmental labeling.

- Subcommittee 4 works on the standard for environmental performance evaluation:

  Working group 1 looks at ways to evaluate the environmental performance of the management system and its relationship to the environment.

  Working group 2 addresses the evaluation of the environmental performance of the operational system and its relationship to the environment.

- Subcommittee 5 creates the standard for life-cycle assessment:

  Working group 1 is responsible for general principles and procedures.

  Working group 2 covers life-cycle inventory analysis general.

  Working group 3 covers life-cycle inventory analysis specific.

  Working group 4 addresses life-cycle impact assessment.

  Working group 5 looks at life-cycle improvement analysis.

- Subcommittee 6 is responsible for the standard for terms and definitions.

Each country gets one vote on each new standard. Many countries form what is called a Technical Advisory Group (TAG). In the U.S., the TAG is run by two groups. The American Society for Testing and Measurement (ASTM) directs the TAG activities for subcommittees 3, 4, 5, and 6, as well as the TAG activities for TC 207 in general. The American Society for Quality Control (ASQC) directs the TAG activities for subcommittees 1 and 2.

Individuals can also participate as observers or active members of a TAG. In the U.S., the points of contact are:

Rose Tomasello
ASTM
1916 Race Street
Philadelphia, PA 19103
(215) 299-5487 (Phone)
(215) 299-2630 (Fax)

and

Patricia Kopp
ASQC
611 E. Wisconsin Avenue
P.O. Box 3005
Milwaukee, WI 53201
(414) 272-8575 (Phone)
(800) 248-1946 (Phone)
(414) 272-1734 (Fax)

These contacts can provide you with copies of working documents, schedules of upcoming meetings, and information on how to join the TAG. For other countries, consult your national standards body on who coordinates your national TAG. By joining a TAG, you will also receive the constant stream of documents and memorandums being used in TC 207. Although at times it is confusing, this is a way to monitor the development and revision of ISO 14000 directly.

THE GOALS OF TC 207

When TC 207 was formed, a set of guiding principles was created for the development of an international standard for environmental management systems. The overall goal of the technical committee was to trade a basic and uniform set of standards that can assist an organization in achieving its environmental objectives, using effective management tools and systems while at the same time protecting against potential negative impact on trade and commerce. The technical committee believes that a large collection of national standards would serve only to impede world trade. So they proposed an international standard that would assist international trade.

This general goal was further defined by ten principles the committees would use in the development of the ISO 14000 family of standards:

1. Advance environmental management through the promotion of uniform, effective, and efficient management techniques.
2. Develop pragmatic and scientifically based environmental management standards that reflect current best practices.
3. Create standards that are cost-effective, nonprescriptive, and flexible, which will add to the value of organizations that use these standards.
4. Discourage the use of an environmental management standard as a trade barrier.
5. Harmonize the international standard for environmental management systems with local and national standards.
6. Avoid setting specific performance levels, goals, objectives, policies, or rates of improvement.
7. Create an environmental management standard that is usable by the internal organization or by an external third-party certification body (registrar).
8. Avoid any environmental management standards that would require a company to divulge its goals, policies, or targets to the public.
9. Build environmental standards through consensus of the interested parties for voluntary adoption by affected organizations to benefit all parties.

10. Harmonize and minimize environmental management standards to avoid duplication and unnecessary expense.

ISO 14000 GETS PLACED ON A FAST TRACK

These guiding principles are then used by the working groups and subcommittees. The process of creating an international standard is lengthy and time consuming. In the case of ISO 9000, it took many years to develop the final standard—even though the technical committee started with an existing national standard. In the case of ISO 14000, the technical committee was placed on a fast track. That meant that the regular procedures and votes used to create a new standard would be retained, but the schedule would be accelerated.

The path to a new international standard takes a course similar to the following. First, a technical committee is established; then subcommittees are proposed to address particular tasks. Each of these tasks is seen as a separate project. The technical committee approves each project. Each approved subcommittee can, if it wishes, divide into working groups.

Usually, each working group holds several meetings to prepare a rough draft of the proposed new standard. For example, working group 1 of subcommittee 1 of Technical Committee 207 would draft the document that eventually becomes ISO 14001—specifications for an environmental management system. Such a document would be discussed thoroughly by the working group before it is released as a Working Group Draft.

The Working Group Draft is sent to the subcommittee for registration as the First Committee Draft. Typically, at least three months of comments are elicited from the technical committee and participating organizations. Those comments and the replies from the secretariat are compiled and published. The subcommittee then considers all the comments and replies. If all comments can be addressed at the subcommittee level, the Committee Draft is now registered as a Draft International Standard. It is also translated into French and other languages. This entire process takes about 24 months.

Once issued as a Draft International Standard (DIS), the document goes into a cycle of votes. Additional comments are collected and a first vote is taken. The DIS is sent to the International Organization for Standardization and to the committee for standards for the European Union. Here it goes through a second and usually final vote. If the international community and the European Union are in agreement, they will jointly adopt the standard. If they disagree, then the European Union is free to develop its own standard.

Once approved, the DIS becomes a true international standard. It is sent out for typesetting and final editing, which takes about one month. The international standard is then sent to the copyright holders within each country. Those organizations then translate the standard into the countries' native languages, if necessary, and may give it a national title. For example, ISO 9000 in the U.S. is called Q-9000.

At the writing of this book, ISO 14000 was a Draft International Standard (DIS). The Committee Draft was already accepted as a national standard by Austria and other countries, allowing them to begin registering companies to the standard. It is anticipated that the final version of ISO 14000 will be similar to the DIS.

THE FUTURE OF ISO 9000 AND ITS IMPACT ON ISO 14000

Like ISO 9000, the ISO 14000 standard was developed using the same technical committee system just described. One of the major goals of this book is to show how these two standards can coexist.

In 1999, the ISO 9000 standard is scheduled for its second set of revisions. This will be a more comprehensive revision of that standard than occurred in 1994. The aspect of this revision that most affects our discussion is the broadening of the ISO 9000 family of standards to include portions of other management issues, such as health, safety, finance, and the environment.

This means that ISO 14000 will move from being a cousin of ISO 9000 to being a full sister to the standard. Companies should be aware of how this will affect the way they plan out their management systems, regardless of the topic being addressed. Exhibit 2-2 shows how several types of management systems can have overlapping common elements.

In addition, the practices of other fields of management are being incorporated with environmental activities. For example, the U.S. Department of the Interior, Fish, and Wildlife Service has a total quality management program and plan. The plan is called "Vision for the Future" (1991).

A management system designed to conform to environmental requirements will have elements similar to a system set up to address quality-related issues. As discussed before, the creation of British Standard 7750 borrowed heavily from British Standard 5750 for quality assurance management systems. This is inevitable because any management system will logically be based on similar elements.

Some of these common elements could be any of the following:

- Management commitment
- Business plans
- Document control
- Use of documentation
- Corrective action
- Preventive measures
- Training

Exhibit 2-2: The Overlapping Nature of Management Systems and Their Common Concerns

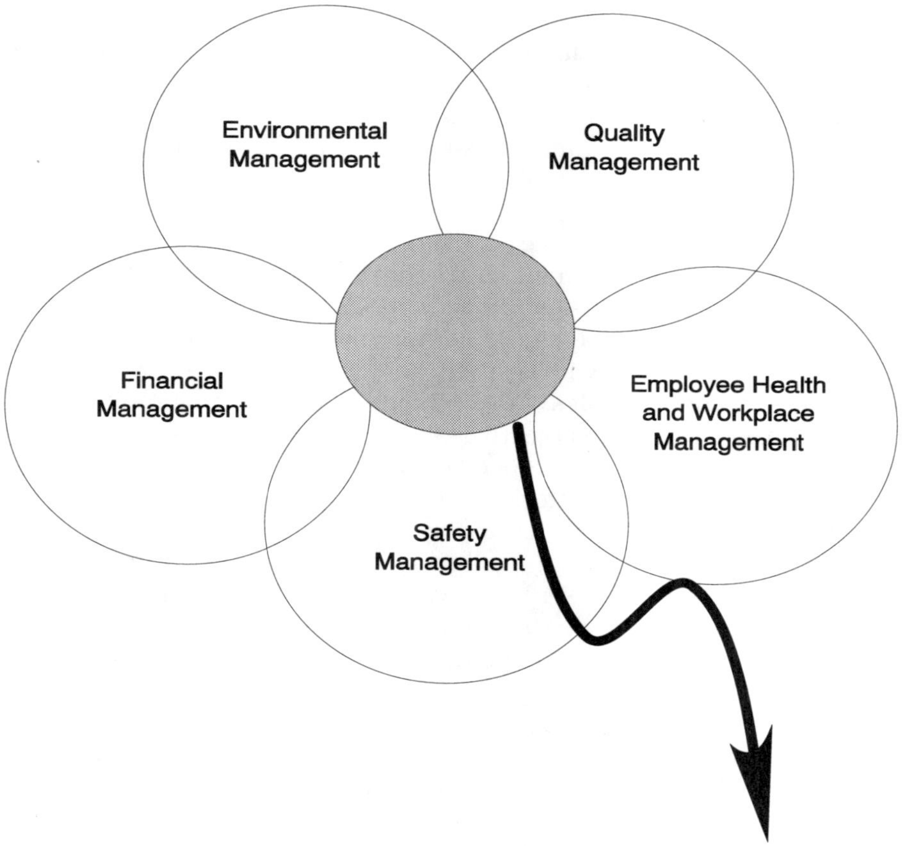

Common Concerns:

+ Management Commitment
+ Management Plans
+ Document Control
+ Corrective Actions
+ Preventive Actions
+ Training
+ Continuous Improvement
+ Supplier Relations

- Continuous improvement
- Supplier relations
- Communication with employees
- Internal audits

As we shall see, many of these elements will be part of your company's environmental management system. However, be aware that other parts of your company's general system of management will have to coexist with the environmental management system. Therefore, do not plan a system that is in any way incompatible with the current management culture. Also, additional paperwork and procedures should be minimized.

The commitment of management to the goals and objectives of any management system is critical for success. Commitment is seen as the dedication of resources, such as time and money, to the implementation of the new system. Managers are expected to assist in implementation, support the program, and convince doubters. Without management commitment, more immediate problems will derail the implementation of your system.

Let's look at some examples. Any company requires a comprehensive business plan. Such a plan lays out the objectives of the company, explains how these objectives will be accomplished, and specifies who is responsible for achieving each objective. For an environmental management system, a company needs only to add its environmental objectives to such a plan.

Crucial to any management system is a way to control critical documents. Such document control is present in any type of organized management system. This is especially true of an environmental management system because many of the documents will be critical for demonstrating compliance with environmental regulations.

In fact, any management system requires the use of documentation. This includes written policies, procedures, and work instructions. It also includes written records of the data obtained while the system is being used. In a management system for quality assurance, such records are called quality records. In an environmental management system, the data collected will be called environmental records.

All management systems require a form of self-examination to determine whether the system as planned is the system being implemented. It should also include an evaluation of whether the system is effective. Internal auditing is the most common way to make such evaluations. Internal audits will look closely at a company's corrective action system because the way it takes corrective action determines how well the management system responds to problems.

One way to evaluate the effectiveness of a management system is to see if there is an established procedure for preventive action. Preventive action means that the root cause of problems are investigated and system-wide actions are taken by management to ensure that the root cause of a problem never occurs again.

Another common element to any management system is the liberal use of training to improve the skills of employees and to communicate the policies of the company. Training should involve a systematic approach to education both inside and outside the company. Besides training, managers should use other methods to communicate policies and instructions to their staff and to the employees at large. These can include methods such as monthly meetings, company newsletters, memorandums, walking around the factory floor, and one-on-one conversations.

A recent addition to the list of characteristics of any management system is the concept of *continuous improvement.* Continuous improvement is the incremental movement of the company toward better methods and higher quality. It means that each day every manager and every employee should be thinking of some way to get their job done a little faster, cheaper, or more effectively. The quality of processes and products should also be improved wherever and whenever possible.

Finally, a good management system should be evangelical in nature. In other words, your company should spread the objectives of its management system to the network of companies that supply your company with goods, raw materials, and services. This can best be implemented through coordinated supplier relationships. In the case of a quality system, you would use the model applied to your company as a requirement for your suppliers. For example, ISO 9000 companies tend to require ISO 9000 compliance from their suppliers. In the same way, your company can involve suppliers in the objective of meeting specific environmental goals.

ENVIRONMENTAL MANAGEMENT SYSTEMS SHOULD BE FULLY INCORPORATED INTO A COMPANY'S CURRENT PRACTICES

In the next chapter, we will look at the specific requirements of an environmental management system under ISO 14001. A management system is not developed in a vacuum. Your company has been in business for some time. Somehow it has managed to get work done, cope with problems, and, perhaps, make a profit. Whether or not it is documented, you have an existing management system.

Thus, the development of your environmental management system will begin by first examining your current system of management. When ISO 14000 was drafted, this was a critical point to be considered—namely, that the environmental management system could be easily integrated into virtually any existing management structure. Later in this book, we will look more closely at companies using ISO 9000 as a model for a management system and see how they can incorporate ISO 14000 rather painlessly.

SUMMARY

The development of ISO 14000 was initiated and completed in a unique atmosphere of several political trends related to the environment. We saw that the drive for world trade played an important role. Also, we learned that ISO 9000 and BS 7750 were inspirations for the form and nature of ISO 14000. As we shall soon see, the requirements of ISO 14000 overlap many requirements of any documented management system. In particular, it shares many elements and a registration scheme with ISO 9000.

Chapter 3

ISO 14004 AND ISO 14001—A CLOSE LOOK AT THE ENVIRONMENTAL STANDARD

In the introduction to this book, I discussed the difference between environmentalism and environmental management systems. Environmentalism is a set of philosophies on how humans should deal with the natural environment. An environmental management system is how a company deals with the immediate environment inside and outside their facilities.

ISO 14000 is actually a collection of standards that present a uniform model for an environmental management system. This family of standards addresses many issues related to the environment. In this chapter, we will look at the two central standards in the family of standards, ISO 14004 and ISO 14001. ISO 14004 is the guideline standard for a family of environmental standards. The others being developed are:

ISO 14001—Specification of Environmental Management Systems

ISO 14010 through ISO 14015—Environmental Auditing and Related Activities

ISO 14020 through ISO 14024—Environmental Labeling

ISO 14031 and ISO 14032—Environmental Performance Evaluation

ISO 14040 through ISO 14043—Life Cycle Assessment

ISO 14050—Terms and Definitions

ISO Guide 64—Product Specifications

In Appendix B is a complete list of the standards already developed and those that are being considered for development.

HOW ISO 14004 SETS DOWN THE GENERAL APPROACH TO AN ENVIRONMENTAL MANAGEMENT SYSTEM

ISO 14004 shares many characteristics with its cousin ISO 9004. For one thing, a company is free to shape its management system to fit the needs of its size, market, and economic situation. Also, some of the elements of a management system are the same.

ISO 14004—Environmental Management Systems–General Guideline on Principles, Systems, and Supporting Techniques is a very important document that you should read first. By studying this standard, you will learn the general approach to an environmental management system. You will also find many suggestions on how to design and implement such an environmental management system.

ISO 14004 is actually a guideline standard intended to help any organization to implement or improve an environmental management system. The goal is to maintain and improve the quality of the environment a company controls and to protect human health. That means looking at the potential impact of the company's activities, products, and services. ISO 14004 points out that concern for the environment is of increasing importance to both internal and external parties to achieve an effective management system approach and a commitment to continuous improvement.

In the introduction of ISO 14004, the standard lays out the basic principles of an environmental management system, which include the following:

- Place environmental management as a top corporate priority.
- Communicate with interested internal and external parties.
- Determine all regulations and requirements that apply to the company and its products.
- Establish management and employee commitment to the protection of the environment.
- Establish clear assignments of responsibility and accountability.
- Consider environmental impacts throughout the product life cycle.
- Establish environmental targets and a disciplined approach to achieving those targets.
- Provide appropriate resources, including training.
- Regularly review the environmental management system while looking for opportunities for improvement.
- Encourage suppliers and subcontractors to also adopt an environmental management system.

The ISO 14004 standard is not intended for use as a registration standard. That is the function of ISO 14001. Instead, ISO 14004 is a guidance standard for any company regardless of size, type, or level of maturity. The standard is structured on a model of continuous improvement following these steps:

4.1 How to Start: Commitment and Policy

4.2 Planning

4.3 Implementation

4.4 Measurement and Evaluation

4.5 Review and Improvement

These are also the major headings in the table of contents. A company starts with commitment by top management and a written environmental policy. Then they plan how they will conform to regulations and customer requirements. This also means the establishment of environmental targets. The plan is then implemented ensuring that adequate resources are available and that management provide supporting actions. When the system is in place, continuous measurement and evaluation take place. The management of your company should regularly review the system for its effectiveness, take corrective actions where needed, and look for opportunities for improvement. The last two steps are repeated in an upward spiral of continuous improvement.

ISO 14004 is really a road map toward an environmental management system. Each detail in the previously shown steps are discussed thoroughly. For example, during implementation there is a discussion about how to ensure that a company has adequate resources for an environmental management system. This is Section 4.3.2 in ISO 14004. It asks questions that can serve as a checklist for your documentation plan, such as does your company have a way to evaluate the environmental resources needed within a particular capital project?

Located in a box under this section is a practical help guide. In the example, the standard suggests that a company with limited resources look into cooperative ventures with interested organizations. This could be the local university, other members of the supply chain, professional societies, chambers of commerce, or government agencies.

As you can see, ISO 14004 is designed as a helpful document for a company's implementation efforts. Therefore, this standard should be consulted first before studying ISO 14001.

ISO 14004 SUGGESTIONS FOR WHAT TO DO DURING IMPLEMENTATION

Registering your company as complying with an international standard on the environment means a huge marketing advantage. Customers like to see this, investors like it, and the local community likes it too. Also, it gives you a single management system to control and track that 20 linear feet of environmental regulations you have lining your desk.

Therefore, begin by looking at your company's current situation. The first goal is to seek and receive full senior management support for implementing such a system. If the company is already ISO 9000 compliant, it will be the expansion of your current system. You also need to know to which external environmental regulations the company must comply.

Next, an internal audit of the company's environmental system is required. Taking your list of environmental regulations, evaluate each for its costs and potential risks of nonconformance. If direct measurement of compliance is possible, collect the data for comparison to your intended targets. For example, if the noise level in your plant should not exceed 102db, test the level of noise at various points and time in the factory. In Chapter 8, we will look at the methods of auditing environmental impacts and the environmental management system in greater detail.

Also look for any written policies, procedures, or work instructions related to environmental concerns. These should be noted for later reference. Be sure to look at your contractual conditions in both customer and supplier contracts too.

Finally, interview the people in charge of conformance. If the plant manager signs off on discharge permits, interview him or her to gain more knowledge of the current system and its flaws. Also look for opportunities for improvement or competitive advantages. For example, if you find that you recycle skids and the competitors don't, then you have a potential market wedge. When interviewing, don't overlook the possibility of talking to local, state, and federal agencies to get up-to-date information on what conformances are expected.

IMPLEMENTING AN ENVIRONMENTAL MANAGEMENT SYSTEM

There are several steps that lead to a cost-efficient and effective environmental management system, which will now be discussed in detail.

1. *Management commitment.* As with ISO 9000, you must seek and receive complete commitment from the senior management of your company. An environmental management system is really just another good business practice that should be embraced by any well-informed management team.

2. *Initial review.* When senior management is committed, you must lead an initial review of your company's current management practices. As with an ISO 9000 internal audit, you want to look at practices, training, record keeping, policies, work instructions, and other resources dedicated to meeting environmental needs. Of course, part of this initial review will be the preparation of a list of the environmental requirements of your company. You will have to dig through regulations, guidelines, and other documents. However, you can always call the appropriate agencies to help you out. In Michigan, the Department of Natural Resources (Environmental Quality) assists businesses in determining which regulations apply. Also, voluntary groups (e.g., local environmental groups) might also be able to help.

3. *Establish a plan.* Armed with the information on what you have to comply with and the general strengths and weaknesses of your current management practices, you can now develop an action plan. In particular, you will want to quantify your requirements, such as decibels of noise allowed in the factory, discharge levels permitted, tons of trash needing disposal each year, scrap rates, and so on. These quantified targets will also show management the opportunities to save money. For example, reducing waste means paying less to have it disposed.

4. *Evaluate the environmental aspects and risks.* Using your list of requirements, prioritize your particular situations. That is, you now have to list the actual environmental aspects (impacts) of your company. To each of these identified aspects, you must evaluate the level of risk involved with conformance and nonconformance. For example, too high a noise level in the factory invites complaints and lawsuits from employees. Meeting the target level means fewer costs but still some minor problems. Reducing noise below mandated levels could mean higher productivity. The cost/benefit ratios must be estimated as closely as possible.

5. *Establish an environmental policy.* Now the company's management can initiate the action plan by writing an environmental policy. You can't just write that you like a clean world with little waste. You must be specific to your company. For example, set specific goals with measurable targets. This will give employees and other interested parties the information they need to know and what they have to do to help achieve these goals.

6. *Implementation.* For an environmental action plan, the first step in implementation is usually to clean up the obvious problems. These are the areas where you already know you are not complying with regulations or customer demands. After that, target areas where you stand to gain greater efficiencies. This includes scrap and waste reduction projects, recycling, and elimination of liabilities. After that, settle into a system of considering environmental impacts during all business decisions, especially those taken in the Design Control phase of ISO 9000. Sustained development and continuous improvement are the watch words.

7. *Monitor for improvement opportunities.* Along with quality control plans, you may want to develop environmental control plans. These plans outline the process of a particular product or service with the identification of critical points for verification of the process. What is being verified is the environmental concern at critical points. For example, the use of a caustic chemical to etch parts would be a point at which worker exposure levels might be continually monitored. With such targets well established, teams can be formed to first meet the targets and then exceed them.

As with any management system, you will need to have adequate resources dedicated to the system. This includes people with the background, education, and experience to cope with environmental issues. Corrective action has to be very proactive and well structured. All corrective actions must be documented and reviewed by management.

In addition, you will need to calibrate and maintain monitoring equipment. Also, internal audits are required to make sure the entire system is working properly. In fact, many of the elements of ISO 9000 can be used in your environmental management system with few modifications. The biggest step may be writing policy statements and control plans. Existing procedures and work instructions for ISO 9000 will need to be slightly expanded to account for your environmental situations.

AN EXAMPLE OF CREATING AN ACTION PLAN

As with ISO 9000, the environmental management system must be carefully planned out to be successful. Eventually, you will develop a complete plan of action for the implementation of your environmental management system. Creating an action plan begins with some preliminary research. Following is a list of the type of activities you should engage in before following the implementation steps just outlined. Pay particular attention to assigning specific top managers to be responsible for developing the following:

1. *Identify environmental regulations and issues.* Typically, the head of engineering or the supervisor of your legal department is responsible for listing all environmental regulations, internal environmental concerns, legal issues, and customer requirements. This involves reviewing all contracts, union agreements, and regulations. Someone has to call all local, state, regional, and national government agencies responsible for environmental issues to determine the regulations that apply to your company. Subscribing to a service that provides this information and updates on a regular basis is highly recommended.

2. *Evaluate the impact of each issue.* For each environmental issue uncovered, you must make a judgment on the impact it poses. For example, if your product is not biodegradable, you have to evaluate the environmental impact of its disposal versus the cost of changing the raw materials, design, or disposal methods.

3. *Develop an environmental policy.* At this point, be ready to draft an initial environmental policy for your company. This should be submitted to a committee of top managers for consideration.

4. *Set initial criteria.* From your database of environmental regulations and issues, you should be able to identify target levels requested by regulations, internal needs, and customer demands. Eventually, this list of initial environmental targets will be considered by a committee of top managers. Each target will be evaluated for its practicality and economic impact.

5. *Establish targets and objectives that are measurable.* For each environmental target and policy objective, the environmental management system manager will have to establish how objective measurements will be taken. That means that some criteria will have to be translated into a form that allows for discrete measurement. For example, if your company states that its intention is to have minimal impact on the floral and fauna of the land it owns, you must devise a way to measure this. Perhaps you will perform an annual census of animal species on your property. Another possibility would be an environmental survey of the land. The environmental issues are likely to involve topics such as noise, discharges, recycling, environmental impact, storage safety, and disposal.

When the issues are identified, create ways to measure their current levels against an established set of targets or objectives. The targets and objectives are frequently set for you in regulations and industrial standards. For example, the parts per million for a specific chemical being discharged into a city sewer system is usually set by law. Using these targets, objectively measure your company's level of compliance.

This database of knowledge on customer requirements and applicable regulations will really assist your implementation efforts. You need this level of knowledge before you read ISO 14001. Later, after you have studied ISO 14001, you will write out a strategic plan on how you will implement an environmental management system to meet your targets and objectives, as well as promote continuous improvement. The market and economic issues involved in your implementation should be clearly addressed. If a new air filtration system costs $5 million, then the impact on profitability must be evaluated.

HOW TO IMPLEMENT A COMPANY'S STRATEGIC PLAN

The next step is to implement your company's strategic plan. Begin where actions will have the greatest benefit for your company. The cost savings and the cleaner conditions will be obvious to all and will create more support for future actions. We shall see how this is done in detail after the discussion of ISO 14001 that comes later in this chapter.

As with ISO 9000, you must assign specific tasks to specific managers. Otherwise, employees will see this as work outside their normal duties and implementation will suffer. At the same time, you now need senior management support to get the people, money, and time resources to complete the job. Also, top management must continually inform everyone about the company environmental policy. As with quality, employees must know how their job affects environmental issues.

The hard part of implementation is to integrate your environmental goals, procedures, and objectives into the everyday operations of the company. What will make this even harder is to point these out as being "environmental issues." That makes the actions look like something unrelated to the process, or it invokes a negative reaction in many people.

A better road to implementation is to take the positive aspect of the change and give it a proper name, such as "waste reduction," "quality of work life," or "community friendly." Environmentalism is a political movement that has created strong opinions. Negative opinions are best avoided by having employees see that ISO 14000 is not environmentalism, it is environmental management—the practical control of items or actions that have a direct impact on the surrounding environment.

CONTINUOUS IMPROVEMENT OF THE SYSTEM

Once your environmental management system is in place, your job is to continually monitor its progress. This can be done through various means, but in general there will be daily measurement of the measurable impacts and an annual audit of the system in general.

This process of monitoring will alert you to conditions that require corrective actions. It will also point out where real improvements have been made. All of this information should be reviewed by top management so that they can update and revise the strategic environmental plan.

The idea is to promote the continuous improvement of the system and the environmental friendliness of the company.

SUMMARY OF THE FORMATION OF AN ENVIRONMENTAL POLICY

The best way to look at an environmental policy is to think in terms of conservation of resources. In other words, you want to waste as little as possible. The result is less environmental impact and better profitability. For example, if your plastic injection machine wastes 100 pounds of resin during setup, you have a considerable loss. The resin must either be reprocessed (using up more energy) or disposed of. However, if the setup method is optimized so that only a few pounds of resin are wasted, energy is conserved and the production run costs less. Taguchi's axiom that quality is measured by the loss to society works equally as well for environmental issues. In Chapter 6, we will examine joint implementation of ISO 9000 and ISO 14000.

ISO 14000 AND THE SMALL BUSINESS

The people working to develop international standards learned a lesson from ISO 9000: As the ISO 14000 standards are being developed, a separate guideline is available for the small business. About 70 percent of the world's economy is fed by companies with fewer than 200 employees. This fact initially escaped the attention of the developers of ISO 9000. Today, registrars are scrambling to develop audit plans and fee structures specifically for these small businesses. The ISO 14000 developers are attacking the issue while the standard is still a Draft International Standard.

WHY BEING SMALL DOESN'T MEAN THAT A COMPANY CAN'T HAVE AN ENVIRONMENTAL MANAGEMENT SYSTEM

A chief criticism of ISO 9000 after its release was that it did not address the special situations and needs of the small business, especially small manufacturing enterprises (SMEs). At the 1994 TC 207 meeting in Vienna, a special group dedicated to creating guidelines for small- and medium-sized enterprises presented a proposed appendix for ISO 14004. These guidelines are being developed to make ISO 14000 more adaptable to the small business owner. The small business owner has many issues and problems to confront everyday. Besides being CEO for the company, he or she is also involved in its ownership and several other tasks. Therefore, the idea of building an environmental management system seems like an expenditure of more time and money. In reality, it doesn't have to be either.

In today's economy, being "green" presents a company with a distinct marketing advantage for its product. In addition, it is already faced with hundreds of regulations related to the environment—from health and safety issues to ecological impacts. Then there is the ever present need to cut internal costs. Add to that the social conscience some owners have and you quickly see the need for a single system to address all these problems. The good news is that an environmental management system does not have to be a separate entity. Instead, if a company has already implemented ISO 9000, it has its environmental management system just about in place.

IMPLEMENTING AN ENVIRONMENTAL MANAGEMENT SYSTEM WITHIN A SMALL BUSINESS

There are several steps that lead to a cost-efficient and effective environmental management system. The proposed appendix of ISO 14004 contains many suggestions on how this is possible. The small business owner may discover that he or she has to talk to suppliers of materials to get a list of possible environmental hazards or the regulations that will apply. The small business owner can also work closely with a larger customer corporation to gain further information by examining the customer's environmental management system. There are also support groups and professional organizations specifically designed to help the small business owner.

The location of the small business in the business chain will determine the level of environmental conformance required. Typically, the small business will be more concerned about short-term planning instead of long-term planning for environmental conformance. Long-term planning is not usually the domain of the small business. Therefore, the small business owner must be constantly aware of regulations and customer requirements.

Implementation of an environmental management system by a small business will proceed in small stages. The implementation rate will be determined by available resources to raise employee awareness and to develop needed procedures. A small business should begin with requirements that will return maximum economic benefits to the company. For example, the reduction of waste represents conformance with several environmental requirements while also cutting the cost of production and the cost of disposal.

The sharing of resources and know-how is an economical strategy for groups of small businesses. For example, the training of employees can be done as a group effort, with the participating companies sharing the cost, resulting in a lower per company cost.

The small business may discover that it has to develop a documented management system as part of a customer's requirements. For example, more than 50,000 small companies have to comply with TE-9000, a customer supplier quality assurance program based on ISO 9001. While developing such documentation, it would be fairly easy to expand the implementation to include an environmental management system.

In short, many of the elements of ISO 9000 can be used in a company's environmental management system with little modifications. In fact, the biggest step may be writing policy statements and control plans. Existing procedures and work instructions for ISO 9000 need to be slightly expanded to account for environmental situations (see Chapter 6).

Most important of all is that massive amounts of documentation are not required for a small business. Many times it will be able to combine work instructions into procedures. In addition, a small business will find that often its procedures can cover many of the requirements for ISO 14001.

SUMMARY OF ISO 14004

A company without an environmental management system and with a poor environmental record is probably going to find it harder to do business in the future. Customers are already not awarding contracts to questionable companies because they fear the bad publicity of an environmental scandal. In addition, banks tend to shy away from companies that may be doing environmental harm. At the same time, they are attracted to companies with well-documented management systems.

ISO 14001—SPECIFICATIONS FOR AN ENVIRONMENTAL MANAGEMENT SYSTEM

ISO 14001 is the standard used when seeking registration or demonstration of an environmental management system. It spells out the actual requirements for an environmental management system. Please keep in mind that these are considered the minimal number of requirements for an environmental management system.

The standard has the actual requirements contained within Section 4, just like ISO 9001. Other parts of ISO 14001 have information on definitions, purpose, and other useful information. Read through these carefully. For now, we will examine only Section 4.

The elements of Section 4 are

- **4.0** General
- **4.1** Environmental Policy
- **4.2** Planning
  - **4.2.1** Environmental Aspects
  - **4.2.2** Legal and Other Requirements
  - **4.2.3** Objectives and Targets
  - **4.2.4** Environmental Management Program
- **4.3** Implementation and Operation
  - **4.3.1** Structure and Responsibility
  - **4.3.2** Training, Awareness, and Competence
  - **4.3.3** Communications
  - **4.3.4** Environmental Management System Documentation
  - **4.3.5** Document Control
  - **4.3.6** Operational Control
  - **4.3.7** Emergency Preparedness and Response
- **4.4** Checking and Corrective Action
  - **4.4.1** Monitoring and Measurement
  - **4.4.2** Nonconformance and Corrective and Preventive Action
  - **4.4.3** Records
  - **4.4.4** Environmental Management System Audit
- **4.5** Management Review

Please keep in mind that we are discussing drafts that are still in transition. However, these working documents will soon become fully approved international standards, most likely at the end of 1996. By looking at them now, we can get a rough idea of what to expect. Even more importantly, we will discover that the ISO 9000 systems already in place at your company will help you dovetail in the 14000 series of standards. Even without an ISO 9000 system you can quickly learn how to implement your management system using both families of standards.

THE ISO 14001 STANDARD EXAMINED IN DETAIL

Many companies today conduct environmental audits of their facilities to see if they conform to local, state, and federal regulations. However, these audits by themselves will not guarantee continuous improvement or future conformance. Only a well-established environmental management system can do that. The thrust of ISO 14001 is to give a company the minimal structure for such a system.

A key point to remember when discussing ISO 14001 is that it shares an important characteristic with ISO 9001—namely, it won't produce an environmentally friendly company by itself. In the same way that ISO 9001 will not make the quality of your product automatically improve, ISO 14001 only establishes the potential for a good system. It is up to your management to set the level of environmental impact to obtain and then seek those targets.

A second key point to remember is that the draft international standard says specifically that an ISO 9000 system can be used as the model of a single management system that addresses both quality and environmental issues. Your health and safety issues can also be wrapped into this same system.

Finally, you can use the proposed ISO 14001 for any of several purposes, such as

- Creating an environmental management system
- Auditing your environmental management system
- Seeking third-party certification
- Seeking customer recognition of your environmental management system
- Declaring your environmental management system to the general public

A BRIEF REVIEW OF DOCUMENTATION REQUIREMENTS FOR MANAGEMENT STANDARDS

As with ISO 9000, ISO 14001 requires a system of documentation. Documentation is the main method of demonstrating the existence of an effective management system. Therefore, documentation will be required within any environmental management system.

As with ISO 9000, companies will be dealing with four levels of documentation. Those levels are

Level I—Policy statements. Policy statements are brief statements as to why your company complies with the requirements stated in ISO 14001. Such statements should also name the job title of the person responsible for ensuring that the particular element of your system is implemented and maintained. Typically, policy statements are published as a group in a manual. Normally, we would call such a book an Environmental Manual. However, if you are already using an ISO 9000 type management system, you should already have a Quality Manual that contains policy statements, your company-wide quality policy, and an organizational chart for the corporation. If you have such a manual, then your policy statements for an environmental management system can be incorporated into it. Otherwise, you will have to create a unique Environmental Manual. Appendix D contains some illustrations of these.

Level II—Standard operating procedures. Standard operating procedures are a description of a specific process. In other words, a process made up of many steps or tasks involving many people. The purpose of an operating procedure is to describe the how, when, where, who, and what of this process. Such procedures are usually placed into standard operating procedure manuals. For example, under ISO 9000, you would have your procedures within a book called the Quality Procedures Manual. The same will be true for ISO 14000. Appendix D contains some illustrations of these.

Level III—Written work instructions. Work instructions are intended to describe the steps taken to accomplish a single task. Typically, this task is performed by an individual. The work instructions can be included with the procedures in a Quality Procedures Manual. Or some or all of the work instructions can be contained in a single procedures manual. Sometimes the work instructions are deployed throughout the company as individual documents. Appendix D contains some illustrations of these.

Level IV—Records. When procedures or work instructions are completed, they create a trail of records. In the case of ISO 9000, these were called the quality records. Under ISO 14000, these will be called the environmental records. Either way, these records are controlled by requirements laid out in the standard.

CREATING THE LEVELS OF DOCUMENTATION WITHIN AN ENVIRONMENTAL MANAGEMENT SYSTEM

Within an environmental management system, you will need to create policy statements, standard operating procedures, written work instructions, and environmental records. This will include a written company-wide policy on the company's position on environmental issues.

The policy statements and an organizational chart of your company showing lines of responsibility will be used to create the Environmental Manual. In later chapters, I will show you how to incorporate these policy statements into an existing quality manual. You must create a set of procedures that meet all the requirements set out in Section 4 of ISO 14001. Many of these procedures would already exist if your company was in compliance with ISO 9000.

You will also have to create written work instructions for particular tasks that will be required under any environmental management system. These work instructions will have to reference the procedures that call out the task being performed. You will also have to establish a systematic and well-controlled method of recording and storing environmental records. Such records will have to be easily retrievable and protected from damage. Detailed examples of each level of documentation are presented in Appendix D. These will serve only as suggestions and guidelines for creating your company's documentation.

THE REQUIREMENTS OF ISO 14001

"The organization shall establish and maintain an environmental management system . . ." begins Section 4 of ISO 14001. As in ISO 9001, Section 4 contains all the requirements you have to meet. Also as in ISO 9001, the word "shall" means you must take this action. You must have a well-documented environmental management system that can be demonstratable to an auditor as being in conformance and effective.

HOW TO SATISFY ELEMENT 4.1–ENVIRONMENTAL POLICY

Senior management must write and make known a company-wide policy on environmental issues. Remember, this is not environmentalism. It is anything that has an impact on your surrounding environment (e.g., noise, quality of work life, discharge, scrap, disposal of products, neighborhood aesthetics, and so on). It should also involve the impacts known during the life cycle analysis of your product or service.

Such a company-wide environmental policy should have the following characteristics:

- Is appropriate to the size, nature, and economy of your company
- Considers the activities, products, and services produced by your company
- Shows your commitment to the prevention of pollution
- Shows your commitment to continuous improvement

- States that you will comply with regulations and customer requirements
- States that you will set environmental objectives and targets
- States that you will review environmental objectives and targets on a regular basis
- Is written, implemented, and communicated to all employees
- Is available to the public

Your environmental policy must be relevant to the size and nature of your company and the impact it has on its environment. It must state that continuous improvement is one of your strategic goals. It must say that you will comply with all relevant regulations. It must state how and when you will review your system, including your stated targets and objectives. All employees have to be aware of your policy, and it has to be made available to the public.

Let's look at an example of a policy. In this case, we are assuming that a large corporation with many manufacturing facilities and facing many regulations and customer requirements has written its environmental policy statement.

> *The XYZ corporation recognizes that it has a responsibility to control, maintain, and improve the environment under its control. Stewardship of the environment is a critical strategic policy for the XYZ corporation. Therefore, each division of this corporation shall have a permanent standing committee of top managers who regularly plan, control, and monitor an environmental management system. The main goal of such systems will be the prevention of pollution, the meeting of all relevant regulations, and the satisfaction of customer requirements related to environmental issues. These committees will establish quantifiable objectives and targets for environmental conformance. Each environmental management system will be committed to the principle of continuous improvement. All goals, targets, objectives, and the EMS system will be completely reviewed by executive level management at least annually.*

As you can see from this statement, most of the requirements for a company-wide policy on the environment have been met. In addition, the statement specifically states the strategic importance of an environmental management system. It is now up to the management to make sure that this company-wide policy is communicated to and understood by all employees. The managers also have to make this policy available to the public. This can be done in any of many ways, such as printing the policy on all company brochures.

HOW TO SATISFY ELEMENT 4.2—PLANNING

Planning begins by defining where your company can control or influence the environmental results of its operations, products, and services. Management has to identify which of these control points have significant impact on the environment.

One way to help in this part of the planning phase is to compile an up-to-date list of environmental regulations and requirements that apply to your company. To this list, you would also include customer requirements that are related to the environment.

For example, in the U.S., parts of the right-to-know law says that your company must submit information on the hazardous chemicals you use to such agencies as the local fire department (for emergency response planning) and environmental protection agencies. Your customer may also ask you to design your products for maximum recycling capabilities. Both of these requirements would go on your list of environmental control points.

Obtaining this information is not always easy. Someone has to read each customer contract and determine which requirements have environmental concerns. The best way to handle this situation is to look for these environmental requirements during contract review and design control phases of your management system. In addition, you must know which environmental regulations apply to your company's activities, products, and services. I strongly recommend regular contact with all local, state, and federal regulatory agencies. I also recommend subscribing to a service that will monitor regulation within your industry and report those that affect your company.

Using this information, begin to set your targets and objectives. You also use this information to create environmental plans. These environmental plans will be similar to the quality control plans required under ISO 9000. Targets and objectives have to be readily measurable. In addition, you have to consider which impacts your company has that can be controlled economically. Also, the concerns of other outside parties have to be considered. At the same time, you have to stay true to your original environmental policy.

As stated before, your environmental plans must designate specific job titles that are responsible for achieving the stated objectives and targets. Such plans also have to spell out the time frame for the accomplishment of each objective and target. This will include a brief description of the means to accomplish these tasks. New projects, products, and processes are expected to be included in the planning phase of your environmental management system.

Exhibit 3-1 shows what such an environmental plan looks like. Exhibit 3-2 is a blank copy of the planning form. Look over the example plan and then use the blank form for your own planning efforts. Note how the items required for environmental planning are broken into columns on this form.

All environmental information and plans have to be kept up to date by your management team. In many cases, your management will set up an environmental planning committee. Such a committee should report directly to top management. It should include managers from each department within your company.

Exhibit 3-1: Example of Environmental Planning Form

Plan Number	Revision		Date	Facility	Authorized
Regulation or customer requirement	Environmental objective	Targets	Who is responsible?	Means or method to be used	Time line
Right-to-know law	Inform all employees of existence, and handling methods for hazardous chemical	Education of all current employees	HRD mgr.	Review of safe handling procedures and use of computer-based training	First quarter of 1996
		Education of temporary employees and new hires	HRD mgr.	same	Third quarter of 1996 and on an ongoing basic
	Inform all local and state agencies as per SARA Title III	Continuous conformance	Eng. mgr.	Section 311, 312, and 313 filings	As required
		Less than 1 spill per year	Eng. and Plant mgr.	Use of cross-functional team to promote proper handling	First quarter 1996
		Zero spills	Eng. and Plant mgr.	Use of auditing and refresher training	First quarter 1998

Notes:

Submitted by: ____________ Customer approval: ____________

Exhibit 3-2: Blank Environmental Planning Form

Plan Number	**Revision**		**Date**	**Facility**	**Authorized**
Regulation or customer requirement	Environmental objective	Targets	Who is responsible?	Means or method to be used	Time line

Notes:

Submitted by: ______________________ Customer approval: ______________________

HOW TO SATISFY ELEMENT 4.3—IMPLEMENTATION AND OPERATION

As with ISO 9000, you must define lines of responsibility and then provide the people and resources to get the job done. You also must have top management assign a manager as the official environmental management system coordinator. This coordinator is responsible for ensuring implementation and then regularly reviewing the environmental management system and reporting to management. All of this has to be documented.

All employees who can have a significant impact on the environment have to be trained to meet identified levels of skills and knowledge. This is similar to the training requirement of ISO 9000. In addition, you must train all employees on the importance of conformance to your environmental policies and procedures, the type of impacts your company has, who has responsibility for controlling which impacts, and the potential costs of nonconformance. Therefore, any employee who holds a position that involves any potentially serious impact on the environment or has a critical role in your environmental management system should be competent. Competency is seen as an appropriate mixture of education, training, and experience. It is up to you to determine this proper mixture and to document it in a training plan and in job descriptions (see Exhibits 3-3 and 3-4).

Internally, you must establish and maintain a standard operating procedure for the communication of concerns related to the environment. Such communication will take one of two forms. The first will be communication between functions and levels within your company. The second will be communication received from customers, regulators, and interested outside parties. Such communications have to follow a standard procedure for receival, documentation, and response. Externally, management must decide how to communicate information about significant environmental aspects of the company. This too can be part of the internal communication procedure.

Each target and objective is then assigned to a specific job title for control and continuous improvement. A specific time frame will have to be created. As new projects or production methods are adopted, the environmental management system plan will have to be changed or expanded to include these developments.

You must document a description of your environmental management system and the interaction between key personnel. This can be accomplished in the Environmental Manual, as previously described. You can also substitute some of the documentation with cross reference charts showing where related documentation describing your environmental management system is located.

Naturally, document control plays a central role in your environmental management system. A written procedure is required. I recommend that the Level II document created to meet the document control requirement from ISO 9000 be used to meet this same requirement. ISO 14001 calls for the following for document control:

- All documents under control must be readily located.
- All controlled documents are authorized before they are issued.

Exhibit 3-3: Example of a Training Schedule and Plan

Job Title	Education or Experience	Training Required to Replace or Supplement Education	Schedule for Training	Date of Completion
Machine Operator	High school diploma or three years experience as a machine apprentice	SPC, blueprint reading, geometric tolerancing, group problem solving, right-to-know overview	Jan., March, June, Oct.	Within two months for new hires or as soon as possible for promotions
Shop Foreman	High school diploma or five years experience as a machine operator	SPC, SPC for supervisors, blueprint reading, group problem solving, handling of hazardous chemicals	Jan., March, June, Oct.	People already having completed required training will be noted in the personnel files
Setup Mechanic	Two-year diploma from a trade school and three years experience as a machine operator	SPC, blueprint reading, basic safety procedures, handling of hazardous chemicals	Jan., March, June, Oct.	

Exhibit 3-4: Example of a Job Description With Environmental Requirements Noted

Job Title: Lift Truck Operator		Revision: 6/6/95
Responsibilities	**Tasks**	**Skills Required**
1.0 Preparation	1.1 Charge lift-truck batteries 1.2 Consult computer schedule	Basic keyboard skills and mechanical aptitude
2.0 Handling Materials	2.1 Obtain location ticket 2.2 Pick up materials 2.3 Properly locate materials 2.4 Safely move materials 2.5 Enter completion of movement	Basic lift-truck instruction training
3.0 Inspection	3.1 Confirm quantity 3.2 Confirm control number for hazardous materials	Ability to read and write
4.0 Maintenance	4.1 Periodically inspect lift truck 4.2 Report potential safety problems 4.3 Clean warehouse areas when required	Basic safety training and right-to-know training
5.0 Paperwork	5.1 Sign received goods bill 5.2 Fill in movement records 5.3 Fill out safety hazard reports when necessary 5.4 Report leaks or other potential chemical spills	Ability to read and write
6.0 Housekeeping	6.1 Clean up spilled materials 6.2 Assist in repairing storage racks	Ability to lift at least 60 pounds and use basic tools

- All controlled documents are periodically reviewed and revised when necessary.
- All current revisions of a document are available at intended locations.
- Obsolete documents are promptly removed.
- Obsolete documents retained for reference or legal purposes are clearly marked as being obsolete.
- All controlled documents must be legible, dated, identified for revision level, clearly identified, and maintained in an orderly manner.
- All controlled documents and data are retained for a specific length of time.

If you are familiar with the document control requirements of ISO 9001, you will realize that these requirements match those stated for ISO 14000. An example procedure for document control can be found in Appendix D. This particular example is an ISO 9000 document control procedure modified to account for the requirements of ISO 14001.

Under the requirements for operational control as stated in ISO 14001, an environmental control plan has to be developed for daily operations. Such a plan would be similar to the quality control plans required in the 1994 version of ISO 9000. You would use a flowchart of your process to identify points where environmental control is required. These environmental control points are situations where the absence of procedures or work instructions could lead to deviation from your environmental policy, objectives, or targets. Each of these points would be listed on the plan along with the criteria to be met and how to react if they are not met. In addition, you should include how to communicate your requirements to suppliers and contractors.

Your environmental operations plan would account for operating criteria used in procedures. It would also call for the establishment and maintenance of specific procedures related to the identified environmental aspects of your processes, products, and services (see Appendix D for an example of this document).

Unique to ISO 14001 is the need for a procedure to cover emergencies. If a company suffers a spill or accidental impact, how will it prevent further environmental damage while also correcting the situation? After any accident or emergency is corrected, management should review what happened and decide how to prevent reoccurrence and determine whether the procedure should be changed. Another interesting requirement for emergency preparedness and response is a team annual test of your emergency response procedure. This would imply mock drills and other similar exercises.

HOW TO SATISFY ELEMENT 4.4—CHECKING AND CORRECTIVE ACTION

Now that you have identified what will be monitored and where the monitoring will take place, you now have to write a procedure on how this is done. First you have to set up a system where key environmental characteristics are measured and recorded. This is done like an SPC system, that is, a regularly scheduled activity is assigned to specific people. Then the written data has to be handled, analyzed, and stored under an ISO 9000 procedure for quality records. In addition, any equipment used to measure environmental targets or objectives must be calibrated and records maintained on equipment maintenance.

You will have to establish a procedure for monitoring and evaluating relevant environmental regulations and customer requirements. As mentioned before, there are services available to provide this information. Otherwise, one member of your staff will have to be dedicated to this task.

As with ISO 9000, you will need a corrective action procedure that identifies when to react, who responds, and what actions are taken. If you already have an ISO 9000 management system, the corrective action and preventive action procedure can easily be modified to include environmental activities. If you need to write a corrective action procedure, be sure that reactions are based on the magnitude of the problem and that you search until a root cause is discovered. Appendix D shows what such a procedure might look like. Please note the methods used to find the root cause of the problem and how a permanent solution is desired to prevent recurrence of the problem.

You will be required under ISO 14001 to maintain records. I have called these the environmental records. They are the reports, data sheets, memos, audit records, training records, control charts, and other information created when you follow your environmentally related procedures and work instructions. You will need a procedure for the proper identification, maintenance, and disposition of such records.

Remember, all records must be legible, identifiable, and traceable back to the process, activity, product, or service involved. They also must be protected from damage or loss. For electronic records, it is necessary to establish a procedure for proper backup of data and protection of the backup. Such a procedure should have the backup data physically separated from your plant so that one natural disaster or human error will not destroy both the data on the computer and your backup. Also, make sure that the time and date on your computer system is always accurate.

For environmental records, you should establish a set period of retention. Typically, this is from three to five years. However, customer requirements and regulations will sometimes specify different lengths of retention. Remember, your environmental records will be a critical part of your ability to demonstrate that you have a working and effective environmental management system. Having written procedures and work instructions will enable you to demonstrate that you have designed an effective environmental management system. However, most auditors will want to see three to six months of accumulated records as proof of the use and effectiveness of your management system.

At least once a year you should perform an internal audit of your complete environmental management system. The procedure for this will be identical to the internal audit requirement under ISO 9000. The key difference is that the internal auditors will need to have knowledge, experience, and/or training in environmental assessment. They need to understand why a particular characteristic is being checked and what potential impacts it could create. Thus, ISO 9000 internal auditor training or lead assessor training is recommended, followed by a seminar on environmental assessments (see Chapter 8 for a complete discussion of auditing techniques).

The purpose of a management audit of the environmental management system is threefold. First, the audit must determine whether the environmental management system conforms to ISO 14001 and the original management plan for the system. Second, the audit must confirm that the environmental management system has been fully implemented and is being maintained. Third, information on the results of the audit must be delivered to your management team so that they can review the effectiveness of the system and look for opportunities for improvement.

The key to any audit program is the audit schedule. The audit schedule is a list of which parts of the management system shall be audited at which particular time. During the course of one year, a company must audit all elements of its environmental management system. However, because of past audit results or the importance of particular elements, some parts of the system will be audited more frequently. This should be reflected in the audit schedule. When an audit schedule is established, it must be adhered to rigorously. If not, the company will be found out of conformance by a registrar.

HOW TO SATISFY ELEMENT 4.5–MANAGEMENT REVIEW

At regular intervals, usually at least once a year, senior management must review the entire environmental management system for completeness and effectiveness. This review will consist of the results of internal audits, reports on new requirements and regulations, and management's discussion of the strategic plan for the company. Then upper management decides whether to modify or change the existing environmental management system to better meet changing needs and targets. All of this must be documented.

Management is responsible for carrying out any major changes in environmental management system. This includes changes in objectives, target, policies, or procedures. To be able to make intelligent decisions on improving the system, management will need accurate and timely information in the form of feedback. This feedback will come from regular audits and reports.

CONCLUSIONS ABOUT ISO 14001

As you can see, the five basic requirements of an environmental management system are a combination of environmental concerns and ISO 9000 requirements. In fact, the most widely used national standard for environmental management system, BS 7750, is very similar to ISO 14001. It would be fair to say that a company that has ISO 9000 in place and has studied BS 7750 would be well on its way to conformance with ISO 14001.

One interesting aspect of ISO 14001 is the proposed idea of written targets and objectives. This would make conformance and improvement obvious to anyone who took the time to look at a series of charts. Employees would gather regular readings of environmental impacts, which could be charted and posted for everyone to see. The target for each chart would be noted; thus, continuous improvement would be a regular part of the environmental management system.

Another interesting aspect of the ISO 14001 standard is Annex A. This guidance provided at the back of the standard reviews how ISO 14001 should be implemented. Therefore, it is highly recommended for your reading list. For example, it clearly points out that an environmental management system should be appropriate for the type of business being run and the economy in which the company operates.

Finally, a warning: ISO 14001 will not help companies when auditors come from organizations like the Environmental Protection Agency (EPA) or the Occupational Safety and Health Administration (OSHA). Conformance to ISO 14001 will not guarantee conformance to regulations. It is up to the management of a company to set targets and objectives to ensure such continuous conformance.

In regulatory situations, ISO 14001 will be a double-edged sword. On the one hand, a company will easily be able to demonstrate its efforts to maintain conformance. On the other hand, the system will leave a paper trail that can be easily followed and used in court if you flagrantly violate the law.

THE USE OF FIRST-, SECOND-, OR THIRD-PARTY AUDITS TO DEMONSTRATE CONFORMANCE

The central concept of a voluntary standard is that a company is given a means to demonstrate its compliance to an established set of criteria. There are three ways to demonstrate conformance.

The first is called a first-party audit: a company performs an internal assessment of its own environmental management system. Similar to an internal audit, the first-party audit involves a complete review of the environmental management system. This first-party audit is conducted by a company's own people within a time frame of a few days. A written report is delivered to management. Some companies than self-declare their conformance.

A second-party audit occurs when auditors from a company's customer review the environmental management system. An example of a second-party audit is a supplier quality assurance audit conducted by a customer. A similar procedure is used for the evaluation of the environmental management system. The customer can then choose whether to issue a company a certificate of compliance. Such a certificate of compliance is good only for that one customer. Recently, with ISO 9000 some industrial groups of customers have banded together to issue certificates good for the group.

A third-party audit occurs when a neutral third party conducts the audit and the results are accepted by both the company audited and its customers. In the case of ISO 9000 and ISO 14000, these independent organizations are called registrars. The registrars are accredited by national government bodies. The accredited registrar can then conduct audits and issue certificates of compliance. A single evaluation of an environmental management system, therefore, satisfies the requirements of many customers.

Examples of registrars for ISO 9000 include organizations such as Underwriters Laboratories, British Standards Institute, Lloyd's of London, National Sanitation Foundation, TUV Rheinland, and ABS Quality Evaluations. In a 1995 survey of ISO 9000 registrars, it was discovered that over 95 percent of North American registrars were planning to issue ISO 14000 certificates.[1]

HOW REGISTRATION WORKS

Registration is a process by which a company submits itself to an audit conducted by a registrar. This audit will confirm the company's conformance to ISO 14001. The registrar will then issue a certificate of conformance. This certificate and the ISO 14000 artwork can be used in a company's letterhead and brochures. The registrar will likely maintain a series of surveillance audits to confirm the company's continuing conformance. After three years, the registrar will want to audit the entire system again, followed by more surveillance. Naturally, a company must pay the registrar for these audits and the certificate.

THE REGISTRATION AUDIT AND WHAT TO DO

The registration audit involves these several distinct steps:

- Signing the contract
- Document review
- Initial visit
- Actual audit
- Corrective action (if needed)
- Award of registration

First, a company must sign a contract with a registrar. The contract will spell out the services the registrar will deliver and the company's obligations. Then the registrar will request the Environmental Policy Manual for review. This is called the document review process. In this process, a lead auditor will examine the compa-

[1] Based on the 1995 North American Registrar Survey, National ISO 9000 Support Group, Caledonia, Michigan.

ny's policies to learn about it and to make sure its policies match the requirements of ISO 14001.

When the document review is completed, the lead auditor will send the company a report on the level of conformance. Then the lead auditor will want to visit the company to see the layout, meet its management team, and glance over its procedures. This initial visit helps the lead auditor to schedule the actual activities for the registration audit.

The registration audit typically lasts from two to five days, depending on the size and complexity of the company. The audit begins with an opening meeting with the company's management. The lead auditor reviews the audit schedule and introduces the auditors to the guides. The guides are people from the company who accompany the auditors to make sure they receive anything they need.

The opening meeting should last less than one hour. Then the actual audit begins. The auditor team will disperse and examine individual departments, interviewing the people within each department. Elements of ISO 14001 that apply to a department will be checked, and environmental records will be sampled and examined. Each auditor will write down any findings and the level of conformance to each requirement. Do not be surprised if the auditor stops someone at random and asks a few questions.

Basically the auditors are trying to answer two questions. First, does everyone know his or her job? Second, does each person know the effect of that job on the environment? Near the end of the audit, the lead auditor will call together all auditors and ask for their reports. These will be compiled into an oral report delivered to management during a closing meeting. Later, a written report will be delivered to the company.

If required because of nonconformances, corrective actions shall be demanded. The company must carry out these corrective actions and report in writing to the registrar. When the company demonstrates all conformance to the requirements, the registrar will issue a certificate of compliance.

After a company receives a certificate of conformance, a regular schedule of surveillance audits will be established by the registrar. Typically, such surveillance occurs twice a year. Only part of the environmental management system will be examined—usually, the parts of the system that showed some minor nonconformances during the registration audit or previous surveillance audit. Either way, the entire system will be examined over a three-year period. After three years, the company must submit to another complete registration audit. This cycle goes on forever or until the company chooses not to conform to the standard.

A BRIEF DISCUSSION OF HOW TO IMPLEMENT ISO 14001

Following is a list of the basic steps a company would take to implement ISO 14001. If you have read a book such as *The Quality Manager's Complete Guide to ISO 9000*[2]

2 Richard Barrett Clements, Prentice-Hall, Englewood Cliffs, NJ, 1993.

or any of the other similar texts, you will recognize these implementation steps. Essentially, the method of implementing ISO 14000 is identical to the system used for ISO 9001. Therefore, we will discuss implementation in detail in Chapter 6.

TWO TYPES OF IMPLEMENTATION

The course to implementation is divided into two paths. Path one is for companies that have been ISO 9000 companies for some years or that have had to conform to previous supplier qualification programs. These companies need only to adjust their existing procedures, write policy statements, and add needed work instructions.

The second path is for companies that are new to the use of a documented management system. Typically, these companies do not have many procedures or work instructions. Nor do they have to have a management system of quality assurance or environmental management in any organized form. These companies, therefore, will have to develop entire processes, procedures, policies, and work instructions. Their implementation process will be intense.

A typical implementation plan might cover the following steps:

1. Establish a steering committee of managers to oversee implementation.
2. Self-evaluate company.
3. Write policies for your environmental management system.
4. Form a written action plan based on management discussions and the baseline audit; assign specific managers specific tasks; form a project management time line.
5. Revise or create your Environmental Procedures Manual (Level II) to reflect the requirements of ISO 14001.
6. Select a registrar if you know you are receiving a third-party audit. Second-party audits will be conducted by your customers.
7. Upgrade or create written work instructions as needed.
8. Conduct a system-wide internal audit when you think your system is in place and compare it to the baseline audit. If few weaknesses are found, take corrective action—otherwise, schedule the actual ISO 14001 audit.
9. Prepare for the audit by reviewing all points of the environmental management system with management and workers.
10. Be audited and respond with corrective actions, if needed.

As you can see, implementation is a project requiring close coordination between departments and managers. It will involve a cross-functional implementation team, and it will take time and resources to complete. This is why management commitment is so critical to the process.

SUMMARY OF THE WAY TO IMPLEMENT ISO 14000

In this chapter, we have looked at the two central standards for an environmental management system, namely, ISO 14001 and ISO 14004. ISO 14004 is the basic guideline to understanding what an environmental management system is and why it is important to your company. ISO 14001 is the standard to which the company will become registered, if registration is required. ISO 14001 also contains the list of system requirements.

We have taken a brief look at the process of registration. We have also taken a brief look at one way to implement an environmental management system. Later chapters of this book will examine implementation issues in depth. Already we have seen what a policy and procedure look like within a documented environmental management system. Therefore, you should have a rough idea of what will be required of your company if regulations or customer requirements say that you have to comply with ISO 14000. You may also find that market pressures or the desire for a marketing advantage will lead your company toward this standard.

As mentioned earlier, a company without an environmental management system and with a poor environmental record will find doing business harder in the future because customers are not awarding contracts to questionable companies for fear of the bad publicity of an environmental scandal. In addition, banks shy away from companies that may be doing environmental harm and are attracted to companies with well-documented management systems.

Therefore, the development of an environmental management system is highly recommended for most small, medium, and large businesses. At the same time, do not lose sight of the fact that most industrialized nations already have environmental management system requirements of one form or another (i.e. EMAS). Don't neglect to investigate these as well.

Chapter 4

GUIDELINE STANDARDS FOR A COMPANY'S MANAGEMENT SYSTEM

Like ISO 9000, ISO 14000 is really a family of standards. The core standard is ISO 14001. This is the standard to which you register your company or which you use in a second- or first-party audit. ISO 14004—Environmental Management Systems–General Guidelines on Principles, Systems, and Supporting Techniques is the primary guidance standard. It provides a road map for environmental management systems.

THE PURPOSE AND USE OF GUIDELINE STANDARDS

To facilitate a greater understanding of a conformance standard and to make it possible for different industries to conform to the same standard, guideline standards are used. In the case of ISO 14000, several guideline standards have already been developed. Several more are being planned. Following is a list of the existing guidelines and the proposed guidelines. The dates in parentheses represent expected dates of final approval.

Environmental Management Systems

ISO 14004—General Guideline (1996)

ISO 14001—Specification With Guidance for Use (1996)

Environmental Auditing

ISO 14010—General Principles (1996)

ISO 14011-1—Management Systems Audits (1996)

ISO 14011-2—Compliance Audits (not yet determined)

ISO 14011-3—Statement Audits (not yet determined)

ISO 14012—Auditor Qualifications (1996)

ISO 14013—Managing Auditing Programs (not yet determined)

ISO 14014—Initial Reviews (not yet determined)

ISO 14015—Site Assessments (not yet determined)

Environmental Labeling

ISO 14020—General Principles (1997)

ISO 14021—Self-Declaration Claims (1996)

ISO 14022—Symbols (1997)

ISO 14023—Testing and Verification (not yet determined)

ISO 14024—Labeling Certification Programs (1996)

Environmental Performance Evaluation

ISO 14031—General Methodology (1997)

ISO 14032—Industry-Specific Indicators (not yet determined)

Life Cycle Assessment

ISO 14040—General Principles (1996)

ISO 14041—Inventory Analysis (not yet determined)

ISO 14042—Impact Assessment (not yet determined)

ISO 14043—Improvement Assessment (not yet determined)

Terms and Definitions

ISO 14050—Glossary

Product Specifications

ISO Guide 64—Environmental Aspects Guide (1997)

This list should give you some idea of the course and intention of the ISO 14000 family of standards. Not only does the family of standards address environmental management systems, but it also addresses the issues of eco-labeling, auditing, life cycle analysis, and performance analysis.

We shall look at three examples of these guideline standards. The glossary of terms, life cycle assessment, and how to include environmental aspects into product standards will be discussed shortly. My intention is to give you a feel for the guideline standards. As new guideline standards are developed, you should be able to select those that will best help you in the creation, and later expansion, of your management system.

WHY THE ISO 14050 GLOSSARY OF TERMS AND DEFINITIONS IS CRITICAL FOR UNDERSTANDING ALL OTHER ISO 14000-RELATED STANDARDS

Central to any set of standards is a collection of terms and definitions that the standards have in common. In the case of the ISO 14000 family of standards, there is ISO 14050, a general glossary of definitions for terms used throughout the standards related to environmental management systems.

By examining several of these definitions, we can quickly see the scope and nature of the vision ISO 14000 has for the issue of the "environment." Thus, a copy of 14050 is recommended if you wish to closely study the ISO 14000 family of standards. However, please note that these definitions are frequently repeated at the beginning of each standard.

The following definitions are not direct quotes from ISO 14050. Instead, they are paraphrased because the final definitions and the exact language for common terms have not been established at the time of the publication of this book.

Continual improvement—A daily improvement in small aspects of environmental performance pursuant to your environmental policy.

Comparative assertion—An environmental claim of the superiority of your product over another.

Environment—The surroundings in which your company operates.

Environmental aspect—Any part of your company's activity, product, or service that interacts with the environment.

Environmental impact—Any adverse or beneficial effect resulting from your company's activity, product, or service.

Environmental management—The parts of your management system that develops, implements, reviews, and maintains an environmental policy.

Environmental management system—Your organizational structure, responsibilities, practices, procedures, processes, and resources for implementing environmental management.

Environmental objective—Your overall environmental goal, quantified when practical.

Environmental performance—The measurable outputs of your environmental management system, based on your environmental targets and objectives.

Environmental policy—A statement by your management of its intentions and principles related to achieving environmental targets and objectives.

Environmental target—A detailed and quantified performance requirement established in relation to a particular environmental objective.

Interested party—Any individual or group expressing concern or having interest in your company's environmental performance.

System boundary—The dividing point between your product or service and the environment it affects.

By no means is this list exhaustive. Instead, it is intended as a sample of terms and general definitions of those terms. You should become familiar with these types of terms if you wish to fully understand the ISO 14000 family of standards. This is particularly critical because the subtle meanings of words can have significant effects on the interpretation of a requirement within a standard.

ISO 14040: GENERAL PRINCIPLES OF LIFE CYCLE ASSESSMENT–A CRITICAL CONCEPT WITHIN ANY ENVIRONMENTAL MANAGEMENT SYSTEM

Any product, service, or activity created by your company will have an impact on the environment. The idea of Life Cycle Assessment (LCA) is to inventory and assess those impacts. The result will be a report used to make decisions and perhaps to share with the public for discussion.

ISO 14040 is a first attempt to develop a methodology for LCA to establish a common way companies can evaluate environmental impacts. LCA is not the only method for addressing environmental impacts. There are also techniques such as risk assessment, quality function deployment, designed experiments, and environmental impact statements.

The concept of life cycle assessment is fairly new. Technical Committee 207 continues to struggle with this concept. Industry demands a standard that clearly defines how a method is used. At this time, ISO 14040 is being supplemented by some examples created by the subcommittees of TC 207. Therefore, life cycle assessment is still a developing technique within environmental management systems.

However, life cycle assessment holds great promise. It can be used to supplement your management system; it can give your company the ability to examine the lifetime effects of its product, services, and activities; it is also flexible enough so that you can use your final report to make product-specific claims or to show conformance to various regulations.

For example, a company could develop a label for its product claiming that its environmental impact has been minimized over its entire life cycle. The life cycle assessment would be the evidence of this. As we shall see in the next chapter, the issue of eco-labeling requires some method of demonstrating claims. Another example would be a government customer that wanted life cycle assessment performed on a company's product or service. Life cycle assessment, as spelled out in ISO 14040, could be used as the standard for defining how the assessment is conducted.

WHAT IS LIFE CYCLE ASSESSMENT?

One of the central concerns of an environmental management system is the environmental impact a company creates with its products, activities, and services. Take the example of a product being manufactured by a company. Depending on the stage of production, the product can create various environmental impacts. Thus, you need to look at the entire life span of the product and how each stage of that product's life affects the environment.

Such an examination is called a life cycle assessment. From the moment raw materials are drawn from the earth, through production and installation or sale, to the point of final disposition, a product creates various impacts. The purpose of a life cycle assessment is to better comprehend and possibly control these impacts. In many cases, you will discover that you can also reduce such impacts. In fact, as we shall see, reduction of environmental impacts will go hand in hand with reducing production costs and improving product quality.

What ISO 14040 does is produce a standard approach to assessing environmental impacts along the continuum of a product's life. Called a life cycle assessment, the method has three distinct stages:

1. *Goal definitions and scope.* In this stage of the process, you begin the life cycle assessment by defining the overall goals of the study, the product involved, the intended audience, the scope of the study, data requirement, and the type of critical review to be conducted.

2. *Inventory analysis.* The life cycle of a product is a series of processes and systems tied together in their common purpose of creating the product. Inventory analysis is a listing of these processes and systems, their boundaries, and the potential impact of each process and system.

3. *Impact assessment.* Taking the list of potential impact from the previous step, you now classify and quantify the expected impacts. This can be a difficult step involving the use of much scientific analysis and careful use of predictions.

Life cycle assessment is a tool for collecting and later interpreting a large collection of environmentally related data for various purposes. The results of the study can be used for decision making, the selection of environmental indicators, marketing, and other management-level activities. The main idea is to get management to integrate environmental information and issues into their normal decision-making process.

Life cycle assessment does not have a fixed methodology. In other words, there is no single way to conduct a life cycle assessment. You have great freedom in the way you wish to conduct such an assessment. However, you also have many choices. Therefore, you should be familiar with scientific methods of investigation and common sense evaluation of complex issues before attending a life cycle assessment.

EXAMPLE OF CONDUCTING A LIFE CYCLE ASSESSMENT

Let's look at a particular product and walk through the steps of a life cycle assessment as outlined in ISO 14040. Specifically, let's look at the life of that small plastic container that holds 35-millimeter film canisters. When you buy 35-millimeter film in the store, the film is inside a small plastic container with a lid. This, in turn, is packaged in a display box.

You would think that the small plastic container would have a simple life cycle. However, by examining such a simple manufactured product, we can see that the life cycle and its environmental impact can become complex.

Step 1: Goal definitions and scope

Life cycle assessment can be a very complex process. Therefore, all assumptions made in your assessment must be clearly communicated to the intended audience. This is why it is important to list your scope of study and its goals.

In the case of the 35-millimeter film container, we want to define the scope of our study as an assessment of its life from obtaining the raw materials, through production and customer use and final disposition. We want to examine all environmental requirements that come from local, state, and national regulations, as well as customer requirements.

In our example, we are the plastic injection firm hired as just one of many suppliers to the film manufacturing corporation. Our contract is to follow customer's specifications for the production of film containers and caps. Thus, we need to buy raw materials from our own suppliers and ship the final product to our customer.

The goals of our study are as follows:

- Minimize the environmental impact in the selection of plastic resins.
- Encourage recycling where possible.
- Discover opportunities to reduce environmental impact.
- Reduce production costs through the reduced use of energy during the life cycle.
- Assist in the future design of the film canister.
- Create a database of environmentally related information on this product.
- Quantify the environmental impacts.
- Assist management's decision making.

The intended audience of this study will be the management and the engineering staff at our company. The assessment will undergo critical review by an outside environmental engineering consulting firm.

The goals list reasons for conducting the assessment, the intended application, the intended audience, the data requirements, and the type of critical review to be conducted. A critical review is how you plan to confirm your results, assumptions, and conclusions. In other words, once the assessment is complete, someone must conduct a critical review of the study. This helps to assure you that you have good data and have made proper assumptions.

The scope of a life cycle assessment lays out the functions of the systems under study, defines functional units, the boundaries of the systems, how you will evaluate environmental impacts, data requirements, basic assumptions being made, and the limitations involved. In short, you describe the parameters of your study.

In this example, the scope may look like this:

> *The scope of this life cycle assessment will involve the life span of part number 475-3, film canister, and part number 647-5, cap for 35-millimeter film canister. It will closely examine the following:*

- Purchase of raw materials
- Production of parts (specifically, the injection molding process)
- Cleaning, trimming, inspection, and packaging of finished parts
- The process of scrapping and regrinding nonconforming parts
- Shipment to customer
- Use by final customer in intended function (protecting film)
- Secondary uses by customer
- Final disposition of product

Each of these items represent separate systems within the life cycle. Please note that all possible systems were not listed—we have produced a description of the limitation of this assessment.

For each of the systems described, you would then describe the system boundaries. These boundaries are the interfaces between the product or service and the potential environmental impacts. For example, the shipment of finished products to the customer would involve the environmental impacts of things like the fuel used to transport the goods, the recycled content of shipping materials, the energy consumption expended in packing and preparing the shipment, and so on. These should be defined well enough to ensure that the breadth and depth of the study will fulfill your stated goals.

You should also consider where data can be collected and the quality of the data you will need. For example, you may find that you have to measure the energy consumption of one system. Will you measure energy in terms of BTUs, electrical costs, or calories?

You should also consider listing the potential methods that could be used within your assessment. This might include such methods as cost/benefit ratios, returns on investment, designed experiments, correlations, species surveys, or any other widely recognized valid method.

A primary way to evaluate a system is to define a particular functional unit within the system. For example, the plastic injection machine that creates the film container cap. This is a single functional unit in your production system. For this functional unit, you can define its various outputs and resource inputs. For example, a plastic injection machine uses raw materials, electricity, water, and various human resources to operate. Its outputs include finished materials, heat, scrap resin, steam, noise, and worn parts of the machinery. By carefully considering such inputs and outputs, you can easily assess the environmental impact of each functional unit. By collecting together these lists within a system, you can evaluate the total impact of the system.

Step 2: Life cycle inventory analysis

Collecting together the inputs and outputs of a system is called inventory analysis. Collect the inputs and outputs into two categories—use of resources and releases to air, water, and land. These, in the next step, will be evaluated for their environmental impact.

A life cycle inventory begins with the well-defined boundaries of your systems under study. The inputs and outputs of each system can be collected and categorized using a flowchart of the system. In our example, we were looking at the plastic injection machine. We could create a chart showing materials and resources flowing into the process and the outputs that resulted (see Exhibit 4-1).

Exhibit 4-1: Inputs and Outputs of a Plastic Injection Machine

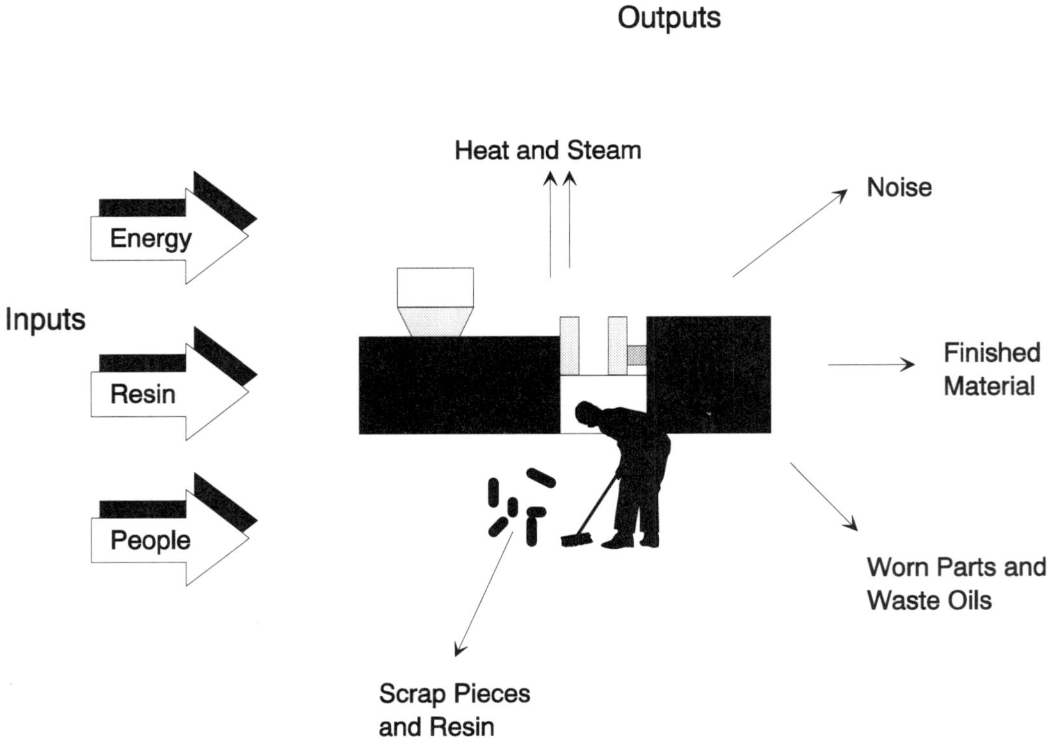

As part of your inventory, you should identify the type of data to be collected. For example, a measurement of energy used by the machine can be measured in kilowatts of electricity. The amount of heat given off by the machine could be measured in BTUs.

Also, you should consider any allocation issues involved when multiple inputs or outputs are involved. For example, the heat generated by the plastic injection machine helps reduce the heating requirements of your facility. Also, some of the scrap created by the machine can be recycled and used again. Such reuse, however, involves the additional use of energy versus savings in resin costs. It will be up to you to precisely calculate these relationships.

Because energy consumption is a critical issue in many countries, you will need a separate page describing the types of fuels used to generate energy and the effect of alternatives. Issues such as the transportation of energy, conversion, and process methods will have to be dealt with separately. Therefore, the inventory analysis ends when you have completely listed out the inputs and outputs of your defined systems within the scope of your life cycle assessment. This detailed list is then the basis for evaluating environmental impacts.

Step 3: Impact assessment

Using your life cycle inventory, try to understand and evaluate the magnitude and significance of each possible environmental impact. Although such evaluation takes place within the scope of your study, you are still free to consider and compare alternatives to the existing conditions. This opens the opportunity for becoming more environmentally friendly, efficiently productive, and capable of higher quality goods.

To conduct an environmental impact assessment, you must conduct three additional tasks. First, you must classify the items listed in your life cycle inventory. Specifically, you should group items according to potential impacts. The general categories to begin with are resource depletion, human health, and ecological impact.

For example, we were discussing the use of energy by the plastic molding process. Energy is seen as a resource you are depleting. Thus, several items from our inventory for the plastic injection process would be placed in this category. The use of electricity for the molding machines, the lights, and the electronic equipment used during the molding process (e.g., measurement gauges, machine controllers, and so forth) would be grouped in this category.

The categories that you actually select would depend on the goal you originally set for the study. For example, one of our goals was to look at ways to save money by reducing energy consumption. Thus, the resource depletion category would have a subcategory on energy usage. Within this subcategory, the impact being studied would be limited to energy consumption and how to minimize it. Other related subcategories may include such issues as raw materials used and human resources required.

Second, you must characterize the extent and effect of each impact identified in the previous task. This involves the use of relevant physical, chemical, biological, statistical, and toxicological data to describe the impact of an inventory item. This can take any of several forms, such as ozone depletion potential, no observed effect levels, calories of energy consumed, and so on.

In our example, you could look at the kilowatts of energy consumed by the plastic molding process during every day of normal operations. We could also look at the BTUs of heat being generated by the process. Such information will assist us in the third and final task of impact assessment.

Third, place a valuation on the impact. This valuation is how you will eventually judge the significance of each impact. Such valuation can involve several parameters, such as cost, personal preferences, environmental disturbances, and social values. These selected parameters should be directly related to the regulations and customer requirements for environmental issues.

For example, it would be fairly simple to calculate the monetary value of the electricity being used by the plastic molding process. However, on another aspect of our example assessment, it would not be easy to place a value; that is, the secondary uses of the plastic film containers.

Many people purchase film every day. When the film is taken out of the container for use, the container and its cap suffer one of three fates—either it is thrown away, saved for recycling, or put to another use. This other use is the secondary usage of the product. For example, some people use the containers to store odds and ends. Others assemble them into useful household objects, such as nail-and-screw dispensers. The point here is that the secondary uses are difficult to predict and evaluate. At the same time, secondary uses can extend the life of the product.

In a landfill, the plastic film container has a considerable negative environmental impact. One of your goals is to avoid this fate for the product. In fact, you have designed the product to use a plastic resin that can be easily and inexpensively recycled. The question will arise as to how you can encourage the final consumers to recycle your product after its intended use or after a secondary use.

USING THE LIFE CYCLE ASSESSMENT IN MANAGEMENT DECISION MAKING

Now that you have created an inventory of environmental items and assessed their impact, it is time to create a report to management outlining what you have discovered and how to improve the situation. Your report to management should include the following:

- Goals and scope of your study
- Methods that you used
- Results of the study (including your inventory and a list of impacts by category)
- Valuation of each item (possibly sorted into order by critical consideration)
- Conclusions and recommendations

Naturally, such a report should be presented in significant detail and clarity so that management can understand, interpret, and use the information for decision making. The use of an executive summary is strongly encouraged.

For each of the critical issues that your assessment has identified, spend some time identifying the effects of possible improvements or alternatives. For example, we have been discussing the use of energy by the plastic molding process. Our study has found that we consume over $800 in electricity every day for the molding process. The process also gives off thousands of BTUs in heat.

One possible discussion would be the concept of using the excess heat to keep the production facility warm in cold-weather months. This would involve installing a system to capture and circulate the heat from the molding machine into areas such as the front office. If such a system would cost $100,000 to install and would save about $20 a day in heating costs, the return on the investment would take about 160 months.

A possible alternative would be to keep the heat within the machine to help speed the process of warming up the barrels of the injection machine and holding down the cost of keeping the barrels warm. Such a system may cost $40,000, but you are not certain of the potential cost savings. You have estimated a daily cost saving of $7. However, you have pointed out in your report that this is only an estimate. The return on investment is approximately 190 months.

As you can see, management will face a difficult decision. Only one of the described options can be implemented. Or, management could decide to reject both possibilities. The return on investment is similar for both possibilities. However, other environmental, engineering, processing, and marketing factors may play a part in this decision.

Another example of a possible discussion of environmental impacts may be the amount of scrap being produced by the injection process. Your report may find that 10 percent of raw material put into the injection system comes out as scrap that is reground and used again. You could detail the cost in extra resin and energy needed to process the scrap.

However, you could also examine the environmental effect of maximizing the efficiency of the process and the quality of the final product. For example, by running a designed experiment, you could identify the causes of variation within your process. Thus, the setup sheets could be modified to virtually eliminate scrap. Also, the design of the mold could be changed to ensure higher molding success. Or quality control charts could identify assignable causes of process variation for elimination. The results of this effort would be lower scrap rates. Lower scrap rates would mean fewer people and less energy needed to deal with scrap. Also, less raw material would need to be purchased.

In this way, you can see that the environmental life cycle assessment involves issues such as efficiency and quality. Therefore, improvement in your process methods and product quality can also reduce environmental impacts. Thus, the life cycle assessment becomes a critical tool for management. It is also seen as the keystone method for an environmental management system.

COMMUNICATION OF RESULTS TO THIRD PARTIES

A controversial aspect of life cycle assessment is communication of your results to third parties. This would potentially involve customers, suppliers, regulators, and the general public. Many companies have little desire to share such information with the public and other third parties. This is understandable. After all, competitors are part of the public. Also, in countries such as the United States, environmental activist groups would love to obtain such information to assist in public pressure and lawsuits. Then there is the issue of the regulators. Some companies do not want to quantify their impacts and publish the results. The fear is that even though the company conforms to requirements and regulations, regulators will insist on higher performance results.

Therefore, your company's management has to decide whether your environmental impact assessment will be communicated to third parties. This includes the decision to use the full report or only portions of the report. At the same time, management must also consider the stakeholders in your company. For example, if you are a publicly held company, should the stockholders receive information on your environmental conformance?

This can be a tricky decision. Announcing actual environmental impacts of your company and the results of efforts to minimize such impacts can be an important marketing tool. It can help attract more capital to your company. However, it can raise expectations to a level beyond the capacity of your company to perform.

A more positive use of life cycle assessment reporting to a third party is the support of any environmental claims your company makes about your product, service, or activity. As we have mentioned before, the report of your assessment activity can be used to support any eco-label claim. We will discuss this further in the next chapter.

A far more likely possibility is that a customer or regulation body will require your company to submit environmental impact statements, a self-assessment of your environmental friendliness, or similar document. Having an international standard on life cycle assessment gives all parties involved a common language and method for describing the exact requirements. For example, a contract with a foreign government may call for your company to state its environmental impact from its product. To assist in such international trade, both parties can agree that a life cycle assessment is the best approach to the requirement and that ISO 14040 is the standard to use.

CRITICAL REVIEW OF THE ENVIRONMENTAL LIFE CYCLE ASSESSMENT

Finally, you should carefully consider a critical review of any life cycle assessment. A critical review is when an outside organization, respected expert, or other qualified individual examines your report. Usually, calculations are checked, assumptions confirmed, and the logic of results evaluated.

When you decide that a critical review will be part of your assessment, this should be spelled out in your goals and scope section. You should identify the scope of the critical review, who will be conducting such a review, and the type of data and method to be used. Particularly important is the level of detail to be examined as part of a critical review. The level of detail should be directly related to the goals first set out in your report.

It is possible to conduct a self-review by an internal expert. It should be done only when it seems to be the most sensible approach. When you are under severe environmental regulations or requirements, or your company is involved with a controversial issue, you should strongly consider an outside review. The review of your study by a disinterested outside party will lend credibility to your conclusions.

Under special circumstances, you may elect to use a committee of outside experts, including some from competitors. This would be used when your company is participating in a forum for your industry. The results of sharing such information between companies can be used to benefit all participants. One example would be a national industrial group using such information to create technologies that can be exported.

SUMMARY OF LIFE CYCLE ASSESSMENT

When using a life cycle assessment, keep in mind that this is not the only way to assess environmental impacts. In fact, you should not use life cycle assessment by itself. Other methods must be used to supplement the assessment, such as risk analysis, cost/benefit analysis, and the like.

Life cycle assessment is still a hotly debated issue within environmental management system standards. For now, there is no pressure to force a company to use life cycle assessment as part of its environmental management system. However, future regulations may call for this technique or one very similar. In addition, life cycle assessment is one of the best methods you can use for planning and decision making within your environmental management system; therefore, you should become familiar with this method and use it for critical products, activities, or services produced by your company.

What is happening with life cycle assessment is that TC 207 is creating a standard for initial use and evaluation in international trade agreements. In other words, the committee agrees that life cycle assessment can be a valuable tool and supplement to ISO 14000 standards. However, the concept is new and the methodology is not yet firmly established. So it seems that the plan is to put into circulation a fairly well-developed standard on the general principles of life cycle assessment (ISO 14040).

The supporting standards—ISO 14041, ISO 14042, and ISO 14043—will be developed as best as possible. Once in use, comments and suggestions will be collected from the community of participating companies. The planned revisions of all four standards for life cycle assessment will then clarify confusing issues and better establish the methodologies to be used. Thus, you should use this standard with a grain of salt.

Use the life cycle assessment standards keeping its flexibility in mind. In the end, you determine how a life cycle assessment will actually be conducted. The standard gives you a firm outline of the issues to address. It also suggests a report format. Thus, you are given a frame on which you can build a life cycle assessment, which includes setting your own limitations, scope, and goals.

ISO 14031–AN EXAMPLE OF THE POSSIBLY TURBULENT FUTURE OF THE ISO 14000 STANDARDS

An example of the turbulent and interesting development of an international standard is found in ISO 14031—Evaluation of Environmental Performance. Now that there are draft standards for environmental management systems and how they are audited, some of the attention of TC 207 is switching to the issue of environmental performance evaluation. That is, how do you measure the environmental performance of your company? Also, how can the TC 207 develop a single approach to performance evaluation for all companies worldwide?

Environmental performance evaluation is seen as a critical tool for companies wishing to assess whether they are meeting their goals and targets. To assist in this effort, subcommittee 4 of TC 207 has been developing a standard for such evaluations. The standard is in a working draft and focuses on planning, implementing, describing, reviewing, and improving a company's methods of evaluating environmental performance. Additional proposed standards plan to give guidance on how to collect, analyze, and report performance data.

The standard has been written and rewritten several times. The chair of subcommittee 4 recently reported that all the key elements for a complete and successful standard have been identified. Now the order and presentation of these elements are being discussed. For example, one element of the proposed standard describes how to select and use environmental performance indicators. Some countries want this to be very explicit. Others want just general principles without confining and specific methodologies.

At the same time, small companies in developing nations want this standard as soon as possible. However, the larger corporations in developed nations want maximum value from the standards for their own interests. Therefore, it will be sometime late in 1996 before a committee draft of the standard will be available. An actual standard may not be available until 1998.

Thus, you can see that some standards, like ISO 14001, are put through committee quickly and become draft international standards within a few years of their conception whereas guideline standards always seem to lag behind. Usually, this is a result of the desire for well-defined guidelines to support the core standard.

Managers must stay in touch with the development of these guidelines and especially their proposed revisions, which will begin around the turn of the century.

ISO GUIDE 64–GUIDE FOR THE INCLUSION OF ENVIRONMENTAL ASPECTS IN PRODUCT STANDARDS

So far we have been discussing reactive management; that is, how your company can react to environmental management system requirements from regulators and customers. However, your company may be the one making the environmental requirements for its suppliers. In such a case, your company is being environmentally *proactive.* Therefore, you will need to know how to state environmental requirements in your specifications and contracts. ISO Guide 64 was developed with this in mind.

ISO Guide 64 states that every product and service has some environmental effect during its manufacture, distribution, use, or disposal. These effects can range from minor to critical. The effects can be experienced at local, regional, or even global levels. Therefore, product standards must reflect the significance of the possible environmental impacts.

Because it is felt that this will be a critical issue now and in the future, ISO Guide 64 was developed. It was developed for the following reasons:

- To raise awareness that provisions in specifications can have environmental effects
- To show the relationship between the product standards you write and their effect on the environment
- To avoid specifications that create environmental harm
- To show that writing environmentally sound specifications is a balancing act
- To recommend life cycle assessment and other scientific methods for developing product standards

Perhaps the most difficult consideration during the writing of a product standard is the balancing of minimizing the environmental impact against other considerations, such as function, performance, quality, safety, workers' health, cost, and profitability. At the same time, you do not want to stifle innovation. Therefore, techniques that encourage the consideration of many dimensions and effects, such as quality function deployment, are encouraged.

Again, we are brought back to the philosophy of Dr. Taguchi; that is, his idea that economies are maximized at the margins. In other words, you want maximum performance with minimal resources. ISO Guide 64 hints that it is possible to achieve your desired engineering outcomes while still assuring minimal environmental impact. The standard recommends that while conducting normal specification creation you should keep in mind the following:

- The types of materials being used, extracted, or processed, with a focus on conserving limited resources such as energy
- The amount of energy input required
- The type and quantities of waste created at each stage of a product's life cycle
- Use of recycled materials for packaging
- Fuel expended in transportation
- Energy and resource usage during distribution
- The possibility of energy recovery, reuse, recycling, or restoration of the product during its useful life
- Options for disposal of the product and any waste generated by the product

THREE STEPS TO TAKE UNDER ISO GUIDE 64

In general, ISO Guide 64 is asking a company to use three basic approaches during the design of its products or services: resource conservation, pollution prevention, and design for the environment.

Step one: Resource conservation. Resource conservation is the minimization of resource depletion; in other words, an encouragement to use renewable resources where possible and minimize the use of nonrenewable resources. For example, the use of timber is a renewable resource; however, you have to consider the rate of renewal in your considerations. If your product uses a great deal of prime timber, there is the chance that the renewable resource will be depleted faster than its rate of replenishment.

Perhaps the most important resource consideration is the conservation of energy. As the world learned with the oil crisis of 1973, basic energy resources lie at the heart of the modern economy. Energy is a key ingredient in the manufacture of products and the delivery of services. Thus, your primary goal in writing specifications is to reduce the loss of inherent energy. In fact, the standard encourages you *not* to specify particular materials in your specifications, to leave open the opportunity for one of your suppliers to find innovative new materials that meet your specifications and accomplish other goals such as energy conservation.

Step two: Pollution prevention. Pollution prevention is described as the human and industrial activities that minimize the release of unwanted materials into the land, air, or water. Pollution can be prevented in any of several ways. For example, there are methods such as source reduction, reuse of wastes, recycling, material substitution, treatment of wastes before release, and so on.

Some issues related to pollution are hard to quantify. Ozone depletion, climatic changes, long-term health effects, and the like cannot be evaluated completely at the moment you write a specification. Therefore, the writer of a specification should first concentrate on local and sector-specific issues and then consider global effects. For example, chlorofluorocarbons (CFCs) are actively discouraged from products.

Step three: Design for the environment. Designing a product for the environment involves techniques such as material substitution, reuse of the product, maintainability, recyclability, and design for disassembly. These activities could easily be incorporated into the design control phase of a management system for quality assurance. This would include methods such as design for manufacturability. While the engineer is considering the best way to manufacture a new product, he or she could consider the design for environmental issues.

Accomplishing these methods is also detailed in ISO Guide 64. First, the specification writer should consider the environmental inputs of the product:

- *Material inputs.* Consideration of the environmental effects of the extraction and use of the raw materials that go into the product's design.
- *Energy inputs.* Consideration of the environmental effects of the use of various energy sources (e.g., fossil fuels, nuclear, hydroelectric, thermal waste, energy recovery, and so on).

The other half of the environmental equation would be the outputs resulting from the manufacture and use of your product. These can be placed into definitive categories such as:

- Air emission
- Water effluent
- Solid waste
- Other releases (e.g., noise, radiation, odor, vibration, and so on)

As you can imagine, life cycle assessment is an immediate and obvious methodology for finding an inventory of environmental outputs that could be placed in these categories.

AN EXAMPLE OF USING ISO GUIDE 64 WITH THE DESIGN OF A SERVICE

Let's take a specific example to illustrate how this is done. This time, let's look at the design of a service and its environmental effect, specifically, the design of an automatic teller machine system—the machine you see in the lobby of most banks.

An automatic teller machine looks like a simple device. In reality, it is actually a service provided by the bank. The service is your ability to directly access and manipulate your accounts. The most obvious portion of the delivery of that service is the automatic teller machine. However, other people, systems, and machines are involved.

We will look only at a portion of the system's design. To make the automatic teller service possible, the teller machine must be electronically connected to the bank's central computer. This is made possible by a modem inside the teller machine. To make the electronic connection secure, a dedicated phone line is installed, which involves a material input. The customer sees the result of communication on a video display unit. Driving the display unit and its modem is a computer. All these components require electrical energy, which would be an energy input. Thus, our list of environmental effects would begin like this:

Inputs:

1. Material inputs
   —Dedicated phone line
2. Energy inputs
   —Electricity

For each input, corresponding outputs are considered. You may find that a single input can affect other inputs and outputs. For example, specifying a dedicated phone line will limit your choice of materials used and how the line is installed because it requires an outside telecommunication company to install the cable.

In our example, we can find several outputs that are a result of our short list of inputs. Thus, our list may begin to look like this:

Inputs:	**Outputs:**
1. Material inputs —Dedicated phone line	1. Air emissions —Minimal fumes from soldering 2. Water effluent —Some runoff during installation 3. Solid waste —Scrap pieces of cable —Asphalt and soil when digging trench up to the building for the cable 4. Other releases —Noise and vibration during installation
2. Energy inputs —Electricity	1. Air emissions —Minimal ozone release 2. Water effluent —None 3. Solid waste —None 4. Other releases —Thermal release and need for minimizing energy usage

From this type of list, the specification writer can point out stages in the implementation of the service where environmental impact can be minimized. For example, the installation of the dedicated phone line can specify the use of horizontal boring equipment to minimize solid waste that would normally be generated if a trench were dug.

In addition, the specification could call for an Energy Star-compliant computer, modem, and video display. Such equipment powers down when not in constant use, thereby saving considerable energy. It also uses low-voltage microchips in its circuitry. By specifying these characteristics, energy can be conserved.

THE BEST WAYS TO USE THE GUIDELINE STANDARDS

You do not have to use guideline standards; however, in the creation of an environmental management system and in supporting such a system, guideline standards are invaluable. At the same time, many guideline standards involve new ideas, concepts, and methods. Thus, they will be maturing as time passes. You will need to use and stay in touch with developments of the ISO 14000 guidelines.

ISO 14004 is one guideline standard you should consult whenever developing an environmental management system. As we have discussed in the previous chapters, this is a central guideline. It explains the nature and composition of an environmental management system. In fact, you should read ISO 14004 before studying the requirements of ISO 14001.

ISO 14050 terms and definitions should be consulted if you are confused by any of the definitions used in the other standards. Much work was done in TC 207 to coordinate definitions of critical terms between standards. The definitions of critical terms are important to the interpretation of ISO 14000 requirements. For example, your environmental policy is part of your environmental management system.

When you have developed an environmental management system, you will find that you will want to use effective environmental methodologies and also gain market advantage. The ISO 14040 set of standards covers the issue of life cycle assessment. Life cycle assessment is an important tool for discovering the environmental effects created by your products, activities, and services.

The ISO 14030 set of standards proposes methods for evaluating your environmental performance. As we have seen previously, an important aspect of your environmental management system is the ability to set goals and targets for your environmental performance based on regulation and customer requirements. The ISO 14030 standards are intended to assist you in this effort.

ISO Guide 64 gives you some guidelines to follow when writing specifications. This allows a company to require environmentally friendly materials, methods, and services from its suppliers. This can assist a company's efforts to develop environmentally friendly products or services.

When a company wishes to make known to its consumers that it has an environmental management system that creates environmentally friendly products, one approach is to use eco-labeling. In the next chapter, we will discuss this issue more fully. ISO 14020 standards can assist you in sorting out your approach to eco-labeling.

Finally, you will find that a critical component of any management system is the ability of management to assess the conformance and effectiveness of their system. That implies the use of internal audits. The ISO 14010 collection of standards will be discussed in Chapter 8. This is the basic approach to auditing for environmental management conformance and effectiveness.

Therefore, you can see that most companies that have or want to develop an environmental management system will eventually need to consult the ISO 14000 guideline standards. These standards are best used when you need to employ a new method or address a new environmental issue. When you have studied a guideline standard, you should seek out advice on the standard from other parties. The easiest way to do this is to consult any of the newsletters or books being published on the implementation of ISO 14000. There are also consultants experienced in environmental assessments, audits, and impact statements who can be of assistance.

HOW TO KEEP UP WITH REVISIONS AND RELEASES OF GUIDELINE STANDARDS

The best way to keep up with developments involving ISO 14000 standards is to become an observer of TC 207. This is a relatively easy and inexpensive procedure. For example, in the U.S., there are two primary contact points for getting on the mailing list of TC 207.

Rose Tomasello
ASTM
1916 Race Street
Philadelphia, PA 19103
(215) 299-5487 (Phone)
(215) 299-2630 (Fax)

Patricia Kopp
American Society for Quality Control
611 East Wisconsin Avenue
P.O. Box 3005
Milwaukee, WI 53201
(414) 272 8575 (Phone)
(800) 248-1946 (Phone)
(414) 272-1734 (Fax)

By contacting either of these two organizations and paying a small fee, you can get on the mailing list. After each critical meeting of TC 207, you will receive minutes of the meeting and copies of draft standards. In other countries, you must identify and contact the organization representing your country at TC 207 meetings. They should offer a similar program.

Consultants, registrars, newsletters, books, and computer bulletin board services related to environmental issues will also be tracking the development and evolution of these standards. Consult the list of these resources in Appendix C. By staying in touch with developments, you can anticipate the future course and requirements of ISO 14000. This will help you with the development of an environmental management system now and the development or maintenance of such a system in the future.

Chapter 5

ECO-LABELING—HOW TO LET THE PUBLIC KNOW ABOUT YOUR ENVIRONMENTAL MANAGEMENT SYSTEM

After you have established an environmental management system, you should use it to obtain maximum benefits for your company. I have already explained the internal benefits of such a system. In this chapter, I shall explain the external benefits, specifically, the marketing potential of the eco-label.

Basically, an eco-label is an environmental claim made on packaging, brochures, or other product literature. Today it is common to see environmental claims being made for a variety of products. For example, you will see the words "dolphin safe," "recyclable," "environmentally friendly," and so on. The problem for consumers is knowing whether these claims are valid.

At the same time, governments have a growing interest in moving away from regulations as a means of protecting the environment. The new movement is toward creating industrial cooperation. Economists believe that the consumer is a better driving force to make industry more environmentally friendly. If the consumer purchases clearly marked products showing environmental friendliness, the industrial world will pursue this market.

Therefore, the current approach within many governments is to use eco-labels, also called green labels. Such labeling is actually just part of the information presented on the product to the consumer. Other information includes safety items, conveniences, performance, nutrition, contents, and so on. Most of these are controlled by federal regulations. A similar approach is being used for eco-labels. Many countries now have eco-labeling regulations, especially those in the European Union. The intention of the ISO 14020 series of standards is to present an international approach to eco-labeling. This will also allow international trade to take advantage of the marketing opportunity eco-labels present.

BACKGROUND

In 1978, Germany began the eco-label movement with the introduction of the Blue Angel seal for selected products. Since then, over 30 countries have adopted similar eco-label programs. In the U.S., there are currently regulations on labeling claims for recycled material content and a few other environmental issues.

Around 1991, the ISO/IEC Strategic Advisory Group on the Environment (SAGE) formed a subgroup to study environmental labeling. This group looked at the existing national programs for eco-labeling. Their mission was to identify whether there was a need for an international standard for such labeling. What they found was a large collection of opinions on what constituted an eco-label. They found even more interpretation of the regulations.

In the European Union, there is an eco-label team already in force. This program is purely voluntary. Under the program, a company can petition for the right to affix a special European Union symbol on a given product to indicate environmental friendliness. The first two product categories affected by this scheme were tissue products and soil improvers.

Obviously, if a company is operating in Europe where customers are extremely sensitive to environmental issues, the eco-label scheme is appealing. This would be especially true for tissue product producers and the makers of soil improvers. However, if your company in North America sells wood pulp to a European manufacturer of tissue paper, you may find that the corporate customer wants to examine your environmental management system.

Therefore, ISO has taken a considerable interest in the idea of an international form of eco-labeling. TC 207 has set up subcommittee 3 to address this very issue. So far they have created committee drafts for two of the four planned standards for eco-labeling:

ISO 14020: Goal and Principles of All Environmental Labeling (planned)

ISO 14021: Self-Declaration Environmental Claims (drafted)

ISO 14022: Symbols Used for Labels (planned)

ISO 14023: Environmental Labeling—Testing and Verification Methodologies (planned)

ISO 14024: Environmental Labeling—Guiding Principles, Practices, and Criteria for Multiple Criteria-Based Practitioner Programs (Type I)—Guide for Certification Procedures (drafted)

Currently, only ISO 14021 and ISO 14024 are moving ahead for approval as standards in 1996. The other standards should follow about a year or so later.

THE CURRENT LOOK OF ECO-LABELS

In 1988, Canada began a program called "EcoLogo." In this program, the Canadian government selects specific product categories for environmental evaluation. The criteria for that product group is established by industry, governmental agencies, and environmental groups. The criteria that is developed gives assurance that the product causes minimal environmental damage.

To get the EcoLogo, a product has to conform to the criteria. In other words, this is an approval-based system in which a single seal on your product assures the customer that the product is friendly to the environment. In the U.S., a similar program is being conducted by a nonprofit group called Green Seal. They have modeled their program on the Canadian system. Industry pays for the evaluation of each product. Underwriters Laboratories conducts many of the certification tests.

A competing program in the U.S. is called the Scientific Certification System (SCS). This is a for-profit group with a different approach to eco-labeling. A company pays SCS to perform a life cycle assessment of a product. The report from the assessment is called an environmental report card. It lists items such as grams of pollutants released through manufacturing, energy used, gallons of water used during production, and so on.

This type of program is not attribute based like the Green Seal. Instead of a single seal, a list of environmental effects are presented along with the product. This has both advantages and disadvantages. Its primary advantage is that the consumer can examine hard data on the environmental impact of the product. Its primary disadvantage is the assumption that consumers will recognize when a product is friendly to the environment; that is, a consumer may see the environmental report card on a product and just assume that it is environmentally friendly when, in fact, it is not.

At the same time, the U.S. Federal Trade Commission is responsible for enforcing truth in labeling. However, they rarely investigate environmental claims. This leaves the consumer in the U.S. overwhelmed with environmental claims on products and the use of terms such as "green" that would lead them to believe a product is environmentally friendly. Yet many U.S. consumers are unaware of the certified eco-labeling programs already in effect.

With this in mind, you can see that the introduction of an environmental labeling standard at an international level will add some confusion. However, the eco-labeling scheme proposed by the ISO 14020 series of standards could lead to greater awareness by consumers and greater usage by industry.

TYPE I LABELS—THIRD-PARTIES VOUCH FOR ENVIRONMENTAL CLAIMS

One of the first moves SAGE took was to categorize eco-labels into logical groups based on existing national programs. For example, there is a group of eco-labels called "Type I." The Type I labels are defined as a "multiple criteria-based third-party eco-labeling program." This means that an official third party is certifying that your product has met most or all of the predetermined criteria that promote environmentally sound purchasing decisions for similar products.

This is distinct from national eco-labeling programs. Under national programs, there will be specific national standards for a product to demonstrate conformance. In the U.S., there is a standard on how you label the amount of recycled material in your packaging and/or product. It is your responsibility first to conform to the standards and laws that apply to labeling and environmental claims.

The intention of the ISO 14020 series of standards is to provide an international approach to common eco-labeling practices. Thus, when you have satisfied your national requirements, you can then conform to the ISO requirements to gain an additional seal on your labels to make your product more appealing to a world market.

The intended use of the ISO 14020 series of standards assumes a lot of cooperation among companies and nations as well as a general consensus on just what makes an eco-label. We are looking at a brand-new area of development in certifications; thus, you will have to stay in close contact with developments in this area to stay on top of opportunities for your company and its products.

Remember, an ISO program for eco-labeling will be purely voluntary, so it will be up to governments and corporations to determine where and when the standard would be used. This includes decisions about which products should have eco-labeling. At the same time, outside organizations such as registrars, government agencies, and certification laboratories will most likely provide the third-party assessment.

HOW ISO 14024 WILL WORK

The primary purpose of such standards as ISO 14024 is to establish the general guideline for how a government or industry can set up a multiple criteria-based, third-party environmental labeling program. It is important to note at this time that standards in the ISO 14020 group are not addressing the use of the ISO 14000 seal or artwork. When you find that you are in conformance with ISO 14001, the registrar will issue a certificate of conformance. In addition, the registrar will also sign a contractual agreement with your company on the use of the ISO 14000 logo and the certification seal of the registrar. That agreement will spell out how you can use such artwork.

A program operating under a standard such as ISO 14024 would apply, in contrast, to environmental claims that a company makes. ISO 14024 is really a guideline to governments and official agencies wishing to internationalize their eco-label programs or who wish to start an eco-label program. ISO 14024 is not a standard against which a company becomes certified. Instead, it is intended to serve as the basis for a company that wishes to initiate an eco-label program. What a company needs to know from this standard is the expectations that will go along with programs that comply with this standard.

For example, suppose that your national government wants to use ISO 14024 to design and develop an eco-label program. The government would begin by identifying the stakeholders in the program. Stakeholders would be the groups with vested interests in an eco-label program—groups such as representatives of your industry, government officials, environmental groups, customer representatives, and environmental scientists.

After these stakeholders are identified, the government agency is supposed to collect their thoughts and feelings about the requirements and scope of any eco-label program. To illustrate this, suppose your government is interested in producing an eco-label for manufacturing firms within your country. They would have to begin by limiting the program to identifiable and specific groups of manufacturers. For example, they may break down all microchip-based product manufacturing into one of three groups, based on the type of product made:

- Semiconductors manufacturers
- Communications equipment
- Related computer hardware

All other product categories would be excluded from this particular program.

When the affected product groups are identified, the next step for your government to take is to determine which phases of the product life cycle will apply to the eco-label program. ISO 14024 recommends that the following stages of the life cycle be considered:

1. Resource extraction
2. Production
3. Distribution
4. Use
5. Disposal

In other words, an eco-label can be developed for each of these phases or a separate label can be established for each phase. For example, during the resource extraction phase of the life cycle, a label program can be developed to mark products that minimize the use of nonrenewable resources or that minimize energy consumption during extraction. Another possibility would be the recognition of products made from raw materials that were extracted with minimal environmental impact.

Against this list of life cycle phases, the government agency has to create a matrix comparing these phases against potential environmental effects. The major effects can include:

- Use of renewable energy
- Use of nonrenewable energy
- Use of renewable material resources

- Use of nonrenewable material resources
- Water contamination
- Air contamination
- Soil contamination

Thus, a matrix can be created that allows the government agency to pinpoint the scope and nature of the eco-label program (see Exhibit 5-1). When organizations inside your country propose an eco-label program, watch for this type of analysis and feedback from stakeholders of the development.

Using this matrix, the government agency would develop the criteria for the eco-labeling program. They would have to give consideration to several issues, such as:

- Identification of relevant areas where the removal of environmental burdens would have maximum benefits
- Creation of levels for each criteria
- Determination of test procedures
- Determination of certification procedures
- Indices to use
- Consideration of impacts on international trade

The objective is to create criteria for the eco-label program that are objective and verifiable. Also, the criteria have to fit the scope and principle of the ISO 14024 standard. That means that interested parties—both foreign and domestic—must be part of the development process.

ISO 14024 spends a considerable amount of time discussing the principles and practices of a conforming eco-label program. The list is extensive and would be difficult to implement completely; therefore, you may find that your national eco-label program may borrow heavily from ISO 14024, but it may not fully conform. A quick look at the suggested principles of a third-party eco-label program shows why:

1. The program must be voluntary.
2. Credibility is established by the involvement of third-party registrars and the development of transparent requirements (that is, requirements developed in public with all interested parties and that are published).
3. Such a program must also conform to relevant environmental regulations within the country.
4. Such programs must use a comprehensive life cycle approach.
5. The levels of criteria must be selective enough to distinguish outstanding products from all other products.

Exhibit 5-1: Matrix of Environmental Considerations

Environmental criteria for the manufacturing of semiconductors. Empty squares indicate area of little concern. Major emphasis for eco-labeling criteria will be placed on minimizing the use of hazardous chemicals and difficult-to-recycle materials during production. Secondary emphasis to be placed upon recycling of used chips.

Environmental Effects	**Product Life Cycle Phases**				
	Resource Extraction	**Production**	**Distribution**	**Use**	**Disposal**
Renewable Energy		Increase use of solar heating for production facilities		Adapt product for solar energy system compatibility	Recycle packaging
Non-renewable Energy	Reduce fossil fuel use during extraction of silica	Reduce use of electricity during production	Reduce fossil fuel use during shipping	Reduce amount of electricity consumed by the chip	Use discarded packaging for energy production
Renewable Material Resources	Use recycled paper for packaging and literature	Recycle production materials	Use recycled paper in shipping containers		Recycle chips
Non-renewable Material Resources	Minimize impact from mining and processing rare earths	Minimize scrap rates		Maximize life of product	Minimize number of hazardous materials in product
Water Pollution	Minimize use of water for material extraction	Minimize contamination of water discharge			Protect ground water after disposal
Air Pollution	Minimize air pollution during mineral extraction	Collect and scrub fumes			
Soil Pollution	Minimize soil impacts from mining	Properly recycle materials for disposal		Discourage customer disposal of chips	Encourage recycling of chips

6. The criteria of the program must be regularly reviewed and updated as necessary.
7. A formal consultation mechanism must be set up among all stakeholders, and such discussions have to be made public.
8. The rationale for the developed eco-label program must be rational and open for examination by the public.
9. Funding for such a program must exhibit that independence from all interested parties exists without conflicts of interest and ensure that financial participation and information is available to the stakeholders.

10. Any conforming eco-label program cannot create barriers to free trade.
11. Conformity assessments have to be possible based on the criteria for qualification.
12. Applications must be available to all parties.
13. Criteria within the program must be based on objective and impartial scientific studies.
14. The cost of applying for an eco-label should be low.
15. Confidentiality is maintained by the registrar in relation to data obtained from a company.
16. The criteria of the program cannot interfere with the function of the product.

As you can see, ISO 14024 lays out many restrictions for any eco-label program. For example, the concern about interference with free trade comes from concerns expressed by developing nations. It is easy to see that a developed nation would have the resources to conduct extensive scientific testing of products. In contrast, developing nations are frequently unable to muster such resources. An eco-label program that required extensive product testing by the manufacturer would make it difficult for a company in a developing nation to conform. Thus, their product would be more difficult to market.

You can see that all interested parties have to be involved, without any one party having undue influence over the criteria or the method of assessment. Previous experience with environmental issues has demonstrated the difficulty of achieving this goal.

HOW A COMPANY WOULD PARTICIPATE IN AN ECO-LABEL PROGRAM BASED ON ISO 14024

Let's assume that your national government has successfully formed an eco-label program based on ISO 14024. What would happen first is that you would contact a registrar who can issue the eco-label. In some cases, a government agency or public organization may be the group issuing the eco-label. Either way, you need to get two items from them. The first is a copy of the general rules for the program. These spell out the products that can qualify and how your company must apply for the eco-label.

The second item would be the specific product criteria. This would be a set of the technical requirements that apply to each qualified product category. Between these two items, you have all the requirements needed for the award of an eco-label. The party that issues the eco-label is actually licensing your company to use such a mark. This implies strict legal relationships between you and the licenser. This also implies that your company, if qualified, would be publicly listed as being in conformance.

Because ISO 14024 does not spell out a specific plan for issuing eco-labels, you will find that schemes between countries can vary considerably. This happens because there are so many factors that can influence the selection of criteria and the choice of a verification procedure. When your company has filed an application for the eco-label of your choice, you will then have to comply with the verification method that applies. ISO 14024 lays out four basic ways you can conform:

1. A self-declaration of conformance based on ISO/IEC Guide 22
2. A review of documentation conducted by the registrar
3. On-site assessment of the manufacturing phase of the requirements
4. Testing of your product against the stated criteria

Through one of these four verification methods, and possibly a combination of methods, you may qualify your product for the eco-label you have selected. Once awarded, it will be the responsibility of your company to maintain ongoing conformance with the criteria of the program. The registrar will make regular examinations of your product and related systems to ensure this ongoing conformance.

You are under no obligation to actually use the seal on your product that represents your awarded eco-label. For example, if you are the supplier to a larger corporation and you can demonstrate that you met the requirements for an eco-label, that may be all that is necessary. In contrast, if your company markets to consumers who are environmentally sensitive, the use of the eco-label seal on your products is critical.

When you evaluate an eco-label program, an important feature to look for in the program is the level of protection given to the winners. A good program will strongly prevent the misuse of the label. We have all seen products that stretch the truth with their labeling. It is important that the public both recognize and respect the eco-label that you choose.

Other considerations you should give any eco-label program include the following:

1. Does the registrar publicly announce your compliance?
2. Are there written procedures for the suspension, cancellation, or withdrawal of the label?
3. Does the registrar allow you to enact corrective actions to achieve conformance?
4. Is there a procedure for the resolution of disputes with the registrar?
5. Is the cost of the program reasonable?
6. Are the criteria for qualification easy to understand and implement?
7. Is the eco-label widely respected by your customers?

SUMMARY OF ISO 14024

As you can see from this discussion, ISO 14024 is still a concept in development. Several countries around the world already have national eco-label programs. However, these tend to be limited to specific products, such as the eco-labeling of fine papers in Norway. In addition, these national programs have had various levels of success.

Therefore, ISO 14024 is handy for evaluating these types of programs. If ISO 14024 catches on with the international community, you should begin to see a more universal approach to eco-labeling.

AN EXAMPLE OF ECO-LABELING LAUNDRY DETERGENT IN THE EUROPEAN UNION

On July 25, 1995, the European Commission adopted a set of ecological criteria for laundry detergent makers that requested an eco-label for their product. The criteria was published and any manufacturer was eligible to apply for an eco-label. The criteria was developed using a very public approach.

The working group that developed the criteria was composed of experts from member states, manufacturing representatives, retailers, consumer interest groups, environmental groups, and scientific experts. They tested 131 types of detergents currently marketed in Europe. This represented 74 percent of the detergent market.

Laundry detergent was one of the selected targets for potential eco-labeling because such products have a significant impact on the quality of water. It was estimated that Europe used 3.5 million tons of detergent per year. It was also felt that an eco-label would be a significant marketing tool for this product line.

A cradle-to-grave life cycle assessment was conducted on laundry detergent. It was determined that the major impact on the environment occurred during the "use" portion of the life cycle. Several characteristics of the product were identified as having significant impacts on the environment:

- Total content of chemicals
- Soluble inorganics
- Insoluble inorganics
- Nonbiodegradable organics
- Toxic substances
- Biological oxygen demand
- Phosphate content

For each of these characteristics, a hurdle point was established. Only a product that can clear these defined hurdles can be considered for an eco-label. The

European Commission also created a database of the existing levels of these criteria within the examined products. As a manufacturer, you can then compare your product against this database to see if you qualify for an eco-label, or you can judge how far your product is from qualification.

Also considered was packaging requirements. The hurdle that was set for primary packaging was 9 grams of total packaging and virgin material per wash. They also encouraged the use of recycled materials and refill pouches. Therefore, you can see that the Europeans have established a well-developed system of eco-labeling based on the suggestions of the ISO 14000 standards.

ISO 14021—HOW A COMPANY CAN SELF-DECLARE ITS ENVIRONMENTAL FRIENDLINESS THROUGH AN ECO-LABEL

When a company self-declares an environmental claim using some form of environmental labeling, this is called a Type II eco-label. ISO 14021 addresses how this should be done. Type II labels can take any of several forms, such as package labels, graphic symbols, statements, product literature, technical bulletins, advertisements, publicity statements, and other marketing devices. These types of self-declaration can be made by anyone who might benefit from such a claim. This would include manufacturers, importers, distributors, retailers, service-based companies, public institutions, and so on. ISO 14021 deals only with the general guidelines for making your own environmental claims. The actual testing and verification of such claims is dealt within ISO 14023 (still under development).

To make things a bit more difficult, ISO 14021 does not allow you to use the following types of terms:

- Environmentally friendly
- Environmentally safe
- Earth friendly
- Nonpolluting
- Green
- Dolphin friendly

Instead, it encourages the company to make very specific and verifiable claims.

In fact, ISO 14021 lists the types of claims you can make by carefully defining the terms you can use in your claim. Here are the specific terms, as addressed by ISO 14021:

1. Recyclable
2. Recycled material

3. Recovered energy
4. Reusable or refillable
5. Compostable
6. Solid-waste reduction
7. Energy efficient, conserving, or saving
8. Water efficient, conserving, or saving
9. Reduced resource use
10. Degradable or biodegradable or photodegradable
11. Disassembly
12. Endorsement by a particular group or support of an environmental cause

ISO 14021 provides a list of criteria and methods for making your own environmental claims. In contrast to ISO 14024, this standard does not depend on third parties or yet-to-be-established national programs. Instead, ISO 14021 is ready to be used today. Therefore, this standard holds the most potential for your company now.

ISO 14021 lays out several criteria for such self-declaration claims. The primary objective of the standard is to contribute to the reduction of burdens on the environment. This is accomplished by making consumers more aware of the environmental impact of specific products. Another primary goal of this standard is to harmonize environmental claims used around the world. Several benefits can be realized from these goals, including:

- Active and verifiable environmental claims
- Increase of market forces for improvement in the environmental impact of products, processes, and the delivery of services
- Creation of good information so that consumers can make informed choices
- Prevention of unwarranted claims
- Reduction of confusion
- Prevention of restrictions or barriers to trade

A less obvious goal of ISO 14021 is the elimination of deceptive environmental claims made on products. This goal will be accomplished by ISO 14021's requirement for accurate, nondeceptive, sustainable, and verifiable claims. Such claims also have to be relevant to the particular product or service. They cannot be trivial or worded in such a way as to be misinterpreted.

Therefore, before a company attempts to make a self-declaration claim, it must follow the rules below:

1. A company should select the specific product and method of publishing its claim. For example, it may select a short statement to appear on the product.

2. When making any claim, a company should provide specific information on the environmental improvement or the environmental benefit created by its product or service. Avoid exaggeration within the claim.
3. Do not use an environmental claim that is literally true but that avoids mentioning a relevant fact. For example, a company might call its product biodegradable, but the batteries contained within are not biodegradable.
4. If a company claims that its product is environmentally superior to competing products, it must be specific and valid in the basis of the comparison. This implies the citing of a published standard or a direct comparison with similar products.
5. When claiming a product is free of a harmful substance, the product must have recently eliminated that substance from the formulation. In other words, a company cannot say that its product is "lead-free" when it never before contained lead.
6. Any environmental claim should not only be in relation to the final product, but it should take into account the life cycle of the product as well.
7. An environmental benefit cannot be claimed more than once.
8. A company must make it very clear in its claim the part of the product, service, component, packaging, or other item to which the claim applies.
9. A company cannot make a claim that has little or no relevance to its product.
10. A company's claim must be relevant to the geographic area in which the environmental effect will occur.
11. Claims must be related to actual, not potential, environmental benefits and be relevant to the intended use of the product.
12. A company must establish and document its methods of verification of its claim. These methods must be reproducible, repeatable, and scientifically sound.

AN EXAMPLE OF HOW A COMPANY CAN MAKE AN ENVIRONMENTAL CLAIM USING ISO 14021

Let's assume that you are the engineer for a company that manufactures washing machines. One of the environmental issues that you have determined to be critical to your product is water conservation. Therefore, you have designed a washing machine that uses far less water than competing models to completely clean the clothes. How would you establish a self-declaration environmental claim?

Using the guidelines within ISO 14021, you would perform the following steps and make the following decisions. First, you would select your washing machine, model 21 D, which marketing has called the "Water Master." This is the specific product for which you want to make a claim. The claim will be published as a large and prominent label on the side of each machine and as a boxed statement in all product literature.

Because you want to avoid exaggeration, you will concentrate on being very specific in your claims and use scientific data to back up your statements. In this example, the environmental benefit that you will focus on will be water conservation. This claim makes sense because you are marketing the machine in such areas as the American West and Europe where water bills are quite high. Also, these same geographic areas have active water conservation programs.

Next, your task will be to demonstrate that your product is environmentally superior to competing products. In this case, you would need to establish the average water usage in competing washing machines. By sampling each of the competing machines and observing the amount of water they consume with an average load, you find that most machines use 120 liters of water. The lowest average you observed was 110 liters and the highest average was 135 liters. In contrast, your new machine consumes an average of 80 liters. Thus, a direct comparison between your machine and comparable competing machines demonstrates a clear reduction in water usage by your product.

To be certain of your superiority, you would conduct a life cycle analysis of your product. What you are looking for is any unusual environmental impact that a normal washing machine would not possess. If the impact is negative, you must compare the benefit of saving water versus this negative impact. If the impact is beneficial, you must decide whether to expand your claims.

By using statistically sound sampling practices and tests of significance, you have established your claim using methods that are repeatable, reproducible, and valid. You have found a statistically significant savings in water usage. This feature is relevant to the product and the geographical areas where you market the product; therefore, you can proceed to produce an environmental claim.

You would begin by documenting the results of your study. Then, with the results in hand, you would meet with your legal representatives and marketing people. You would have to point out that the claim cannot exaggerate the benefits of the water savings. Therefore, your team decides to make the following claim and print it on a label for each machine and to include it in all related literature:

> *Water Master, the revolutionary washing machine that can reduce the water used per load by up to one third.*

This represents the center of your claim and is printed in large type on the machine. In smaller type, the following information is also given:

> *The average washing machine in this size category uses an average of 120 liters of water per load. The Water Master uses an average of 80 liters per load. This is a reduction in water usage of one third. Therefore, this machine can save you water and money. It is also recommended for use in areas encouraging water conservation.*

Below these claims appears a chart comparing the cost of water in three representative cities. For example, a typical four-member family in Phoenix has a water bill of $59. Assuming that such a family does 12 loads of laundry each week, the chart shows that this washing machine should save that family an average of $3 per week in water charges. Therefore, the machine should pay for itself within four years.

By including such a chart for the consumer, you point out the economic benefit of the environmental benefit of your product. The thought is that environmentally concerned consumers will go for the water-saving feature. Otherwise, customers will be attracted to the cost-saving feature of the machine.

A SECOND EXAMPLE OF A SELF-DECLARATION: A SERVICE-BASED PRODUCT

Metropolis, Ohio, is a medium-to-large city. We will assume that you are the Chief Traffic Engineer for Metropolis. One of your largest problems is that traffic is often delayed or even halted on three major freeways. The freeways all lead to the downtown region where they join together. In the suburban areas, commercial districts dominate both sides of the freeways. Thus, from 7:00 A.M. until 9:00 A.M. there are frequent traffic jams. The same is true for the period from 5:00 P.M. until 7:00 P.M.

These traffic problems represent economic, political, and environmental problems. Politically, there is a strong demand by local businesses to build a bypass around the city. The cost of such a project for your department would be in the hundreds of millions of dollars. Environmentally, the major effects of stalled traffic is the waste of fuel and the added pollution to the air.

Putting together several new technologies, you develop a new service called Street Smart. The system is a collection of video cameras placed at strategic locations throughout the city. Also, a collection of traffic sensors will be placed on the freeways and major secondary roads. The information from these sources are fed into a central computer that contains a recently developed traffic model that can predict traffic flows five and ten minutes into the future based on current data.

Another part of your plan is to put the system together and present it to the public as a new service. Specifically, you will set up a low-power FM radio station that will constantly report existing traffic conditions based on the data from the computer. This radio station will report on existing problems with traffic, expected problems, and suggestions for alternative routes. The goal is to make the traffic move more efficiently and thus prevent the need for a bypass.

The cost of setting up this system is just over $1 million. Annual operation will cost more than $2 million. Thus, the suggested service is far less expensive than a bypass and potentially less than the cost of fuel wasted and air polluted. However, these are only potential benefits. You will have to establish baseline data on traffic flow and pollution levels so that you can establish the exact environmental benefits.

The city council agrees with your logic and approves a three-year pilot study of the system. The entire system will be installed and monitored over the three-year period. You must propose what data will be collected during this time frame. To make your self-declared environmental claims you will need to begin by measuring the current problem and deciding the specific aspects of your new service that will produce benefits. Therefore, you decide to focus on the reduction of air pollution and the conservation of fuel. The specific aspects of your new service to monitor will be the effectiveness of the radio reports on traffic flow. Also, you will study the effect of changes in traffic volume, weather, and business developments along the freeways. Each of these has been shown in previous studies to be significant factors affecting traffic flow.

Next, you obtain information on traffic flows during the past three years and the level of air pollution experienced. You want to correlate air pollution levels associated with traffic delays and traffic jams. You also want to establish how often delays and jams occur. Particularly, you want to know how many cars are involved and how long they are delayed. With such information, you can estimate the amount of fuel being wasted.

When you have that information in hand, you can establish a baseline for comparison. This should be reported to the city council before your system is installed and active. As the system is used, you can sample the same information as outlined above to make a direct comparison with your baseline data. This comparison will be the basis for your environmental claims.

The actual environmental claims would be made as part of an annual report made to the city council. This report would focus on all aspects of the Street Smart system, such as its environmental, political, monetary, and environmental effects. The environmental claims would be in a section of the report focusing on environmental benefits of the system. Here you would establish the scope of the environmental effects. In our example, this would be a study of the environmental effects of the service component of the system; specifically, the radio station's effectiveness.

Here you would compare the baseline data with the information you have collected over the previous year. For example, you may find that traffic delays have been reduced from an average of 49 per week to less than 5. In addition, outright traffic jams have been eliminated. You estimate that this has shortened the average commuter's travel time by 15 minutes. You further estimate that this has saved over 100,000 gallons of fuel per month.

However, you must report on other potential factors. For example, development along the highways during the past year was very low. Also, employment did drop slightly. The estimated effect of the outside factors was calculated to be slightly significant, but they were estimated to have little contribution to the improvement noted in traffic flow.

Finally, you establish that reduced traffic jams and faster commute times have reduced air pollution by an average of 7 percent. You note that this claim is only an estimate based on observations of actual pollution levels during the period of study and that it is possible that other factors were involved. Therefore, your environmental claims are actually findings included in a report to your city government.

When you make such statements, you can say that you used ISO 14021 as a guideline for the claims. If this is part of a report, you will want to explain that ISO 14021 establishes internationally accepted criteria for environmental claims. For example, the system likely put off the need to build an expensive bypass. However, you cannot make an environmental claim about this because it is only a potential benefit. You cannot know at this point whether the bypass could ever be financed or approved.

By using ISO 14021 and statistical methods of comparison, you have established valid and reproducible claims. In addition, the standard has forced you to be very specific about the aspect of the new service associated with environmental benefits. To complete your environmental claims, you should look at the life cycle of the service and the highway system. For example, you should examine the potential decline in interest in the system by drivers, the environmental impact of the system, and issues such as the replacement or disposal of the system. At the same time, you should look at the life cycle of the existing highway system. Perhaps you will find additional environmental impacts that should be addressed in future reports.

CONCLUSIONS

As we have seen, ISO 14024 and 14021 are already drafted and on track to be approved as standards. They are the beginning of the proposed ISO 14020 series of standards for eco-labels and related claims. Having an environmental management system alone is not creating the maximum economic benefit to your company. Instead, you need to market the advantages gained by having such a system. Eco-labeling is one area in which major economic benefits can be realized by tapping the environmental concerns of your customers.

However, eco-labeling is a relatively new practice in the world. Right now the eco-label schemes are national in nature and have had mixed success. The introduction of an international standard will have an unpredictable result. But the potential for this group of standards is quite high. If accepted in major markets and found to be effective by customers, these standards could form the core of eco-labeling worldwide. Therefore, you should monitor the progress, usage, and success of the ISO 14020 set of standards and be prepared to fully deploy the standard within your company.

Chapter 6

HOW TO IMPLEMENT ISO 14000 USING ISO 9000 AS A GUIDE

The ISO 9000 standard introduced to business a common approach to implementing a management system. It does not matter whether you are familiar with ISO 9000. Instead, we shall see that ISO 9000 established the path to implementation for ISO 14000.

Determine the exact nature of your business and the scope of your proposed environmental management system. A small business, for instance, would have different priorities from a large manufacturer or a medium-sized service-based firm. Therefore, as we review the steps to implementation, we will make notes about how specific businesses would apply each step.

Before proceeding further, take a moment to assess whether your company needs a documented environmental management system or is able to use the resources available to your company. For example, time is a critical resource. If there is no pressing demand for an environmental management system and everyone is extremely busy, perhaps implementation can wait or be spread out over a longer time frame. If you know that you have no additional personnel to assist you, you should look at the possible benefits versus the cost of a qualified consultant.

SUGGESTED STEPS TO IMPLEMENTATION

As I briefly discussed in a previous chapter, there are ten steps in the model for the implementation of ISO 14000. These steps are not set in stone. They are flexible. You can expand the list of steps to better fit your particular situation or reduce the number of steps if this is appropriate for your particular corporate culture.

The order of the steps can also be changed if that suits your situation. Some of the steps can be carried out concurrently. In short, these steps to implementation should be used as a starting point for your company. Study these suggested steps and the exceptions noted against your knowledge of your company to create the actual implementation plan you will develop.

Your goal in this chapter is to create a plan for implementation of ISO 14000. In the next chapter, we will see how you can implement ISO 14000 with and without ISO 9000. In this chapter, ISO 9000 is used only as a passing reference to the path to implementing a management system.

The following steps assume that your company's top management is committed to implementing ISO 14000 and that you have been selected to develop an action plan for implementation. It also assumes that you have read the previous chapters so that you are familiar with the standard ISO 14001, its guideline standards, and related documents.

STEP 1: ESTABLISH A STEERING COMMITTEE OF MANAGERS TO OVERSEE IMPLEMENTATION

This first step in implementing ISO 14000 is perhaps the most critical step. One of the best ways to accomplish this step is to form a steering committee of top managers. Such a group would represent the highest senior officials in your company. The committee would have several benefits, the most important of which would be a demonstration of the commitment of top managers to the formation of your environmental management system.

Another key advantage is that such a committee would be able to draft the policy statements needed, also called the Level I documentation. Not only are these managers the best people to write such policy statements, but by writing the statements themselves, they will be familiar with the environmental management system being created.

It is difficult for a committee to implement a consistent management system. Committees are good for forming policies and overseeing implementation. However, an individual is best for the day-to-day task of implementing the plans of the committee. In this case, the individual would be a management representative.

Task 1: Appoint a Management Representative As Implementation Leader

This person would be identified as the official spokesperson of the program. He or she would be responsible for leading the implementation effort and for serving as liaison to the customers and regulators. Later, this management representative could be the liaison to a registrar if your company chooses to become officially registered to the ISO 14001 standard.

By appointing a management representative, your company has established a particular individual identified with the implementation project. That gives all other managers and the employees an identified source for information and guidance. The management representative must be a person with executive-level authority and experience in implementing management systems or other similar projects. The management representative is expected to draft an action plan for implementation that the executive committee will approve. This same person is expected to carry out the action plan by assigning tasks to specific people within the company; therefore, this person must be a leader with clear communication abilities.

Task 2: Begin Training Internal Auditors

The ISO 14001 standard requires that an internal auditing team be established. This team of auditors will perform several functions during and after implementation. They will perform an initial gap analysis, regular system reviews, then regular internal maintenance audits; therefore, you must establish and train the internal auditors as soon as possible. Auditors should be people with technical education and experience. They should be capable of clear communications and be able to work with any personality within your company. Chapter 8 will discuss qualifications for internal auditors in detail.

The number of auditors needed within your company will vary depending on the size and complexity of your organization. For example, a small manufacturing firm with one site and 150 employees may need only one or two auditors. In contrast, a large corporation with many manufacturing sites and thousands of employees may need several audit teams that travel to many locations.

Whatever your needs for internal auditors, select your audit team leader and the members of the team early in your implementation. This team should be experienced with environmental issues and they should receive training on how to conduct management audits. The ISO 9000 lead assessor training is adequate for this purpose.

Task 3: Establish a Means to Document the Environmental Management System

ISO 14001 states that your environmental management system has to be documented, implemented, maintained, and communicated to all employees; therefore a company-wide policy will have to be published and placed in strategic locations around your company. However, a company-wide policy will not be enough. You must also establish a documented environmental management system. This can easily be incorporated into an existing management system, such as ISO 9000, or be made into a free-standing management system.

The best way to do this is to use the ISO 9000 system of documentation, namely, a three-tier system. Level I policy statements on each element of Section 4 in ISO 14001. Level II would be standard operating procedures to implement the Level I policy statements. Level III would be work instructions to support the standard operating procedures.

APPLYING STEP 1 TO DIFFERENT TYPES OF COMPANIES. The small business might have only one top manager, the owner, or it might have only a few managers. In either case, these managers would form the steering committee. A service-based firm, such as a law firm, would be confronted with a different set of environmental priorities. Because a law firm is not machine intensive, issues tend to focus on the use of such resources as energy, materials, and people. The top managers could be the partners. If they were active partners, they would form the steering committee. Otherwise, the duty would fall to department or service area managers.

In most cases involving manufacturing companies, an engineering or quality manager would be the management representative, especially if such a manager has training in environmental auditing. Such training and experience is critical for the management representative.

In the case of a very small business, one of the owners or partners could be the management representative. This same person could also lead the steering committee, if one exists. In many cases, the owner or partner of a fairly small business will assume many of the management roles needed for ISO 14001 implementation. In a service company, a customer quality manager or a technical manager or a public relations manager could serve as the management representative. As mentioned earlier, such a person needs experience and training with environmental matters.

STEP 2: SELF-EVALUATE THE COMPANY

Three components of the business must be assessed before you form your action plan for implementation. The first component is an audit of the environmental impacts created by your company's activities and products.

Task 1: Conduct an Environmental Impact Audit

This audit is usually conducted by an experienced environmental consulting firm. Most cities now have environmental engineering firms available that have extensive experience in these types of audits. These audits will be examined in detail in the next chapter (also see Appendix E).

The purpose of an environmental impact assessment is to select baseline information on your company. This includes the level of current discharges, noise levels, safety violations, employee health issues, and other related topics. The database of information created will be used to set the objectives and targets of your company's environmental management system.

Task 2: Examine the Existing Management System

This could range from a nonexistent system to a management system that is so complete and well documented that compliance with ISO 14001 would be easy to achieve. The purpose of examining your management system as it now exists is to determine how much of the documentation you will need—policy statements, operating procedures, and work instructions—are already in place. You will also have to evaluate the effectiveness of these documents as they are currently being used.

Part of this assessment would be a gap analysis. A gap analysis is an analysis that compares your company's current system against the requirements of ISO 14001. Such an analysis should be done to determine which processes in your company will need the most attention to bring them into conformance with ISO 14001.

It is suggested that you create a checklist of the processes that are near conformance and the systems that need attention. This information will help prioritize tasks within your action plan.

A gap analysis is traditionally conducted by the internal audit team. In many cases, an outside expert is hired to train the internal audit team. Then, as part of their training, the new internal auditors accompany the expert on a gap analysis. In this way, the internal auditors can both gain experience and witness an experienced expert conducting a proper audit.

Task 3: Review All Applicable Regulations and Customer Requirements

This is frequently called a regulatory review. Such a review will provide additional information on the environmental targets that must be achieved.

Element 4.2 of ISO 14001 requires a company to establish a plan for the environmental management system that takes into account the environmental aspects of the company, related legal requirements, and the objectives and targets of the system. The three assessments just described create the information needed to fulfill these planning tasks. In the next chapter, we shall see examples of how this information is collected and used.

APPLYING STEP 2 TO DIFFERENT TYPES OF COMPANIES. A small business will discover that it is difficult to establish all the regulations that apply. Therefore, the small business owner must take a proactive stance and contact local, state, and federal agencies to establish the regulations that apply.

In addition, the small business owner usually has to interview customers to establish their environmental requirements. A few may appear on contracts (e.g., requiring the use of recycled materials). Probing customers for their needs may reveal further environmental requirements and should increase your marketing profile by meeting needs beyond those that a customer requires.

A small business will most likely discover that the weakest point in its system is the lack of written policies, procedures, and instructions. Many small businesses like to be as flexible as possible, especially companies such as software producers. To maintain flexibility while writing procedures, you can combine policy and work instructions into your standard operating procedures. After all, usually one person carries out the procedures.

For a service-based company, environmental regulations and customer requirements will be especially difficult to establish. Usually, worker health issues are the most obvious environmental requirements. However, service-based companies must also address the use of recycled materials, conservation of energy, recycling programs, and other such issues. Discharges into the office air from copy machines, laser printers, and the like are other possible issues. Considerable research is required to establish base levels for these types of issues.

Service companies may discover that they lack documentation to support an environmental management system. If written procedures and work instructions are present, however, you can usually incorporate the environmental requirements into these existing documents.

STEP 3: WRITE POLICIES FOR THE ENVIRONMENTAL MANAGEMENT SYSTEM

Your company must establish a firm policy on why it has an environmental management system. Perhaps it is to meet regulatory requirements, customer requirements, limit liability, or to conserve resources. Whatever the reason for establishing an environmental management system, it is critical that a company-wide environmental policy and supporting set of related policies be established.

Task 1: Write the Company-Wide Environmental Policy

Both ISO 14001 and 14004 say that such a company-wide environmental policy is the first step in establishing an environmental management system. As discussed earlier, this policy is the result of a company's self-evaluation and should express the reason the company has an environmental management system, as well as its nature, scale, and appropriateness to the environmental impacts created by your company. The company-wide policy should state your commitment to continuous improvement and the prevention of pollution. Naturally, you would state that you will comply with regulations and customer requirements related to the environment.

Appendix D contains an example of a company-wide policy. Part of this policy should be a framework of environmental objectives and targets. Therefore, at the beginning of implementation, management must assess where the company is now and where it wants to go environmentally. Management should assess the current environmental state of your company and its products. An environmental assessment by an outside consulting group may be a good idea. The findings of such an assessment can help your steering committee determine both objectives and targets for your environmental management system. Appendix E contains an example of an environmental audit that you can study to see where such objectives and targets are drawn.

Task 2: Write the Level I Documents for the System

After creating the company-wide policy, the steering committee would now draft the Level I documents and place them in a book to be called the Environmental Management Manual.

Each policy statement should be less than one page in length and should reflect the requirements within each numbered element of Section 4 of ISO 14001. To review, the following elements make up Section 4 of the standard:

4.1 Environmental Policy

4.2 Planning

- **4.2.1** Environmental Aspects
- **4.2.2** Legal and Other Requirements

- **4.2.3** Objectives and Targets
- **4.2.4** Environmental Management Programs

4.3 Implementation and Operation

- **4.3.1** Structure and Responsibility
- **4.3.2** Training Awareness and Competence
- **4.3.3** Communications
- **4.3.4** Environmental Management System Documentation
- **4.3.5** Document Control
- **4.3.6** Operational Control
- **4.3.7** Emergency Preparedness and Response

4.4 Checking and Corrective Actions

- **4.4.1** Monitoring and Measurement
- **4.4.2** Nonconformance and Corrective and Preventive Action
- **4.4.3** Records
- **4.4.4** Environmental Management System Audit

4.5 Management Review

For each numbered element of Section 4, create a checklist of requirements. Then, to write each Level I document, explain why your company will comply. For example, under Element 4.4.2 the standard says that you have to establish a procedure that defines the responsibilities and authorities for handling and investigating nonconformances. In addition, you have to take action to reduce the impact from the nonconformance and initiate both corrective and preventive actions.

Therefore, your Level I policy would begin by naming the person ultimately responsible for this element, such as, "the engineering manager shall be responsible for corrective and preventive actions." Then you need to state your company's policy on this part of the requirements, such as,

> *A documented system of preventive and corrective actions shall be established and maintained. This system will be initiated wherever a nonconformance is discovered within our operations. Actions shall be taken to reduce the effect of the nonconformance, to investigate the root cause of the problem, and to prevent recurrence.*

As you can see, you are almost paraphrasing the requirements. The important point to remember is to describe as accurately as possible how your environmental management system operates and the unique character of your company. All of this has to be done with a minimal number of words. Appendix D contains examples of such Level I documents.

APPLYING STEP 3 TO DIFFERENT TYPES OF COMPANIES. For very small businesses, the writing of the company-wide environmental policy and the Level I documents would most likely fall upon the owner or the primary manager. Such Level I statements can be short and to the point. They may also be published in a booklet that could also be used for advertising purposes.

Larger corporations may find that they need a corporate-wide environmental policy with each corporate site writing its own Level I documents. This allows a single approach for the corporation with flexibility to adapt to the particular circumstances of each manufacturing location.

STEP 4: FORM A WRITTEN ACTION PLAN BASED ON MANAGEMENT DISCUSSIONS AND THE BASELINE AUDIT; ASSIGN SPECIFIC MANAGERS SPECIFIC TASKS; FORM A PROJECT MANAGEMENT TIME LINE

The assessments carried out in Step 2 will create a considerable amount of information. It is up to the steering committee to discuss this information in light of the strategic objectives of establishing an environmental management system. In other words, the steering committee first has to establish a consensus on where the company now stands environmentally. Then they have to develop a vision of where the company should be one, five, and ten years from now.

Task 1: Develop a Written Implementation Action Plan

The written action plan should be a combination of the steps needed by the company to achieve conformance with ISO 14001 and to achieve the strategic goals of the company. Thus, the action plan is a description of how the company will first achieve conformance to the ISO 14001 standard and then move toward its own goals and continuous improvement. As mentioned earlier, it is suggested that the management representative review the assessments and draft the action plan for discussion and approval by the steering committee.

Exhibit 6-1 shows what a written action plan can look like. Specific people are given specific tasks with exact time lines for each task. The creation of a written action plan requires considerable skill and experience. The management representative must study the available information and balance the needed tasks against the available resources within your company. Typically, political situations within your company also have to be considered.

Task 2: Incorporate Project Management Techniques Into the Action Plan

Project management techniques are highly recommended for ISO 14001 implementation efforts. This includes the use of a time line and a GANTT chart to track each phase of your implementation. You should also constantly monitor the completion of tasks assigned to other personnel. As a task completion date approaches, you should check with the affected people to match the amount of work completed against expected results. Regular meetings to find and eliminate bottlenecks in implementation are also suggested.

Exhibit 6-1: Example of Implementation Assignment Form

ISO 14000 Implementation Assignment Plan			
Element	**Manager Assigned**	**Time Lines**	**Task/Deliverables**
4.1 Environmental Policy	T. Peters	Jan 1 to Feb 28	Research and write company-wide policy
4.2 Planning	J. Rocker	Jan 1 to March 30	Oversee evaluation
4.2.1 Environmental Aspects	B. Marley	Feb 1 to Feb 15	Audit report
4.2.2 Legal and Other Requirements	P. Collins	Feb 1 to Feb 15	Audit report
4.2.3 Objectives and Targets	M. Hooper	Feb 1 to Feb 15	Audit report
4.2.4 Environmental Management Program	T. Peters	March 1 to March 30	Organizational chart
4.3 Implementation and Operation			
....			
4.4 Checking and Corrective Action			
....			
4.5 Management Review			

Applying Step 4 to Different Types of Companies. For a small business, the implementation plan will likely be a shorter version of the plan presented in this chapter. The smaller business will discover that it needs fewer documents and related processes. For example, management review could be part of an annual review of all company functions. Standard operating procedures, in many cases, will also serve as work instructions.

A service-based company will have to develop an implementation plan that takes into account the service plan of the organization. A service plan is a detailed description of how your company delivers its primary services to its customers. For example, a stock brokerage would develop a plan on how stock transactions and account services are delivered to the customer. This would include every possible interface between the company and its customers with a description of the service qualities critical at that point.

Environmental issues would be related to the service plan. For example, if written account sheets are sent to customers each month, the use of recycled paper could be evaluated, or the use of electronic customer accounts access could be evaluated against the cost and environmental impact of monthly paper statements.

STEP 5: REVISE OR CREATE AN ENVIRONMENTAL PROCEDURES MANUAL (LEVEL II) TO REFLECT THE REQUIREMENTS OF ISO 14001

After a Level I document manual is created, you are ready to proceed with the creation of Level II documents (standard operating procedures). In some companies there will already be existing written procedures and you would review these procedures to be sure that they conform to ISO 14001. However, most companies will find that they need to write additional procedures or amend existing procedures to achieve compliance with ISO 14001.

In most cases, you can assign the creation of a standard operating procedure to someone in the appropriate department. The management representative should not write more than one or two procedures, if any. Instead, it is recommended that managers in specific departments write the procedures so that they become more familiar with the new environmental management system. Also, a manager within that department will know more about the target process.

Task 1: Review Existing Written Procedures Using Flowcharts

If a company has any existing procedures, you must review the compliance of these procedures against the requirement of ISO 14001. This can be done by using a checklist of compliance items from the standard. You should also draw a flowchart of the flow of the existing procedures. Later that flowchart could be used to further evaluate the draft procedure.

Exhibit 6-2 is a list of the potential procedures that would be required under ISO 14001. If you already have a management system based on ISO 9000 or are planning to implement such a system, you will recognize many of these procedures.

Exhibit 6-2: Comparison of Policy Requirements Within ISO 9001 and ISO 14001

Elements of ISO 9001	Elements of ISO 14001
4.1 Management Responsibility	4.1 Environmental Policy
	4.5 Management Review
4.2 Quality System	4.2 Planning
	4.2.1 Environmental Aspects
	4.2.2 Legal and Other Requirements
	4.2.3 Objectives and Targets
	4.2.4 Environmental Management Program
	4.3.1 Structure and Responsibility
	4.3.4 Environmental Management System Documentation
4.3 Contract Review	4.2.2 Legal and Other Requirements
4.4 Design Control	
4.5 Document and Data Control	4.3.5 Document Control
4.6 Purchasing	
4.7 Control of Customer Supplier Product	
4.8 Product I.D. and Traceability	
4.9 Process Control	4.3.6 Operational Control
4.10 Inspection and Testing	4.4.1 Monitoring and Measurement
4.11 Control of Inspection, Measuring, and Test Equipment	4.4.1 Monitoring and Measurement
4.12 Inspection and Test Status	
4.13 Control Nonconforming Products	4.4.2 Nonconforming and Corrective and Preventive Actions
4.14 Corrective and Preventive Actions	4.4 Checking and Corrective Actions
	4.5 Management Review
4.15 Handling, Storage, Packaging, Preservation, and Delivery	
4.16 Control of Quality Records	4.4.3 Records
4.17 Internal Quality Audits	4.4.4 Environmental Management System Audit
4.18 Training	4.3.2 Training, Awareness, and Competence
4.19 Servicing	
4.20 Statistical Techniques	
	4.3.3 Communication
	4.3.7 Emergency Preparedness and Response

Task 2: Flowchart Processes in Need of a Written Procedure

If gap analysis reveals the need for additional written procedures, you must prepare a flowchart of the process requiring a procedure. For example, you may find that you need a corrective action procedure. You would follow the activities involved in the current system of reporting and correcting nonconformances, summarized as a flowchart. The flowchart would help you to see where needed actions were missing or where confusion occurs in the process (Chapter 9 will show this method in detail).

Task 3: Review Flowcharts to See If the Procedures Are Effective

Now it is time to look at the issue of effectiveness. Many companies have written procedures; however, not all of these procedures are effective. In many cases, the procedure doesn't even make sense, or the people performing the process are doing something different from what the procedure says.

Therefore, you need to review your flowcharts with managers, technical experts, and the people performing the procedure. Together, you must determine whether the flowchart represents the best way to perform the process. In many cases you will discover that a process can be improved. This could involve fewer operational steps, less paperwork, or more efficient work flows. This can result in higher quality, faster processing, and lower costs.

As you can see, a review to determine effectiveness can be profitable to your company. Therefore, we strongly suggest this type of review in addition to assessing each procedure for conformance.

Task 4: Draft the New and Revised Procedures

When your team establishes a better process or approves the existing procedure, translate the flowcharts into written procedures. Again, Chapter 9 will elaborate on how this is done.

The draft procedures should be presented in a standard format. Based on the lessons learned from ISO 9000, the procedures should be numbered and titled. In addition, they should have a space for the date of approval, authorized signature, revision number, and page number.

Task 5: Steering Committee Approves New Procedures

As each procedure is found acceptable in its existing form or is drafted as a new procedure, it should be submitted to the steering committee for approval. There is no need to wait for all procedures to be written—you can approve each document as it is completed. However, you should discuss which procedures might share common activities. For example, the process control procedure and the proper disposal of hazardous chemicals procedure may have similar activities. These similarities should be identified and assigned to the same team for co-creation.

The steering committee must review each procedure to assure that it conforms to the requirements of ISO 14001. They also need to review each draft procedure for accuracy, sensibility, and applicability. Caution should be exercised to make sure that authorities and functions do not overlap. As each procedure is approved, the steering committee should note which requirements of ISO 14001 have now been satisfied. When all procedures have been approved, the committee determines whether all requirements of the standard have been met. New procedures will mean that some training has to take place.

APPLYING STEP 5 TO DIFFERENT TYPES OF COMPANIES. This step applies equally as well to manufacturing firms as it does to other companies such as small businesses, software companies, and service-based organizations. The only difference might be that smaller companies could use the same person to write many of the needed documents.

STEP 6: SELECT A REGISTRAR IF THE COMPANY IS RECEIVING A THIRD-PARTY AUDIT; SECOND-PARTY AUDITS WILL BE CONDUCTED BY THE CUSTOMERS

While the procedures are being written, other implementation activities can be taking place. For example, you can take the time to select a qualified registrar if registration is part of your action plan. If you are going to be audited by your customer (second-party registration) or performing a self-audit, you can skip this step.

Task 1: Obtain a List of Qualified Registrars

Qualified registrars will be third-party organizations recognized by national approval bodies as registrars for ISO 14000. The list of qualified registrars is available from any of these national bodies, particularly the Registrar Accreditation Board (U.S.), RvA (Netherlands), and the UKAS (United Kingdom). Appendix C has full contact information for these groups.

In particular, you should look for a registrar with experience in issuing ISO 14000 certificates for companies in your industrial group. Each registrar is supposed to publish the scope of industrial categories it covers. For example, if you are a heat-treating facility, you will want a registrar that has certified other heat treaters. Call or write each of the prospective registrars and ask for their ISO 14000 registration information and application.

Task 2: Create a List of Your Company's Needs

While you are waiting for the registrar to respond to your request for information, list the needs of your company; specifically, what your company expects from contracting with a registrar. This would include how the registration audit will be conducted, the cost for services, amount of support expected from the registrar, the expected qualifications of the auditors, and other similar issues.

As described earlier, the registration process is formal and legally binding; therefore, you will want to read the application form, contract, and information packages from each registrar carefully. Your steering committee should be aware of how a registration process proceeds, then they can be queried as to the expectations they have for the registrar. The resulting list of expectations and needs should be written down so that each prospective registrar can be evaluated using objective measurements. You should also note that the lowest priced registrar may not be the best choice if another registrar with a slightly higher price offers more services and a better reputation.

Task 3: Select at Least Three Registrars for Further Review

After you receive literature from all the prospective registrars, reduce the list of candidates to three. This is not a hard and fast rule, but you should always attempt to get at least three or more good candidates. This will improve your ability to negotiate a better contract and price with the winning registrar.

From the three registrars selected, you should ask for references from previous clients. All the references should be contacted and interviewed. You are looking for the level of professionalism displayed by auditors from the registrar, how well the registrar met customer needs, and how the registrar handled problems. This information should be summarized in a written report that also summarizes the terms and conditions of the registrars' proposed contracts. This report is then presented to the steering committee for review and comments.

Task 4: Select the Best Registrar and Sign a Contract

Now the steering committee votes on the best registrar. Once selected, a contract with that registrar must be negotiated. At this point you want to make sure that all understandings about your relationship with the registrar are placed in writing. For example, you will want a "quit clause" in the contract which allows you to fire the registrar at any time and not owe the remaining expense. You will also want to finalize the price for the registrar's services. Typically, a three-year contract is signed.

The first year involves reviewing your documentation, an initial visit, the registration fees, and the expense of the registration audit. The second and third years will involve the expense of surveillance audits. All expenses should be itemized on the contract so that if you need additional services from the registrar you already know the price. From the moment you sign a contract with a registrar, the registrar starts working with your company to prepare for the registration audit.

APPLYING STEP 6 TO DIFFERENT TYPES OF COMPANIES. The unique nature and size of your company is a primary consideration when selecting a registrar. Also critical to the selection process is the legal status of your company. For example, if your company is part of a larger holding company, this information should be shared with your registrar. There is the possibility that another member of the holding company's properties has used one of the registrars for consulting purposes. By knowing this, you can prevent an unintended conflict of interest.

If your company is a nonprofit organization, you should seek a registrar with experience assessing similar nonprofit companies. Likewise, a software firm would look for registrars that have auditors with considerable software programming experience. A service-based company would also seek a registrar with experience certifying similar organizations.

In all cases, you will want to get copies of the résumés of the audit team from the registrar assigned to your company. Examine these carefully to make sure that an auditor from a competitor is not on the team. Also confirm the qualifications of the auditors to understand how your company works. For example, if you are a powder-coating facility, at least one auditor should have experience with this process.

STEP 7: UPGRADE OR CREATE WRITTEN WORK INSTRUCTIONS AS NEEDED

As standard operating procedures are approved, you may begin writing the related work instructions. As with operating procedures, you can assign specific work instruction creation to particular people. Also, much of the writing of Level II and Level III documents can occur at the same time.

Task 1: Study the Activities Described in the Related Procedure and the Paperwork Involved

Each standard operating procedure will undoubtedly refer to specific work instructions, such as lab procedures, forms to complete, inspection instructions, specific tests, process checks to perform, and so on. In many cases paperwork related to these specific tasks will exist.

You should first create a list of work instructions that are either referred to in a procedure or are known to be part of that procedure. The paperwork associated with such tasks should be examined. This will give you a good picture of some of the activities a person will have to complete as part of a specific task.

Task 2: Create a Flowchart of the Task Being Performed

Let's take the example of a procedure that calls for the machine operator to inspect five pieces each hour for acceptability. Knowing that the criteria for acceptability is available as photographs of known defects and that a process control sheet is filled in after each inspection, you can begin a flowchart of the steps required to complete this task.

The machine operator selects the five pieces at random during the previous hour of production. Then he or she compares the selected pieces against a set of photographs of known defects. The operator will note the number and type of defects seen on the process chart. Then each piece is measured for a critical dimension. In this case, it is the outside diameter of the part. These measurements are written into the statistical process control chart area. If statistical control is lost, then a reaction plan is invoked.

You trace out these actions as a flowchart. Then, working with a group of machine operators, you discuss whether this is the best approach to the task of inspection. When this group has established a system they like to use and one that is effective, then a final flowchart of the process is created.

Task 3: Draft the Work Instruction

Using the flowchart from the previous task, draft the work instruction. Like the method that you used for writing operating procedures, you write out a description of each step of the task. You note who conducts the activity, when it should occur, equipment to be used, and how to fill out the appropriate paperwork.

It is also recommended that when paperwork or computer screens are to be filled out by an employee, examples are provided. This can be as simple as a picture of what the completed form or screen would look like. In most cases, you will want to provide such an example along with lists of codes or other items that could be used to fill out particular fields on the form or the screen.

Task 4: Submit a Draft to the Appropriate Department Manager for Approval

This is done to ensure that the work instruction meets that department's requirements and that it does not conflict with other existing instructions.

After the department manager approves the work instruction, the draft should be forwarded to the steering committee for final approval. Naturally, all work instructions are considered controlled documents and should be treated as such. Any work instruction created as part of the implementation process requires the training of employees in its usage. Be sure to include such training in your overall plan for implementation.

APPLYING STEP 7 TO DIFFERENT TYPES OF COMPANIES. Typically, standard operating procedures are written for cross-functional activities, whereas work instructions are for one person performing a single task. In most small businesses, activities involve just one person at a time; therefore, Level II and Level III documents can be easily combined.

Software companies will have to write work instructions that remain flexible. Typically, this involves a system of work instructions called "best practices." The idea is to document the best way to accomplish a task. As a person discovers an easier or more effective way of accomplishing the same task, this new method is documented and replaces the previous method. In this way, if a company wishes to make a dramatic change in the way tasks are performed then it merely publishes the newest method.

Service-based companies will find that work instructions are critical to their success, especially when a large number of people carry out the same task or there is a high rate of employee turnover. Take the case of a telemarketing company. If several dozen people take orders over the phone, then it is critical that they all make consistent entries on the order form. Therefore, you would write a detailed work instruction so that each new employee could be quickly trained on what to do. In addition, you would provide a list of proper entries for each field on the order form, to create consistency and rapid assimilation of the task.

STEP 8: CONDUCT A SYSTEM-WIDE INTERNAL AUDIT

When you think your system is in place and you want to compare it to the baseline audit, an internal audit of the complete system is conducted. If few weaknesses are found, you schedule the actual ISO 14001 audit. If many weaknesses are found, you delay the registration audit and take corrective action.

This is a critical phase in the implementation of ISO 14001. First, you have to assure the management team that the company is ready for a registration audit. This internal audit should produce enough information so that management can decide whether the company is ready. Second, you must show evidence that you have an internal audit system being used within your environmental management system. By conducting a complete internal audit, you will create the evidence of a system in place and its effectiveness.

Task 1: Plan for and Conduct the System-Wide Internal Audit

When all documentation has been created, employees have been trained, and evidence in the form of environmental records has been collected, a company is ready for a complete internal audit. Planning for such an audit involves informing key managers that they will be interviewed and establishing an audit schedule. The audit schedule will specify which department will be examined at which times. Conducting the internal audit involves interviewing managers and employees, sampling the environmental records, and confirming that procedures and work instructions are being properly followed. Chapter 8 will discuss in detail how this is done.

Task 2: Prepare an Audit Report for Management Review

When the audit has been completed, the auditors should submit their written findings to the lead auditor. The lead auditor, in turn, creates a written report on the level of conformance of the company to ISO 14001. This conformance is determined by the completeness of the system and the effectiveness of its usage.

The audit report is then sent to the management committee of the company for review. This first audit report should also be copied for the steering committee for their review. Any deficiencies found within the system should be corrected. It is up to the management committee to assign specific people to the task of completing these corrective actions. It is also the responsibility of the management committee to change the system when needed to achieve a higher level of conformance. At the same time, do not lose sight of the constant search for opportunities for improvement. When these opportunities are discovered during an internal audit, they should be noted on the audit report and brought to the attention of the management committee.

Task 3: Decide When to Schedule the Registration Audit

The audit report should have a section called "conclusions." In the audit reports created during implementation, this section should express the auditors' feelings on the level of conformance the company has to ISO 14001. The management committee needs this information to determine whether your company is ready for a registration audit or if further actions are required.

If management decides that further development of the environmental management system is required, they should develop a plan of additional actions. Like your initial action plan, this plan will identify particular tasks to be performed by specific people. Only when the management team is convinced of your company's conformance to ISO 14001, or feel that conformance will soon be achieved, should the registration audit be scheduled. The registration audit is scheduled by your management representative, who contacts the registrar and secures a time when the registrar's audit team is available and your key managers will all be on site.

Applying Step 8 to Different Types of Companies. The conduct of an internal audit and the report on the audit results will be similar no matter which type of company is involved.

STEP 9: PREPARE FOR THE AUDIT BY REVIEWING ALL POINTS OF THE ENVIRONMENTAL MANAGEMENT SYSTEM WITH MANAGEMENT AND WORKERS

Now that the registration audit has been scheduled, you must prepare your company for the upcoming activities. The better prepared your company is, the smoother the audit will proceed and the greater the likelihood that your company will receive registration quickly.

Task 1: Inform All Employees of the Coming Audit

One of the first things to plan and conduct is overview training for all employees. The employees should understand what is involved in an ISO 14001 audit and why the company is seeking registration. By this point, you should have been training employees in the revised or new procedures and work instructions. As part of that training, you should have mentioned why the company is developing a documented environmental management system.

As part of this overview training, you are reminding all employees of the importance of your company's environmental management system. At the same time you must prepare the employees for any possible contact with the auditors from the registrar. In particular, employees have to be able to explain your company's environmental policy. They also have to understand that when questioned, they should give truthful answers and should provide information only to questions that they were asked.

Task 2: Prepare Your Management Team for the Audit

Along with the employees, you will need to prepare your managers for the audit. Managers will have to be familiar with all policy statements related to the environmental management system. They also have to know the procedures used within their department. A controlled copy of the policy manual and the manual of standard operating procedures for your company's environmental management system must be present in each manager's office.

The managers should be interviewed during your initial internal audit. This should be accompanied by training on proper interview techniques. Managers should be made aware of how they should answer auditor questions—for example, when asked how they look for continuous improvement, each manager should be ready to show written memos and other internal communications reporting opportunities for improvement. Then they should produce their own memos instructing particular people to take advantage of the opportunity.

Finally, the managers should receive some instruction on the steps that occur during a registration audit. They should be made aware of the proposed audit schedule so that they know when they will be audited and how long their department will be examined. It is critical that key managers in your system be available during the entire audit.

Task 3: Select Guides for the Registrar's Auditors

One of the responsibilities of your company will be to provide guides for the auditors provided by the registrar. Guides are employees who are very familiar with operations and your environmental management system. Select guides based on their ability to think quickly on their feet, take notes, and be polite at all times.

The guides are provided so that auditors can be quickly moved to the locations and the people they wish to examine. The guides do not answer interview questions for other people. They do not interfere with the audit. They do help the auditors in locating what they need and in fostering communication with key people in your facility. For example, if a safety violation is observed, the auditor may request that your management representative come to the site of the violation to correct it immediately. The guide would call the management representative while noting the situation.

A guide can be a great resource for your company. Besides helping to make the audit flow smoothly, a guide can note all questions asked by an auditor and the responses heard. These notes will later prove invaluable. You can use them to make appeals on findings reported at the closing meeting. You can also use them to further the education of your internal audit team.

APPLYING STEP 9 TO DIFFERENT TYPES OF COMPANIES. For the small business, it is likely that the management representative will also be the guide for the auditors. Small businesses can usually prepare both staff and managers at the same time. Because individual responsibilities tend to be greater within a smaller company, employees need complete preparation for the audit. It is far more likely in a small company that an employee will be interviewed by an auditor.

Service-based companies will perform preparations similar to those described earlier. Software companies will need to have guides who are also familiar with your system of programming. For example, if you use a waterfall approach, the guides should be familiar with how your company works with this technique. That way they can suggest to auditors the best person to interview for an issue that might arise.

STEP 10: BE AUDITED AND RESPOND WITH CORRECTIVE ACTIONS IF NEEDED

The last step in implementation is the actual registration audit. Sometime before this, the registrar should have sent a lead auditor to perform an initial visit of your site. This visit would help the lead auditor to understand your facilities and to meet some of your top managers. In addition, the lead auditor would have reviewed your Level I documentation. This desk review of your documentation helps the registrar to better understand your company and assists in the creation of an audit plan. Before the actual registration audit takes place, you should receive the registrar's audit plan for your company.

Task 1: Take Responsibility for Hosting the Registration Audit

Getting ready for a registration audit requires communication between your company and the registrar. For example, the registrar will submit a proposed audit plan a few weeks before the audit. The management representative will serve as host for this audit; therefore, the management representative should review the proposed audit plan with the management team of your company. Changes should be made if necessary.

If you are the management representative, you have several responsibilities as host. You should greet the auditors when they arrive on site and introduce the auditors to your management team. You are responsible for arranging a meeting room for the opening and closing meetings of the audit. The auditors will need a private meeting room with food catered. You will also have to be on site during most of the audit. Larger companies will discover that the auditors will want to check all three shifts; therefore, you should set up meetings with the auditors each day during each shift. If a problem occurs during the audit, the management representative will be contacted first. Also, if an auditor requests to file a complaint with your company president, then as management representative, you should escort the auditor to the president.

Task 2: Take Corrective Actions If Needed

When the audit has been completed, the auditors will hold a closing meeting to list any corrective actions they feel are necessary for your company to demonstrate conformance. If such corrective actions are called for, you should meet with the steering committee to establish a written plan on how the corrective actions will be completed.

This corrective action plan should note the original problem, how the root cause will be determined, the person assigned the task of correcting the situation, and the time line until completion. This written report should be prepared within a week of the audit. It should then be forwarded to the registrar.

Task 3: Confirm All Corrective Actions and Receive Registration

Next, your internal audit team leader will take responsibility for tracking and reporting on the success of the corrective action plan. This team leader must make sure that the people assigned the task of corrective action are carefully tracked on their progress. As each corrective action is completed, the team leader should note this and sign off on the corrective action plan.

When all corrective actions have been carried out, the registrar should be informed. In most cases, the lead auditor from the registrar will want to visit your site again to confirm the corrective actions. Once confirmed, your company will be recommended for registration to ISO 14001.

Task 4: Use the Registration to Its Maximum Benefit

A commonly forgotten portion of implementation is to take advantage of the registration. Your registration seal indicates that your company has a confirmed environmental management system. Your management team should now disband the implementation steering committee. Next, they should begin to actively address how the registration will be marketed to new and existing customers. They should also remember that a registered environmental management system with well-set targets will always be in conformance with regulations. Therefore, they should investigate opportunities for continuous improvement to continue the assurance of conformance to regulations and to increase the efficiency of the company. In the next chapter, we will examine some of the marketing benefits that can come from registration.

APPLYING STEP 10 TO DIFFERENT TYPES OF COMPANIES. In a small company, it is not unusual for the management representative to also be the company owner or president. Therefore, the owner or president serves as host to the auditors from the registrar. It is also not unusual for the owner or president of a small firm to lead the corrective action plan.

In a service-based company, corrective actions are likely to involve cross-functional activities. For example, the auditors may find that you are deficient in internal communication between departments. It will, therefore, be necessary to have several departments work on this problem. If this is the case, you should appoint a top-level manager to lead a cross-functional team in the exploration of a root cause and its correction.

THE CRITICAL NEED FOR TOP MANAGEMENT COMMITMENT

Throughout the implementation process it is critical that you get and maintain top management commitment. By commitment, I mean the dedication of the managers at the executive level in terms of time, effort, resources, and promotion of the environmental management system. I also mean the commitment of the proper amount of resources, such as human capital, money, and time.

Management commitment should be obtained as soon as possible in the implementation project. In fact, as I have said earlier, management commitment should be your first priority. Without the support of your top management, the implementation project will stall as other daily problems and commitments interfere with your efforts to install an environmental management system.

As you can see, the top managers are involved with either a management team or a steering committee. This level of involvement makes them responsible for the creation of policy statements, review of procedures, and approval of changes in the implementation plan. It is a good idea to find one executive-level manager highly interested in the project and make this person the management representative for the system. In that way, you have a representative who can motivate other managers to participate while maintaining the ability to work daily with top managers.

Furthermore, if you are in charge of implementation, you will find that from time to time you need extra support to clear out a roadblock to your action plan. With a committed executive team, you can call on them to assist you when all other actions fail.

USING YOUR ACTION PLAN AND ORGANIZING PEOPLE, MATERIALS, AND TIME

Once you have established your action plan for implementation, you will find that you need a systematic method for organizing people, materials, and time. I recommend that you use the successful method demonstrated in project management techniques. This would involve the establishment of time lines, task assignments, and work flowcharts.

As you can see from the discussion in this chapter, each step in implementation is broken down into tasks. When you create your own implementation action plan, you should break each step into assignable tasks. Typically, each task should be a small part of the implementation with an identifiable outcome that a single manager can assume responsibility for completion.

For example, you may find that the creation of standard operating procedures looks fairly overwhelming for your company. In such a case, you can break up the creation of Level II documents into a series of easier tasks. As an illustration, let's assume that you have identified 20 operating procedures you need to write as part of the creation of your environmental management system. Instead of assigning all procedures to a single person, assign one or two procedures to the managers they most affect.

As a further clarification of this example, assume you have assigned the document control procedure task to the office manager. He or she, in turn, must survey the use of important documents within the company and draft a standard procedure for the control of critical documents. Thus, the assignment of this task would become part of your project management time line.

Today, there is a wide selection of software available to assist in project management. Typically, these packages ask you to describe the overall job to be done. Then you break the job into identifiable milestones you must achieve. In the discussion of implementation in this chapter, I have identified the milestones as the 10 steps shown above. Each of these steps are then broken down into identifiable tasks. For each milestone and task, identify when they should be completed. Naturally, some of the tasks and steps will occur concurrently or somewhat overlap each other. Your job as implementation leader is to coordinate all activities so that maximum efficiency is achieved with the available resources.

This can be a demanding balancing act; therefore, I recommend that you obtain training in project management techniques or feel comfortable with your level of experience with projects of this size. At times, implementation of a new management system can be a bit overwhelming. However, if you have had the experience of implementing ISO 9000, you can use that for the creation of an environmental management system. In the next chapter I will discuss this in detail.

Whether you use software or do your project charts by hand, one of your goals should be the creation of a GANNT chart to show the sequence, tasks, and time line of the project. You should also create a PERT chart to see the flow of the project. A PERT chart can also be used to find the critical path of implementation. The critical path is the sequence of tasks that must occur for other tasks to be completed.

REVIEWING LOCAL, STATE, AND FEDERAL REGULATIONS

Taking a cue from BS 7750, you should also begin creating a library of applicable regulations drawn from local, state, federal, and other government sources. In addition, I recommend that you subscribe to a service that will keep your company up to date on changes in regulations and the issuing of new regulations.

When you use outside environmental consultants, be sure to inquire as to which regulations will apply to your company. Feel free to ask them to create such a list. In this way you can obtain copies of the needed regulations. However, you should still investigate whether there are additional regulations for your company. The resulting library of regulations is used to help your management team develop objectives and targets for your environmental management system.

Part of this library should also be the reports submitted after environmental audits by external and internal audit teams. This will allow you to track compliance with past and current requirements. In addition, you may want to review contracts with your sales and engineering staff to list all customer requirements related to environmental issues. This will allow you to see the "big picture." In other words, all the environmental requirements for your company would be in one place.

The existence of this library of information should be known to all staff at your company. This allows various people to access this information when they need it. For example, a plant engineer wishing to install a new ventilation system could consult the library to determine the local, state, and federal requirements for vent placement and air discharge allowable limits.

In a larger company or a company dealing with many environmental issues, there will be a need for a staff member with environmental knowledge. For example, an environmental engineer or technician could maintain the library, create a monthly newsletter that updates all managers on changes in environmental regulations, and could take accurate samples for measuring environmental targets.

HOW TO SELL ISO 14000 TO MANAGEMENT

One of the most difficult first steps in implementation could be the convincing of management that an environmental management system is needed. To convince top managers (or if you are the company president, to convince your managers), you need to be well educated in ISO 14000 and prepare a solid argument for implementation. There are three levels of argument that can be made for implementing ISO 14000. These appear in order of importance:

1. *The customer requires it.* This is a convincing argument to most managers. However, presenting this argument as a "no choice" option will not foster complete cooperation from the managers. Instead, you should point out that several customers would like to see your company comply with ISO 14000. This pressure usually comes from customers that also have to comply with the standard. You can point out that compliance means customer satisfaction, which is a primary goal of your company. Later you can point out the internal benefits and expected cost savings to reinforce your argument. The point here is that forced compliance should be stated in positive terms and cooperation should be fostered.

Sometimes regulations or trade requirements will force your company to adopt ISO 14000. In such cases, you again have to put all this into a positive light and convince managers that conformance makes good business sense. This can be a sensitive issue in a company bombarded by other regulations and requirements; therefore, you need to present the implementation of ISO 14000 as a solution to more than one problem.

This book shows how you can implement ISO 9000 and ISO 14000 together to save money and effort while solving two problems. Some companies face many types of environmental audits. An ISO 14000 system of environmental management would assure continuous compliance with all audits while also continuously improving the efficiency and effectiveness of your management system. Perhaps a company has always wanted greater discipline in areas such as document control and work instructions. Such a company would solve several problems with the introduction of a single documented management system.

2. *Implementation represents a considerable marketing advantage.* If your business trades in Europe or you have customers sensitive to environmental issues, implementation of ISO 14000 can represent a considerable marketing advantage. By having a certification saying that you have a verified environmental management system, you can demonstrate to customers your company's dedication to protection of the environment.

As we saw in the earlier discussion of eco-labels, such information has been shown to increase sales. If ISO 14000 becomes as widely used as ISO 9000, you can expect similar benefits from being registered. For example, many companies have reported that they obtained large contracts solely because they were ISO 9000 registered. In making your argument to management, look for success stories from companies already conforming to either ISO 14000 or BS 7750. These success stories, especially from competitors, are usually fairly convincing to managers.

3. *ISO 14000 will help the company run better and reduce worry during environmental audits.* An organized and documented system of management will help any company run more smoothly and efficiently if properly designed. Therefore, if your company does not currently have a documented management system, it can only benefit from implementing ISO 14000, providing you design the management system to fit your method of operations.

In addition, when properly implemented, ISO 14000 can take much of the worry out of compliance to regulations. If your management reviews all regulations related to your company and then sets targets and objectives to meet these requirements, they will have little to worry about. Once your company is in compliance with all regulations, management will be informed and the system should maintain or improve your level of compliance. Therefore, your company will always be ready for an audit. If you review Chapter 1, you will find a list of individual benefits that can be used to bolster your argument.

A FINAL WORD ABOUT LIABILITY

Finally, I should caution you about the issue of liability. With ISO 9000 there is the chance that someone will falsify a lab result or certificate of compliance to a product standard. This is fairly rare and usually deliberate. In contrast, an improperly functioning ISO 14000 system can result in failures during audits that result in fines, restricted production, or legal penalties. Such failures can be unintentional, such as the result of a poorly understood procedure; therefore, environmental systems tend to have a higher degree of risk.

In addition, you will be dealing with environmental regulations that require some knowledge of chemistry or other technical subjects. You will need to have knowledge on site about hazardous chemicals, air pollutants, water contaminants, noise sources, environmental countermeasures, and so on. For example, when attempting to neutralize a sulfur dioxide emission you cannot make guesses—you must have someone available who has knowledge and experience with the particular issue. Therefore, I strongly recommend that you seek out experts in the environmental field to meet your needs. The economic and market penalties for environmental mistakes are too high to allow you to design an inadequate environmental management system.

Chapter 7

EXAMPLES OF IMPLEMENTING ISO 14000 WITH AND WITHOUT ISO 9000

Because ISO 9000 and ISO 14000 are both management system standards and share many characteristics, they can be implemented concurrently. In fact, with ISO 9000 registrars planning to also offer ISO 14000 registration, it is assumed that joint audits will be conducted. This should allow a company to obtain both certificates with one audit and possibly at a lower cost. Many of the current registrars are also offering services for certifying product standards and industry-specific standards, such as QS-9000.

Therefore, we shall examine the three most likely scenarios for your company. The first scenario is a company already registered to ISO 9000 that wishes to also obtain ISO 14000 certification. The second scenario is a company wishing to implement ISO 9000 and ISO 14000 concurrently. The third scenario is a company disinterested in ISO 9000 but highly interest in obtaining ISO 14000 certification.

If your company is interested in complying to ISO 14000 without obtaining a third-party certification, you can read these scenarios and ignore the discussion involving registrars.

REQUIREMENTS SHARED BY ISO 9000 AND ISO 14000

Previously, I discussed the suggested procedures needed to comply with ISO 14001. I have also discussed the policy statements needed to conform. If you look at the policy statements and procedures recommended for ISO 9001, you can see that there is considerable overlap (see Exhibits 6-2 and 7-1). Because of such overlapping, it is possible to expand existing documentation to include the requirements of ISO 14001. In later scenarios, you shall see that it is also possible to create a single document to cover ISO 14001 and another standard such as ISO 9001.

As an example, you can examine the overlap of policy statement requirements in ISO 14001 and ISO 9001 (see Exhibit 6-2). Although there are overlaps, you still have to decide whether a single set of policies for both standards makes sense for your company. You may discover that the quality function and environmental management functions are fairly separate and that two Level I documents would make better sense for your company. Or you might find that incorporating environmental management concerns into your Level I document for your quality management system is both efficient and effective. The smaller your company is in size, the more likely you will find this possibility to apply.

The following sections discuss how to incorporate both standards into a common set of documents. What I will illustrate is only one way of achieving this goal. For your particular company, you should use these examples as a guideline. Then you should consider more effective ways to combine documentation for your particular situation. You can also expand your implementation plans to include eco-labeling and life cycle analysis.

FIRST SCENARIO: A PLATING COMPANY WITH ISO 9002 CERTIFICATION SEEKS ISO 14001 CERTIFICATION

In the first scenario, we will examine a metal-plating company. This company is already ISO 9000 certified. This scenario can be used by any company already possessing ISO 9000 certification or that is in compliance with the standard. This would include companies using a standard similar to ISO 9000. Examples include QS-9000, the Good Manufacturing Practices of the Food and Drug Administration, Military Standard 9858A, and so on.

The approach to implementation is to use the 10-step program described in Chapter 6. The main objective is to implement ISO 14000 by taking advantage of the management system already documented for another standard. We will also seek to minimize the cost of implementation while avoiding redundancy in our documentation. At the same time, we want the minimal amount of documentation to achieve conformance.

Now let's look at Queen Inc., a metal-plating company specializing in putting chrome onto various metal parts supplied by a variety of customers. Queen is located in the U.S. and does some work for companies that supply parts to European customers. Because they have a connection to the European market, they sought out ISO 9002 registration. This helped them to run a more efficient shop while also increasing their market appeal to current and future customers.

Because Queen works with dangerous chemicals (e.g., cyanide) and creates heavy-metal wastes, they are heavily regulated by local, state, and federal agencies. This includes their need for obtaining water discharge permits, conforming to OSHA requirements, high risks for employee health, disposal issues, and a host of other environmental concerns. Therefore, the company is highly interested in forming an environmental management system to assure constant conformance. Because they went through ISO 9000 implementation, they look favorably upon implementing ISO 14000.

Exhibit 7-1: Overlapping of Environmental and Quality Assurance Procedures

ISO 14001 Elements	Environmental Procedures	Quality Assurance Procedures
4.1 Environmental Policy	Environmental Policy Review	Quality Assurance Policy Review
4.2 Planning		Quality Control Planning
4.2.1 Environmental Aspects	Identification of Environmental Aspect	Contract Review
4.2.2 Legal and Other Requirements	Establishment and Control of Library of Customer Requirements and Environmental Regulation	Design Review
4.2.3 Objectives and Targets	Setting and Monitoring Environmental Targets and Objectives	Management Review
4.2.4 Environmental Management Program		
4.3 Implementation and Cooperation		
4.3.1 Structure and Responsibility	Organizational Chart	Organizational Chart
	Management Job Descriptions	Management Job Descriptions
4.3.2 Training, Awareness, and Competence	Training Plan	Training
	Employee Job Descriptions With Competency Checks	Employee Job Descriptions With Competency Checks
4.3.3 Communication	Internal Communications	
	External Communications	
4.3.4 EMS Documentation	Creation and Updating of Environmental Management System Procedures	Quality System Documentation
4.3.5 Document Control	Data and Document Control	Data and Document Control
4.3.6 Operational Control	Process Control	Process Control
	Environmental Operation Plans	Quality Control Plans
	Purchasing	Purchasing
	Statistical Techniques (If Needed)	Statistical Techniques
		Product I.D. and Traceability
		Inspection and Test Status
4.3.7 Emergency Preparedness and Response	Emergency Site Plan	
	Emergency Response Plan	
4.4 Checking and Corrective Action		
4.4.1 Monitoring and Measurement	Calibration of Monitoring Equipment	Receiving Inspection
	Environmental Monitoring and Inspection	In-Process Inspection
		Final Inspection
		Inspection, Measuring, and Test Maintenance and Calibration
4.4.2 Nonconformance and Corrective/ Preventive Action	Corrective and Preventive Action	Corrective and Preventive Action
	Control of Nonconforming Goods	Control of Nonconforming Goods
4.4.3 Records	Control of Environmental Records	Control of Quality Records
4.4.4 EMS Audit	Internal Environmental Management System Audit	Internal Quality Audits
4.5 Management Review	Annual Management Review of Environmental Management System	Management Review
Quality Procedures Only		Product Handling
		Storage
		Packaging and Delivery
		Service and Warranty

STEP 1: ESTABLISH A STEERING COMMITTEE OF MANAGERS TO OVERSEE IMPLEMENTATION

Queen employs 500 people at two sites in the same town. The main site handles all plating operations. The second site employs about 30 people responsible for cleaning, sorting, and preparing special pieces for plating. The company is privately owned by a holding company, which has appointed a president in the company to run all management activities.

The holding company obtained Queen about six years ago. Most of the key managers were retained. Formal departments were organized into the following areas: operations, finance, sales, purchasing, engineering, quality, and shipping. The company had operated like a job shop, using distinct batches of parts. Now, it has been reorganized into a just-in-time system of continuous processing eliminating the need for a warehouse. Instead, parts are plated, dried, packed, and shipped to the customer in a continuous operation that does not allow storage of work in progress.

Thus, when the company's president decided to pursue ISO 14001 certification, his first step was to convince the managers of key departments the importance of this concept. When that was done, they formed a steering committee of the managers in the engineering, quality, purchasing, and operations departments. These four departments would be most affected by the creation of an environmental management system. The remaining top managers would be kept informed of the activities of the steering committee.

Task 1: Appoint a Management Representative as Implementation Leader

Because of the small-to-medium size of Queen, it will require only a single management representative. Larger companies with multiple sites would have to consider the possibility of appointing a management representative for each site, depending on the level of independence given to each site and whether each site would try separately to become ISO 14001 certified.

In the case of Queen, the engineering manager was selected as the management representative. This decision was made because the engineering manager had previous environmental management experience and she was a key player in the creation of the ISO 9002 system already in place. Therefore, she would have complete knowledge of the existing management system and would be fairly familiar with environmental issues related to the operation of the company. Also of great importance is that she holds an executive-level position with the company.

Task 2: Begin Training Internal Auditors

Very early in the implementation process you must evaluate your existing level of conformance to ISO 14001. This gap analysis is critical in determining how much time and effort you can expect to spend in bringing your company into conformance with the standard. Therefore, it is strongly recommended that your internal audit team be selected and trained early in the implementation process.

First, this internal audit team will help conduct the initial gap analysis. Later, as implementation proceeds, the internal audit team will examine portions of your system to ensure that it now conforms to the standard and is being effectively implemented. Finally, the internal audit team will review the entire environmental management system to ensure that you are ready for registration.

As discussed in the next chapter, the members of the internal audit team must be selected carefully. I recommend that at least one member of the team be familiar with environmental management practices—either from experience or additional training. The internal audit team should also receive extensive training in management system auditing. ISO 9000 courses on registration auditing techniques is one source of such training.

In addition, you should investigate the use of an external consultant as a role model for the internal audit team. In our example, Queen Inc., selected the engineering supervisor as audit team leader and one person from the quality department and another from the operations department to serve as internal audit team members.

This team of three auditors received ISO 9000 lead assessor training and training in environmental assessments. They also were briefed by an external consultant on the finer points of ISO 14000. This represented their formal training. Next, they would follow the external consultant as he or she conducted a gap analysis of the company. By observing this person's technique and the questions asked, the team members would gain both knowledge and experience.

Task 3: Establish a Means to Document the Environmental Management System

The steering committee was now ready to begin drafting the structure of the company's environmental management system. The environmental policy should be posted throughout the company as soon as possible. At the same time, the president should hold monthly meetings with employees to explain the reasons the company is seeking registration and the meaning of the company-wide environmental policy.

The steering committee decided that the three-tier documentation system they used for ISO 9000 will be retained for the environmental management system. Part of this decision was to make the current document control procedure effective for environmental management system documents. In this way, as documents are created for the environmental management system, they will go through the same approval process and issuing method already established at the company.

STEP 2: SELF-EVALUATE THE COMPANY

The steering committee began by requesting that the engineering manager obtain a list of all regulations involving environmental issues within the company, all environmental requirements from customers, and an overview of health and safety issues related to the plating industry. This would be presented within 30 days to the steering committee as their list of environmental issues.

Task 1: Conduct an Environmental Impact Audit

The next step the company took was to hire a professional environmental engineering firm to conduct an environmental audit of the company. Such an audit will examine all regulatory issues related to the environment. The contracted firm then delivers a complete report on the company's compliance to all applicable regulations. This information will help the management team to refine their targets and objectives for their environmental management system. An example of such a report is found in Appendix E.

Task 2: Examine the Existing Management System

The existing management system at Queen is already well known to the management team. However, they ordered a complete system review to be conducted by the existing internal audit team. The mandate for this special audit is to examine the existing ISO 9002 system with some consideration for ISO 14001.

The internal audit team will report the results of their assessment to the management team. In a way, this will be a gap analysis. One of the consultants from the contracted engineering firm will provide instructions on what to look for in ISO 14000. This gap analysis will provide the information the management team needs to outline their plan of action.

Task 3: Review All Applicable Regulations and Customer Requirements

The engineering manager then reports back on all regulations and customer requirements involving environmental issues related to the company. This library of information will form the core of the database used by the management team in setting objectives and targets for the environmental management system.

STEP 3: WRITE POLICIES FOR THE ENVIRONMENTAL MANAGEMENT SYSTEM

After the presentation of the list of environmental concerns (which was extensive), a lively discussion within the steering committee followed. The goal of the discussion was to draft a short but comprehensive environmental policy for Queen. After two more meetings, a final environmental policy was drafted.

Task 1: Write the Company-Wide Environmental Policy

Using the information from the initial assessment of the company, management drafted the following statement:

Queen, Inc., recognizes that metal plating and its related activities represent potentially harmful impacts on the environment. The environment is seen as the surrounding ecology and the internal health and safety conditions within our facilities. Therefore, this management is dedicated to minimizing the negative environmental impacts of our operations and the products we create. This objective will be achieved through conformance with all relevant environmental regulations and the continuous improvement of our environmental management system. Each year the management team will review the company's list of objectives and targets for the environmental management system. These targets and objectives will be based on existing regulations and customer requirements. We shall also involve all employees in our efforts to prevent pollution.

Task 2: Write the Level I Documents for the System

Because this company already has a Level I document for its quality system, it now has to make a critical decision, namely, whether to incorporate the ISO 14001 requirements into the existing policy manual or whether to create a separate policy manual just for the environmental management system.

The decision is not an easy one. In some companies, the environmental policies can be amended into the existing quality system policy manual. This is usually the choice for small- and medium-sized companies where department managers share many cross department responsibilities. For example, the quality manager may also supervise the technician who monitors environmental factors within the plant. It would then make sense to place the environmental policy statements (Level I documents) within the existing quality system policy manual. In larger companies, however, where functions for departments are clearly defined, a separate environmental policy statement manual would make more sense because the environmental management system is fairly independent from other management procedures and activities.

In the case of Queen, management has decided to amend existing quality policy statements and to add, where necessary, additional environmental policy statements written by the key managers of each department. Each statement would cover each numbered paragraph in Section 4 of ISO 14001.

Because Queen already has an ISO 9002-based management system in place, the management team has some idea of the policies, procedures, and work instructions already in place. Therefore, the bulk of their concern will be focused on environmental issues.

STEP 4: FORM A WRITTEN ACTION PLAN BASED ON MANAGEMENT DISCUSSIONS AND THE BASELINE AUDIT; ASSIGN SPECIFIC MANAGERS SPECIFIC TASKS; FORM A PROJECT MANAGEMENT TIME LINE

The management team at Queen now has all the information they need to form a plan for implementation. The gap analysis shows where additional processes and procedures must be put in place. The results of the environmental audit will give the management team feedback on the current level of conformance with regulatory requirements. At the same time the engineering manager has confirmed all the regulations that should apply to the company and has listed customer requirements related to environmental issues. This gives the management team a fairly complete picture of the company's environmental position. From this point, they can draft their action plan.

Task 1: Develop a Written Implementation Action Plan

It is vital that the management team discuss and document their plans. For example, it is highly encouraged that a management team list and prioritize the relevant environmental issues. In addition, the management team should clearly lay out the structure and intention of the environmental management system. This can be done with a few explanatory paragraphs at the beginning of the written plan.

The targets and objectives of the environmental management plan should be listed. Then the relationship of the proposed processes and procedures to the targets and objectives should be clearly shown. Exhibit 7-2 shows how this can be accomplished.

The implementation action plan should be unanimously agreed upon by the management team before its release. As discussed in the previous chapter, the action plan will assign specific tasks to particular people. Without complete endorsement by the management team, implementing the action plan will prove difficult.

Task 2: Incorporate Project Management Techniques Into the Action Plan

To assist in the implementation of the action plan, project management techniques can be used to clearly communicate the intention and activities of the action plan. This would include a drawn out time line chart that can be reviewed by the action plan administrator and by the people given specific tasks to perform. The administrator can use such a chart to keep the project on target and to ensure that milestones are accomplished in a timely fashion. The people assigned specific tasks are able to see the relationships between their activities and the other activities required to complete the implementation plan.

STEP 5: REVISE OR CREATE AN ENVIRONMENTAL PROCEDURES MANUAL (LEVEL II) TO REFLECT THE REQUIREMENTS OF ISO 14001

In the case of Queen, there exists a Level II procedures manual for the management system for quality assurance. Therefore, a great deal of the work that lies ahead for the company involves revising these procedures to include activities related to the environmental management system.

Exhibit 7-2: Relating Targets and Objectives to the Implementation Plan

Environmental Effects	**Targets or Objectives**	**Procedure or Process Involved**
Renewable Energy	No objective	
Nonrenewable Energy	Reduce electrical use by 20 percent	Process Control
Renewable Material Resources	Reduce water use by 10 percent within one year	Process Design
Nonrenewable Material Resources	Reduce chrome scrap rate to 0.5 percent of production	Process Design and Process Control
	Reduce copper loss to 1 percent of production	Process Design
Water Pollution	Zero cyanide release	Cyanide Capture System
	Reduce average discharge to 10,000 gallons per day	Waste-Water Treatment System
Air Pollution	Reduce in-house fumes to less than 1 part per million	Process Design and Air Scrubbing System
	Reduce discharge to the outside air to less than 3 parts per million	Process Design and Fume-Capturing System
Soil Pollution	Eventual complete recycling of all heavy-metal wastes	Storage and Shipment Scheduled Maintenance
	Reduce heavy-metal wastes to less than 3 tons per year by 1997	Process Design

Task 1: Review Existing Written Procedures Using Flowcharts

The method of writing procedures based on flowcharts of the process under study is described in greater detail in Chapter 9. For the revision of existing procedures, the process is a bit easier. The company has already conducted a complete audit of the existing management system; therefore, any faults found in the procedures can be corrected as part of the revision process. More importantly, the accuracy of the procedures in describing actual activities has been confirmed; therefore, for conforming procedures, you only need to flowchart the existing procedure.

Task 2: Flowchart Processes in Need of a Written Procedure

As we saw in Exhibit 7-1, there is considerable overlap in the requirements of ISO 9000 and ISO 14000. However, an existing ISO 9000-based management system will not automatically fulfill all the requirements of ISO 14001. For example, your procedure for reacting to an emergency will likely be a new document.

In such cases, you will have to flowchart the existing process. If a company such as Queen had no emergency procedure or process, the process would have to be designed. The management team would assign the task of developing such a process to a particular manager. When the process has been designed and established, you can flowchart to create the written procedure.

Task 3: Review Flowcharts to See If the Procedures Are Effective

With both new and revised procedures, the management team should review the related flowcharts to see whether this is the most effective way to accomplish the process. The management team in larger companies may assign subcommittees of experts on particular processes to review such flowcharts. Where greater efficiencies, higher quality, and more effective methods are discovered, they should be incorporated into the new procedures. This will support your commitment to continuous improvement and will also help to reduce costs and frustrations within your operations, benefiting the company directly.

Task 4: Draft the New and Revised Procedures

When the manager of the particular department accepts the new processes and requirements, it is time to formally draft the new or revised procedure. This is a task normally carried out by the manager of that department or a person assigned the task by that particular manager.

The new or revised procedure is drafted directly from the flowchart. The details on who does what, when it is done, the equipment used, the records to be kept, the related work instructions, and so on are filled in. The idea is to clearly and effectively communicate what has to happen in as few words as possible. You may even decide to test the drafted procedure for clarity and completeness. (See Chapter 9 for further examples.)

Task 5: Steering Committee Approves New Procedures

When the manager assigned the task of writing a new or revised procedure feels the document is in its best possible form, the draft should be submitted to the steering committee for approval. The steering committee should review the submitted procedure against their expectations and the content of other existing procedures. Their job is to ensure that the procedure is clearly written and that it does not conflict with other existing or planned procedures. When the new or revised procedure has been approved, it is put into force by submitting it to document control. Also, the people affected by the procedure are informed of its creation and, quite possibly, will also receive training in how to use the new document.

STEP 6: SELECT A REGISTRAR WHEN RECEIVING A THIRD-PARTY AUDIT; SECOND-PARTY AUDITS WILL BE CONDUCTED BY THE CUSTOMERS

As the Level II procedures are completed, the Queen company has decided to search for a registrar for ISO 14001. The steering committee has also decided that any registrar they select should have experience in the plating industry, have issued ISO 14001 certificates to similar companies, and be competitively priced. Next, the steering committee charges the management representative with the task of finding a suitable registrar.

Task 1: Obtain a List of Qualified Registrars

The management representative begins by obtaining a list of registrars from around the world qualified to issue ISO 14001 certificates. Because the list of such registrars can change and grow rapidly, the management representative will call a few of the national accreditation bodies, such as the RvA in the Netherlands and the UKAS in the United Kingdom, to ask for the current list of approved registrars. This will help her obtain a complete list of registrars.

Task 2: Create a List of the Company's Needs

The steering committee has already given the management representative a list of company needs. However, these are needs as seen by top management. She needs to add to the list the concerns and needs for herself and other areas of the company. Her list of further needs looks like this:

1. Cooperative auditors
2. Qualified auditors
3. Good references
4. Clearly written contracts and other instructions
5. Low travel expenses
6. Reduced price for combined ISO 9002 and ISO 14001 audit

This last item refers to the fact that the company is already registered to ISO 9002. The management representative would like to synchronize these registration audit cycles so that they can be conducted concurrently. This would eventually save both time and money for the company. It would also encourage the incorporation of the two management models into a single system.

Task 3: Select at Least Three Registrars for Further Review

Because Queen is already registered to ISO 9002, their existing registrar is automatically considered to be on the final list. If this registrar can also perform ISO 14001 audits, it is placed on the list of finalists.

The management representative would reduce the list of all registrars by first removing any registrar without national accreditation from bodies such as the RvA. Next, the registrars that have no experience with the plating industry are also removed, reducing the list considerably. If necessary, the list can be further reduced by eliminating registrars in other countries that would not offer a marketing advantage because they are not in an area where you do a significant amount of business.

The objective is to get a short list of finalists with at least three meeting your requirements. Your list of finalists should not have more than six or seven names on it because you will be contacting these companies for quotes and extensive review of their information packages.

Task 4: Select the Best Registrar and Sign a Contract

When you have contacted the finalists, you will want to get a quote from each candidate. In addition, you will begin to take extensive notes on how each registrar reacts to your requests. The quotes provided will help shorten the list to only one or two candidates.

The final candidates should be carefully reviewed by checking their references and perhaps by meeting the registrar personnel face to face. In the case of the Queen company, only two registrars could be found with experience in plating. Therefore, the company interviewed each registrar. The current ISO 9002 registrar for Queen did not offer ISO 14000 certification.

When a final decision was made on a registrar, a formal contract was signed. Queen insisted on a "quit clause" and a synchronized schedule for dual audits. The registrar agreed to conduct the ISO 14001 audit and an ISO 9002 initial assessment at the same time. The agreement would allow the new registrar to reaudit and recertify the company when the current ISO 9002 registrar's contract expired.

STEP 7: UPGRADE OR CREATE WRITTEN WORK INSTRUCTIONS AS NEEDED

While the management at Queen were searching for a registrar, the task of creating the needed documentation for an environmental management system continued. When each written procedure was approved, the related work instructions were either reviewed or, when necessary, were created.

Task 1: Study the Activities Described in the Related Procedure and the Paperwork Involved

Many of the procedures for an environmental management system require written work instructions. As discussed before, written work instructions are intended for individual people performing a particular task called out in the written procedures.

The number of work instructions should be the minimal amount needed to complete the tasks called for in the written procedures. The work instructions should contain just enough information to be clear and useful. For example, a highly experienced work force with low turnover would need only brief instructions. In contrast, a company like Queen with a high turnover and the frequent use of temporary employees would need complete written instructions. The work instructions are created by observing the task to be completed and the related paperwork. If you wish, you can create a flowchart of the steps required to complete the task. (See Chapter 9 for specific examples.)

Task 2: Create a Flowchart of the Task Being Performed

Such a flowchart would detail each step. For each step, you would note the equipment to use, related standards, how to complete the step, and other such information. If a form or data record has to be completed, you would also note this and eventually attach an example of the form to the written work instruction.

Task 3: Draft the Work Instruction

Using the flowchart, draft out the work instruction. Typically, the task of creating the flowchart and drafting the work instruction is assigned to a technical-level person by the manager of that particular department. The person writing the work instruction should be totally familiar with the task being performed and should use simple language and as few words as possible. The work instruction in draft form should then be given to someone who has never performed the task. If this person can successfully complete the task using only your written instructions, the draft can be considered effective.

Task 4: Submit the Draft to the Specific Department Manager for Approval

When the draft has been tested, it should be submitted to the appropriate manager for approval. He or she, in turn, will ensure that the work instruction is complete and effective and agree on its form and presentation. Then the manager must ensure that it does not conflict with existing procedures or other work instructions.

After securing the approval of the department-level manager, the work instruction is submitted to the steering committee for final approval and submission into the document control system. The steering committee confirms that the work instruction fulfilled a portion of the action plan. They also track the creation or revision of work instructions to ensure that the appropriate people will receive training in the new instructions.

STEP 8: CONDUCT A SYSTEM-WIDE INTERNAL AUDIT

Armed with an internal audit team already experienced with ISO 9000 and trained for ISO 14000 and all procedures and work instructions in place, Queen is ready to conduct a system-wide audit. A registrar will want three to six months of evidence of usage before conducting a registration audit. Your company does not have to wait that long to conduct an internal audit, however.

Task 1: Plan for and Conduct the System-Wide Internal Audit

Because Queen is already registered to ISO 9002, the internal audit team should coordinate their existing internal audit schedule to permit a system-wide audit of ISO 9002 and ISO 14001. The reason for combining these audits is to confirm the health of the existing management system and the newly implemented environmental management system. Queen is planning to combine registration audits in the future, so internal audits should also adopt this approach as soon as possible.

The internal audit should confirm that the ISO 9002 system has improved since the previous internal audit. The ISO 14001 requirements should be blended into the auditors' checklists. In this way, an audit of both systems is possible. The findings collected by the auditors should be reported separating for the quality system and the environmental management system. Chapter 8 will discuss auditing techniques in more detail.

Task 2: Prepare an Audit Report for Management Review

After conducting the internal audit, the audit team must prepare a written report of their findings. This report will be used for a critical management decision—namely, whether to proceed with the scheduled registration audit. If the report indicates the company is close to or completely within conformance to ISO 14001, then the scheduled registration audit should proceed. Management would assign last-minute tasks to particular people to bring the company into full compliance.

Task 3: Decide When to Schedule the Registration Audit

If the internal audit report indicates one or more major nonconformance in the environmental management system, the management team should consider delaying the registration audit. Such a delay should be avoided if possible. Such action should be taken only if you cannot correct the system before the scheduled audit.

STEP 9: PREPARE FOR THE AUDIT BY REVIEWING ALL POINTS OF THE ENVIRONMENTAL MANAGEMENT SYSTEM WITH MANAGEMENT AND WORKERS

When the registration audit is scheduled, it is usually time to make sure that all employees and managers are thoroughly familiar with the new environmental management system. The tasks described next can be conducted concurrently.

Task 1: Inform All Employees of the Coming Audit

One of the most critical tasks in this step is assuring that all employees are aware of the environmental management system. In fact, you should be striving for employee ownership of the system. Employees should be constantly aware of the environmental impacts related to their jobs.

The most common way to do this is to hold meetings for all employees to inform them of the coming audit. Queen did this by having one member of the management team meet with small groups of employees for about 45 minutes each. This type of orientation meeting introduced the principles of the new environmental management system and each employee's responsibility. In addition, each employee was briefed on what they were expected to do during an audit.

Each employee was told that they must know the company-wide policy on environmental management, the responsibilities of their job, and the effect their job has on environmental issues. They were told to tell the truth when asked a question by an outside auditor. Also, they were told to offer information only to questions they were asked.

Task 2: Prepare the Management Team for the Audit

The management representative at Queen met with each key manager, reviewing the policies and procedures directly affecting each department. Then she reviewed what would happen during an audit and how to respond when interviewed. She also reminded each manager to be on site during the period of the audit. That meant that they had to be ready at any time to answer auditor questions. At this time, she had a proposed audit schedule from the registrar. With each manager, she confirmed their availability during the proposed times for interviews.

Task 3: Select Guides for the Registrar's Auditors

Guides were selected from the operation, administration, engineering, and quality control departments. Each would be assigned a separate registrar auditor to guide. These people were selected because among the four of them they were completely familiar with all plant operations and procedures. These guides received instructions on what to do and how to handle any problems that might arise. They were also instructed to take detailed notes on what occurred during the audit.

STEP 10: BE AUDITED AND RESPOND WITH CORRECTIVE ACTIONS IF NEEDED

Queen was now ready for a complete registration audit. All personnel had been informed of the coming audit, all managers were prepared, and the steering committee was confident of the conformance of the company to ISO 14001.

Task 1: Take Responsibility for Hosting the Registration Audit

Queen took all the usual responsibilities of a registration audit: They provided a private meeting room for the auditors, they catered lunch every day, they held an opening meeting with the registrar's auditors, company management, and guides, and they conducted a brief tour of the company. Then the auditors were allowed to do their work.

As the registration audit progressed, managers were always available, questions were answered, documents were made available for examination, and auditors were allowed to inspect equipment anywhere in the plant. Each evening, the management representative met with the lead auditor to discuss the day's findings.

At the end of the audit, the auditors held a closing meeting with Queen's management to review their findings. Management was well armed with the notes made by the guides so that they could argue a few of the findings. After about 30 minutes of discussion, the auditors presented their written findings and management signed the initial report.

Task 2: Take Corrective Actions If Needed

As it turned out, Queen had only one major nonconformance in the area of training. The auditors did not feel that employee training on environmental matters was sufficient. In addition, several minor problems were also identified. The auditors, during the closing meeting, asked management for an initial plan of corrective action.

Queen replied that they would assign the human resources director the task of improving the training of employees. It was felt that three months would be required to correct this problem. The minor problems could all be corrected by other managers within one month. Later, Queen would put all of this into a written action plan for corrective actions.

Task 3: Confirm All Corrective Actions and Receive Registration

As each corrective action was completed by Queen, the management representative reported this to the lead assessor at the registrar. When all corrective actions had been taken, the lead auditor returned to confirm the conformance of the environmental management system to ISO 14001. In turn, the lead auditor reported to the board of governors at the registrar that Queen was ready for registration. The board then issued the certificate of compliance.

Task 4: Use the Registration to Its Maximum Benefit

For Queen, the registration now allowed the company to achieve several benefits, some of which had already been realized. For one, employees now knew that they had an active role in preventing pollution and improving the environment of their workplace. Also, management could now be more confident during audits by regulators.

With certificate in hand, Queen would actively market their new environmental image to corporate customers. They would target existing and potential customers that had indicated their own interest in environmental management registration. Queen would offer their experience and expertise with ISO 14001 as a new service to customers.

Also, Queen would encourage their managers to offer their knowledge and experience with implementing ISO 14000 to various professional societies. This would enhance the image of the company and the egos of the managers. Next, Queen made sure that the local press and a few trade magazines knew of their registration to increase their potential for attracting new business.

THE BENEFITS OF THE APPROACH USED IN THIS SCENARIO

This example used the implementation plan I outlined in the previous chapter. For small and medium-sized manufacturing firms, individual sites of a larger corporation, and service-based companies, this approach can be effective.

The primary benefit from this approach comes from implementation using a structured plan. By carefully planning in the first implementation steps, you will find that many problems are avoided downstream. For example, by assigning specific tasks to particular people and then showing all involved individuals their role in the overall plan, you promote a greater understanding of purpose and clearer lines of communication.

Another benefit of this type of approach is its linear nature. Because one step follows another, you can conduct some tasks concurrently knowing what outcomes are expected. In addition, the approach presented is designed so that one individual can control and monitor the entire process. In most cases, that individual will be the management representative or the implementation team leader.

Finally, this approach breaks up the challenge of implementing ISO 14000 into manageable tasks and takes advantage of an existing documented management system, such as ISO 9000. Thus, the goal of this approach is maximum efficiency in creating an effective environmental management system.

HOW DIFFERENT COMPANIES WOULD USE THIS TYPE OF IMPLEMENTATION

As we shall see in the next example, very small companies can also use this approach with modifications. Specifically, some steps can be combined. For small companies with fewer than 75 employees or most software firms, the written procedures and work instructions can be combined into a single document.

For a large corporation with many sites seeking blanket ISO 14001 certification, this approach could also be used. However, chances are that a corporate ISO 14000 steering committee would coordinate implementation at each manufacturing site. Policies would be written by the corporation and procedures and work instructions written at each site. Therefore, each manufacturing site would use many of these steps. Project management would be handled by the management representative, who would also report to the corporate steering committee.

Service-based companies could also use the approach shown in our example. Companies such as banks, insurance firms, law offices, and the like will discover that there are few outside regulations for environmental issues. Customer requirements or concerns for environmental issues will be more important. Therefore, service-based companies have to look toward their community to develop environmental requirements. Such requirements would include recycling, energy conservation, work at home, reduction of paper usage, use of biodegradable inks, quality of the workplace, quality of the air in the office, and so on.

HOW TO IMPLEMENT ISO 14000 AND ISO 9000 CONCURRENTLY

In this example, we will look at a company that wishes to implement both international standards at the same time. DrisCo is a distribution company selling chemicals, gases, and rare minerals to a variety of companies. DrisCo purchases these goods in bulk quantities, then breaks the bulk quantities down into smaller packages for resale. For example, they may purchase carbon tetracycline in five-gallon containers. Most of their customers—small to medium-sized manufacturing firms—purchase such chemicals in one-quart or one-liter quantities. Therefore, DrisCo is both a redistribution center and a provider of a service.

For the past three years, DrisCo has been finding that more and more of their customers are adopting ISO 9000. Their purchasing people have been getting hints that they should encourage DrisCo to become certified as well. At the same time, the president of DrisCo has become interested in the environmental perception of his company in the marketplace and has also been investigating the idea of implementing ISO 14000.

At a recent management meeting, these two ideas were both discussed. After much discussion, the management team decided that the company should implement both of these standards within the next two years. Further discussion revealed that it would be more efficient to implement both standards at the same time because some of the documentation would overlap.

Therefore, in this example, we shall examine how both standards can be implemented together. This means that some of the tasks in our model of implementation will be altered. We will also examine how to write one set of documents to meet the requirements of both standards.

STEP 1: ESTABLISH A STEERING COMMITTEE OF MANAGERS TO OVERSEE IMPLEMENTATION

DrisCo is somewhat unique in that the company only has one senior manager—the president who is also the owner. After the president there is a supervisor of operations, six order-entry people, three inspectors, and nine warehouse and processing personnel.

At the same time, the company is highly automated. The warehouse personnel pick and place materials according to instructions given by a computer system. These same people are responsible for filling orders and preparing the goods for shipment, specifically, breaking down larger quantities of goods into smaller containers.

The order-entry people receive requests for items from a host of customers. Customers can place orders verbally by making a phone call, in writing using a fax transmission, or through electronic mail. The order-entry people confirm the availability of the desired goods, and their computer software calculates discounts, shipping cost, and keeps the purchasing history. The software also notifies the order-entry people when it is time to reorder a particular material. Upon receipt of goods, an inspector confirms the quantity and quality of the material. In most cases, chemicals and gases are accompanied by a certificate of purity issued by the supplier.

Thus, we have a company in which written documentation is not needed for some functions. At the same time, any written documentation created by management needs to be minimal. With only one senior manager, the management representative and the steering committee leader are the same person—the president.

This opens some new possibilities. One is to involve the operations supervisor in the steering committee. However, there is a more interesting possibility—namely, the enrollment of all employees into a single implementation team. Thus, the president would control the management of the project, but the employees would have some freedom in designing their own system. Again, the small size of DrisCo means that the president is the only person available as a management representative. The operation supervisor would have been another possibility, but his heavy workload prevents this.

Task 1: Appoint a Management Representative as Implementation Leader

Because the president is also the management representative, he has to serve as implementation leader. Naturally, the president of a company is a very busy person. In a situation such as this one, the president must dedicate time to the project. He also has to design a very simple plan of implementation and documentation to minimize the amount of time required for effective participation.

Task 2: Establish a Means to Document the Environmental Management System and Management System for Quality Assurance

DrisCo already uses a computer system designed around a local area network (LAN). This opens the possibility of creating documentation for the two management systems on the computers.

DrisCo's president decides to take such an approach. Using Lotus Notes, the company will combine procedures and work instructions into common documents available at the click of a mouse button. The Level I documents will be produced in written form to aid auditors from the registrar. The existence of a written set of policies covering both ISO 9003 and ISO 14001 will enable the company to demonstrate to potential customers their commitment to quality and environmental improvement.

Task 3: Begin Training the Internal Auditors

Because of the small size of DrisCo, there is need for only one internal auditor. The first-shift inspector is selected for this role. This inspector has much experience with quality assurance procedures. Therefore, his training will include a course on internal auditing for ISO 9000, a second seminar on auditing ISO 14000, and some individual training by an outside consultant.

STEP 2: EVALUATE THE COMPANY'S EXISTING SYSTEMS

DrisCo's environmental management system will integrate the environmental needs of its customers. Therefore, when evaluating its existing system, it will also have to consider the needs of its customers' environmental management systems.

Task 1: Conduct an Environmental Impact Audit and Review Applicable Regulations

Because of time restraints and the shortage of available personnel and knowledge, DrisCo's president elects to hire an environmental engineering firm. The first task of this firm is to conduct an environmental impact audit and review applicable regulations.

A second consultant is hired from a quality assurance consulting firm. The primary goal of this consultant is to identify all regulatory issues involving DrisCo and to evaluate the company's current conformance level to these regulations. At the same time, the order-entry people will search through previous contracts to discover any customer requirements related to the environment.

A database of knowledge will be created that will help the president identify and document the targets and objectives of the environmental management system.

Task 2: Examine the Existing Management System

The quality assurance consultant, with the assistance of the environmental consultant and the company's internal auditor, examines the current management system at DrisCo and prepares a written report comparing current levels of conformance to ISO 9003 and ISO 14001. The report is delivered to the president of the company, who uses the information to develop an action plan for implementation.

STEP 3: WRITE THE COMPANY-WIDE ENVIRONMENTAL POLICY AND LEVEL I DOCUMENTS

As before, any company should begin by examining their current situation. It is important for setting targets and objectives for the environmental management system.

Task 1: Write the Company-Wide Environmental and Quality Policy

The first place where implementing the two standards changes the approach to implementation is in writing the company-wide policies. Because DrisCo is implementing two management systems, there is no reason the company-wide policies for quality and the environmental management system cannot be combined.

So the president took the strategic plan for the company and began to connect the requirements of ISO 9003 and ISO 14001 with the goals and objectives of the company. This resulted in the following statement:

> *DrisCo is dedicated to the goal of becoming a world leader in the field of delivering customized quantities of chemicals and gases to the manufacturing community. This includes the concepts of satisfying our customers by delivering high-quality service, continuously improving our service and operation, preventing pollution, enhancing the environment in which we work, and continuously improving profits to the stakeholders in this company.*

As you can see, this short, simple policy statement combines the strategic goals of the company with the overall requirements of a management system for quality assurance and an environmental management system. Combining these requirements will be repeated several times in this scenario of implementation.

Task 2: Write the Level I Documents for the System

Normally, the key managers within a company would write the Level I documents. In the example we are examining, the president and the supervisor of operations will write the Level I statements. These will be fewer than those of the previous example because ISO 9003 has fewer requirements and there is still overlap with the requirements for ISO 14001 (see Exhibit 7-3).

Exhibit 7-3: Comparison of Policy Requirements Within ISO 9003 and ISO 14001

Elements of ISO 9003	Elements of ISO 14001
4.1 Management Responsibility	4.1 Environmental Policy
	4.5 Management Review
4.2 Quality System	4.2 Planning
	4.2.1 Environmental Aspects
	4.2.2 Legal and Other Requirements
	4.2.3 Objectives and Target
	4.2.4 Environmental Management Program
	4.3.1 Structure and Responsibility
	4.3.4 Environmental Management System Documentation
4.3 Contract Review	4.2.2 Legal and Other Requirements
4.5 Document and Data Control	4.3.5 Document Control
4.7 Control of Customer Supplier Product	
4.8 Product I.D. and Traceability	
	4.3.6 Operational Control
4.10 Inspection and Testing	4.4.1 Monitoring and Measurement
4.11 Control of Inspection, Measurement, and Test Equipment	4.4.1 Monitoring and Measurement
4.12 Inspection and Test Status	
4.13 Control Nonconforming Products	4.4.2 Nonconforming and Corrective and Preventive Actions
4.14 Corrective and Preventive Actions	4.4 Checking and Corrective Actions
	4.5 Management Review
4.15 Handling, Storage, Packaging, Preservation, and Delivery	
4.16 Control of Quality Records	4.4.3 Records
4.17 Internal Quality Audits	4.4.4 Environmental Management System Audit
4.18 Training	4.3.2 Training, Awareness, and Competence
4.20 Statistical Techniques	
Only ISO 14001 Requirements ------------------->	4.3.3 Communication
	4.3.7 Emergency Preparedness and Response

STEP 4: FORM A WRITTEN ACTION PLAN BASED ON MANAGEMENT DISCUSSIONS AND THE BASELINE AUDIT; ASSIGN SPECIFIC PEOPLE SPECIFIC TASKS; FORM A PROJECT MANAGEMENT TIME LINE

The president of DrisCo has a difficult task—to develop an implementation plan to ensure full conformance with two separate standards while keeping the plan simple.

Task 1: Develop a Written Implementation Action Plan

Using the audit report as a guideline, the president divides the tasks to be completed into manageable groups. Then he assigns each group to a small team of employees. Each of these teams receives some training in preparing documentation. The quality assurance consultant and the environmental consultant provide this training and assist in document preparation.

As an example of one assignment, writing procedures for the inspection process, care of inspection and test equipment, and inspection and test status are assigned to the three inspectors. It will be their task to create a single document describing the procedure for all three requirements and to also include the work instructions.

Task 2: Incorporate Project Management Techniques Into the Action Plan

At the same time, the president will post a project time line chart for all employees to see. The chart will list out the tasks assigned to the various employee teams. In this way, each employee can see what tasks he has to participate in and the relationship between each of the teams.

STEP 5: REVISE OR CREATE AN ENVIRONMENTAL PROCEDURES MANUAL (LEVEL II) TO REFLECT THE REQUIREMENTS OF ISO 14001 AND ISO 9003; COMBINE PROCEDURES AND WORK INSTRUCTIONS INTO A SINGLE DOCUMENT

DrisCo has never really documented its standard operating procedures; therefore, the creation of standard operating procedures and written work instructions will be a major portion of the implementation effort. At the same time, procedures will include the work instructions. This is possible because the procedures are carried out by individuals; thus, there would be little difference between a procedure and a work instruction.

Task 1: Review Existing Written Procedures and Work Instructions Using Flowcharts

DrisCo has to review any existing procedures or work instructions. These are found to be handwritten notes kept by the employees. In most cases, each employee has a slightly different way of accomplishing the same task. For example, each of the order-entry people confirm an order in a different way.

The president places all six order-entry people into a single team. The quality assurance consultant leads this team in a group problem-solving exercise. Specifically, the team brainstorms for ideas about how they can create the best way to confirm orders.

Task 2: Prepare Flowcharts of Processes That Need Written Procedures/Work Instructions

As described in our previous example, you can flowchart the specific processes to assist in creating the needed documentation. In the case of the order-entry team, they flowchart the process of taking and confirming an order. To this flowchart they note the requirement for contract review and environmental requirement review. By flowcharting the process and adding in the requirements from the two standards, they begin to create a single procedure. As part of this process, each order-entry person shares his or her particular method. By mutual agreement, the team develops a single approach that all order-entry people will use.

Task 3: Review Flowcharts to See If the Procedures/Work Instructions Are Effective

The flowchart created by the order-entry team is redrawn to reflect the new, single method. Then the team examines the effectiveness of this method by discussing its ease of use and its ability to accurately record information. This should result in a method that is both effective and acceptable to all order-entry people. This process is repeated with different employee teams for each of the documents that needs to be created.

Task 4: Draft the New and Revised Procedures/Work Instructions

Using the final flowchart, each team then drafts a combination of procedures and work instructions. For example, the order entry team drafts a description of why order entry is important, what has to be accomplished, who does this work, when the work should be done, and what computer software is used. Then the next few paragraphs describe how the order confirmation screen is filled out. An example screen with applicable codes is also included. This, in turn, is placed into Lotus Notes as a help screen. The actual order confirmation screen is already in Notes. Thus, if an order-entry person is curious about how to fill in a particular field, a single mouse button click opens the copy of the procedure/work instruction.

Task 5: President Approves New Procedures/Work Instructions

Before the drafted procedure/work instruction is entered into Notes, the president and operations supervisor review the team's work. Then the document is placed into the document control system. In our example, the document control procedure involves approval by the president and entry of the approved document into the computer LAN.

STEP 6: SELECT A REGISTRAR IF A COMPANY IS RECEIVING A THIRD-PARTY AUDIT; SECOND-PARTY AUDITS WILL BE CONDUCTED BY THE CUSTOMERS

Because DrisCo is seeking dual registration, the process of selecting a registrar is a bit more involved. They must find a registrar with accreditation for ISO 9000 and ISO 14000. At the same time, they need a registrar who is willing to conduct both audits at the same time and who offers a discount to very small businesses.

Task 1: Obtain a List of Qualified Registrars

The quality assurance consultant obtains the current list of qualified registrars that can handle both standards.

Task 2: Create a List of the Company's Needs

Working with the two contracted consultants, the president draws up a list of company needs, which looks something like this:

1. Low cost
2. Dual registration
3. Experience with companies like DrisCo
4. Experienced auditors
5. Only one surveillance visit per year
6. Quit clause in the contract

Task 3: Select at Least Three Registrars for Further Review

Because of the special nature of DrisCo and the list of needs, only two registrars could be identified. Therefore, the company proceeded to ask for quotes and references at the same time.

Task 4: Select the Best Registrar and Sign a Contract

The president of DrisCo decides that both registrars are equally qualified and have similar quotes; therefore, he begins a process of trying to get one registrar to bid against the other. The objective is to obtain a favorable contract and a lower price. Part of the success in this effort was an agreement that if a nonconformance was discovered in just one system, it would not stop certification for the other system.

STEP 7: CONDUCT A SYSTEM-WIDE INTERNAL AUDIT

While the negotiations were being conducted with the registrars, the internal auditor proceeded with examining the results of the new system of documentation.

Task 1: Plan for and Conduct the System-Wide Internal Audit

This time the internal auditor would lead the audit; the quality assurance and environmental consultants would only observe. The objective would be to assure that the internal auditor now knew how to conduct these audits.

The internal audit would review the management system that was now supposed to cover both the issue of environmental management and quality assurance. Documentation was reviewed against the two standards. People were interviewed, and records were examined.

Task 2: Prepare an Audit Report for Management Review and Decide When to Schedule the Registration Audit

The findings of the internal auditor were prepared as a written report for the president. These findings were reviewed by the president to decide whether the company was ready for the registration audit. He felt that the company would be fully prepared after three months of quality and environmental records had been created under the new system; therefore, the registration audit was scheduled for three months hence.

STEP 8: PREPARE FOR THE AUDIT BY REVIEWING ALL POINTS OF THE ENVIRONMENTAL AND QUALITY MANAGEMENT SYSTEM WITH MANAGEMENT AND WORKERS

Because management and the employees were all involved in the creation of the new management system, little additional work was required to prepare them for the audit.

Task 1: Inform All Employees of the Coming Audit

This company took a unique approach to preparing their personnel. All employees were informed of what an environmental management system was at the beginning of the implementation process, after which the employees were formed into teams to design and implement the new system. Through this process the employees became very aware of the quality and environmental responsibility and consequences of their work; thus, all that was needed was to educate each employee on what to do during an audit.

Task 2: Select Guides for the Registrar's Auditors

Because of the small size of the company, the registrar has decided to send two auditors. One auditor will examine the quality assurance system while the other examines the environmental management system. Where the two systems overlap, both auditors will work together; therefore, two employees will serve as guides. As described in our previous example, these two people are thoroughly trained for their role as guides.

STEP 9: BE AUDITED AND RESPOND WITH CORRECTIVE ACTIONS IF NEEDED

Like any registration audit for these two standards, an opening meeting is held, the audit conducted, and the results reported during a closing meeting. In the case of DrisCo, all of this is done in a single day.

Task 1: Take Responsibility for Hosting the Registration Audit

As before, the company must take full responsibility for hosting the auditors. The president, as management representative, plays the part of host. He greets the auditors, provides a private meeting place, and ensures that all employees are available for interviews if necessary.

Task 2: Take Corrective Actions If Needed

When the audit has been completed, the auditors will inform the company whether corrective actions are required. Should DrisCo receive many corrective action requests, they are to respond within one week with a written action plan. This should be sent to the registrar.

Task 3: Confirm All Corrective Actions and Receive Registration

As each corrective action is completed, the registrar should be informed in writing. When all corrective actions have been completed, the registrar may elect to confirm these by a site visit. When the management system is found to be in compliance with the two standards, dual registration should result.

Task 4: Use the Registration to Its Maximum Benefit

Armed with ISO 9003 and ISO 14001 registration, DrisCo can now begin an active campaign of advertising their new status. For example, all company literature will now feature artwork of the two registration seals. In addition, the order-entry people are instructed to inform all customers that the company now has a documented system for quality assurance and environmental management.

Because the company depends on outside sales representatives, these representatives are brought to the company to learn about the new system. In turn, they will make the environmentally proactive and quality assurance aspects of the company a central part of their sales presentation. An advertisement in *The Wall Street Journal* will announce the company's new status as a general way to promote new business.

The president will further this effort by frequently addressing professional societies and local business groups to point out the benefits he has seen from adopting ISO 9003 and ISO 14001. This helps to increase the positive public image of the company and attract new customers.

THE BENEFITS OF THE APPROACH USED IN THIS SCENARIO

The approach used in this example is designed for the small to very small company—that is, any situation in which a company has procedures that are basically performed by an individual. A software company would probably find this to be a good approach.

The primary benefit of this approach is that one entire step is eliminated by combining the writing of procedures with work instructions. Another benefit comes from being able to reduce the number of tasks performed within some of the steps. The benefits of a structured and linear approach also apply to the scenario used in this example.

You should examine the size, nature, and complexity of your own company to see if such reductions in the steps and tasks is possible. This will be especially true for companies seeking ISO 9003 co-registration or for companies wishing to comply only with portions of ISO 14001 and not planning to be registered. Our next example will examine a company that wants full compliance with ISO 14000 without seeking registration.

HOW TO IMPLEMENT ISO 14000 BY ITSELF

In some cases, companies will not be under any pressure to implement ISO 9000 along with ISO 14000. However, they may be greatly concerned about their environmental image with customers, both corporate and end-users. Thus, they will be interested in implementing just ISO 14000.

Although we have used ISO 9000 as a model for ISO 14000 implementation, when a company chooses to use only ISO 14000, many of the tasks remain the same. For example, a company may already have a total quality management system in place and wish to establish an environmental management system. Or a company may have a well-established system of overall management and wish to incorporate the principles of environmental management into their best practices.

Our example this time is Pavewell, a hot-mix asphalt producer. Hot-mix asphalt is produced by applying oil-based adhesives to locally obtained aggregates. The resulting asphalt is used for paving roads, parking lots, playing surfaces, and so forth. Pavewell is a medium-sized processing plant that supplies asphalt to several states. The process of creating the asphalt is highly automated. Process and quality control are built into the process; thus, Pavewell has never felt that ISO 9000 was needed at their site.

However, they are seriously concerned about their environmental image. The process of creating asphalt requires great quantities of energy. It also involves the use of nonrenewable resources such as oil. Some of the chemicals involved in the process require special handling and disposal. Naturally, the company wants to control the environmental impact of these characteristics of the business. At the same time, there are environmentally friendly aspects of asphalt, such as its ability to be recycled, which the company wants to emphasize.

STEP 1: ESTABLISH A STEERING COMMITTEE OF MANAGERS TO WRITE THE LEVEL I DOCUMENTS AND OVERSEE IMPLEMENTATION

Pavewell is under no customer or regulatory pressure to register to ISO 14000. Instead, their top management has decided that ISO 14001 represents a good model for an environmental management system. The first step for the company was to form a steering committee. The operations manager, plant manager, and chief engineer formed this committee. The steering committee began by attending a few seminars on environmental issues and on how to implement ISO 14000.

Task 1: Establish a Means to Document the Environmental Management System

The steering committee quickly moved on to the issue of how to document the environmental management system. Here they faced an unusual problem. The entire operation of the company's processes was controlled by computer-based process control units. These computers automatically adjusted and controlled the mixing process—very little was done manually. What was controlled by humans was carefully documented in work instructions. No standard operating procedures existed for most processes within the company.

Therefore, the steering committee had to decide whether to create standard operating procedures or to enhance the existing work instructions. The final decision was to use standard operating procedures for the few processes that require them, such as company-wide environmental planning, training, document control, and internal auditing. Other processes would be addressed through extended work instructions. For example, the calibration of the sensors used in the process was handled by an outside firm. Thus, the work instruction for calibration called for the operations manager to regularly schedule an outside firm to provide the calibration service.

Task 2: Write the Level I Documents for the System

The steering community also had to decide whether to create a Level I document. Because they were not seeking registration, there would not be a registrar requiring a Level I document. After much discussion, the steering committee decided that it would be in their best interest to create the policy manual. In that way, they could have a brief document to explain their environmental management system to suppliers and customers. In addition, the policy manual would assist in educating employees about the environmental management system.

Task 3: Begin Training Internal Auditors

At the same time, two engineering technicians were selected as internal auditors. Here the company had a clear advantage: Both technicians were certified as environmental auditors. They had been hired by the company to help monitor environmental impact and to design systems to control pollution; therefore, these two individuals needed only a week of training on how to conduct management audits related to ISO 14000.

Task 4: Appoint an Implementation Leader

A normal early task would be to appoint a management representative; however, this company is not seeking registration. Therefore, they can dispense with that step and proceed to appointing an implementation leader. In this example, they appoint the operations manager to this task. He will be responsible for carrying out the implementation action plan.

STEP 2: CONDUCT A BASELINE AUDIT OF THE EXISTING SYSTEM TO DETERMINE THE AMOUNT OF ACTION REQUIRED TO CONFORM TO ISO 14001

Before the implementation action plan can be formed, the company needs to assess its current management system and level of compliance with ISO 14001. Luckily, because of its existing level of environmental concern and available human resources, Pavewell will need little or no outside assistance.

Task 1: Conduct an Environmental Impact Audit

First, the internal auditors conduct a complete environmental impact audit. All possible sources of pollution or other negative environmental impacts are listed. Then the audit team examines each source and measures its level of impact. For example, the energy consumed at each processing step is measured by the kilowatts of electricity used per ton of asphalt created. Also, the level of fumes is measured at the source and is recorded as parts per million per cubic centimeter of air.

The results of this study are reported to management in the form of an environmental impact statement. The auditors have been preparing such statements every two years for the past several years; therefore, this steering committee has very detailed information and historic data upon which to base their targets and objectives.

Task 2: Examine the Existing Management System

Using their new-found knowledge of auditing management systems, the internal auditors also examined the existing procedures and work instructions. They also interviewed key process people to gain a measure of their knowledge of the effect of their jobs on the environmental impacts the company creates. This information is reported to the steering committee in the form of a written audit report.

Task 3: Review All Applicable Regulations and Customer Requirements

The internal auditors have been responsible in the past for tracking all applicable environmental regulations. They have subscribed to a service that keeps them informed of which regulations affect the hot-mix asphalt industry. In addition, their existing job functions include tracking customer-related environmental requirements. Thus, the internal audit team already has a list of applicable regulations and customer requirements. They only need to make sure the list is up to date before submitting it to the steering committee.

Pavewell is in a unique position in that the internal auditors were fully qualified to conduct all three tasks within this stage of implementation. This saves the company considerable money because they do not have to hire an outside consulting firm. However, any company with the slightest concern about assuring that all environmental impacts, applicable regulations, and customer requirements have been found should consider an outside consultant to confirm their work.

Task 4: Write the Company-Wide Environmental Policy and Level I Documents

The steering committee quickly realized that they needed to write a company-wide policy for their environmental management system. First, they studied the environmental issues related to their type of company. They found that they needed to address the issues of recycling, discharge to the air, usage of water, worker safety, the handling of chemicals, and energy conservation.

Because the main objective of the company is to establish an environmental management system as a preventive measure against regulatory fines and to constantly reduce the environmental impact of their operation, the company-wide policy would address all these issues. Next, the steering committee drafted a general environmental policy stating that the company was dedicated to preventing pollution, improving their immediate environment, and promoting the responsible use and reuse of hot-mix asphalt. This was followed by the drafting of Level I policy statements for each element of Section 4 in ISO 14001.

STEP 3: FORM A WRITTEN ACTION PLAN BASED ON MANAGEMENT DISCUSSIONS AND THE BASELINE AUDIT; ASSIGN SPECIFIC MANAGERS SPECIFIC TASKS; FORM A PROJECT MANAGEMENT TIME LINE

The steering committee has a considerable task before it, namely the conversion of the reports submitted by the internal auditors into an action plan for implementation. The steering committee quickly realizes that many environmental regulations and customer requirements apply to Pavewell. For example, they are regulated by the Environmental Protection Agency, the State Occupational Health and Safety Administration, the Department of Natural Resources, the Department of Labor, the State Department of Labor, the County Environmental Health Administration, and local zoning ordinances for industrial sites.

Task 1: Develop a Written Implementation Action plan

The steering committee decides that the approach they will use is to form their list of targets and objectives for the environmental management system. Armed with such a list, they will then assess whether the current management system adequately addresses these targets and objectives.

This approach discovers that there are many gaps and overlaps in their system. In other words, a systematic environmental management system would not only provide compliance with ISO 14001, but would probably make the management of the company more efficient.

As with our other examples, Pavewell designs an implementation plan in which specific tasks are assigned to particular people. Also, time lines for completion are given with each task assignment. This is all written down into a formal action plan. Naturally, such a plan is a living document that can be changed as the steering committee discovers needs for additional tasks or better ways to accomplish earlier assignments.

Task 2: Incorporate Project Management Techniques Into an Action Plan

Also as before, project management techniques figure strongly in the company's plan of action. A time line chart is created and a critical path analysis is conducted to assure that just the right amount of resources are dedicated to each task.

STEP 4: REVISE OR CREATE AN ENVIRONMENTAL PROCEDURES MANUAL (LEVEL II) TO REFLECT THE REQUIREMENTS OF ISO 14001

Because they do not plan to create a complete Level II document, the efforts expended in this step will be less than those seen in our first example.

Task 1: Review Existing Written Procedures Using Flowcharts

As before, existing written procedures have to be modified to adjust to the new environmental management system. The original gap analysis conducted by the internal auditors is used to identify the existing procedures that must be modified. Pavewell discovers that there are few written procedures in existence; therefore, they have to create several new procedures.

Some of the new procedures will be written as work instructions because only one person will carry out the prescribed activities. The remaining procedures are drafted by the steering committee. The members of the steering committee begin by drawing a flowchart of those processes. For example, document control does not currently exist, so the steering committee drafts a proposed system of document control using a flowchart.

Task 2: Review Flowcharts to See If the Procedures Are Effective

When the new procedure is drafted as a flowchart, the steering committee reviews the proposed system for effectiveness and efficiency. Because they are using ISO 14001 just as a model for an environmental management system, they have more latitude in the creation of processes and their related procedures.

In this example, they not only consider the effectiveness of the procedure, but they can look at the cost efficiency. They even have the freedom to combine procedures for greater efficiency. When they are convinced that the new procedure will not be a burden on the company and will promote an effective environmental management system, the flowchart is approved.

Task 3: Draft the New and Revised Procedures

Next, the steering committee uses the flowchart to draft an actual procedure. Chapter 9 will examine how a flowchart can be used to draft the final procedure.

Task 4: Steering Committee Approves New Procedures

When the new procedure is written, the steering committee at Pavewell will test it with the people who have to carry out its specific activities. The steering committee wants the employees of the company to accept the new procedure. When the steering committee feels that the procedure is fully developed and in final form, a vote is taken on whether to approve the new procedure.

STEP 5: UPGRADE OR CREATE WRITTEN WORK INSTRUCTIONS AS NEEDED

Because Pavewell is highly dependent on written work instructions, this is where the bulk of document writing will take place.

Task 1: Study the Existing Work Instruction and the Paperwork Involved

Unlike the previous examples, Pavewell already has a well-developed system of written work instructions. Only a few new instructions will have to be developed to complete the environmental management system. The remaining work instructions also require some modifications to fit into the new system.

A member of the steering committee teams up with a person who has to carry out a specific work instruction. These two-person teams work to incorporate the requirements of the environmental management system smoothly into existing written work instructions. In this way, the steering committee member can provide guidance on what is needed to comply with the new system. At the same time, the other person can provide information on what can be done effectively and with as little change as possible to the current system.

Task 2: Create a Flowchart of the Task Being Performed

To assist in this effort, communication between the two members of the team are improved by creating a flowchart of the existing work instructions. Then these two people discuss what has to be included for compliance with the environmental management system. Next, they discuss whether the instructions can be rewritten for greater clarity and more efficiency.

Needless to say, this can be a long and involved process; therefore, the steering committee has to put explicit time limits on the effort. At the same time, management has to encourage these two-person teams to settle differences quickly and fairly. At Pavewell, if a team cannot decide an issue, then a member of management comes to the meeting to settle the issue.

Task 3: Draft the Work Instruction

When agreement is reached, the flowchart and team notes are converted into a draft work instruction. Again, the newly proposed instruction is tested on the people who have to carry it out. Naturally, the draft is reworked until all parties feel they have a complying instruction that is also effective and sensible.

Task 4: Submit the Draft to the Steering Committee for Approval

The final draft is submitted to the steering committee for approval. In the previous examples, the appropriate department manager made the final approval of the work instruction. In the case of Pavewell, the steering committee gives the approval because there are no department managers per se in the company.

STEP 6: FORM SYSTEMS TO PASS ENVIRONMENTAL REQUIREMENTS ONTO SUPPLIERS

This step represents an addition to the implementation plan. In the case of Pavewell, the management has decided that their own company's environmental targets and objectives will require the cooperation of key suppliers. Therefore, they add tasks to their implementation plan to accomplish this goal.

Task 1: Adopt Additional ISO 14000 Standards for Internal Use

Pavewell appoints a small team comprised of an engineer, purchasing representative, and a member of senior management to use ISO Guide 64. That is, they are developing a system for incorporating environmental aspects into their purchasing agreements and product standards.

Another small team of engineers examines ISO 14040 to see how life cycle assessment can be incorporated into their process and product design operations. The plan is to use the standard and other conservation engineering techniques to design a more efficient process that creates a more environmentally friendly product.

Sometime in the future, Pavewell will petition its industrial group and government officials on criteria for an eco-label for hot-mix asphalt. Such a move will give the company a considerable advantage when marketing to corporations and governments. The company is especially interested in impressing government agencies because they represent its primary group of customers.

Task 2: Develop a Program to Encourage Suppliers to Consider Environmental Management Systems

Local aggregate is used in the process of creating hot-mix asphalt. This aggregate comes from many local sources represented by several suppliers. One of the early projects will be the creation of a product standard that not only specifies the physical properties desired in the aggregate, but it will also encourage the suppliers to minimize impacts on the environment and to conserve energy.

STEP 7: CONDUCT A SYSTEM-WIDE INTERNAL AUDIT

When an environmental system is in place, Pavewell will want to examine its effectiveness during usage. Also, management will want to know whether the company is in a position to make a self-declaration of its compliance.

Task 1: Plan for and Conduct a System-Wide Internal Audit

Unlike the previous examples, Pavewell is not seeking third-party regulation. Therefore, in place of the internal audit to confirm its readiness for an outside assessment, it is conducting an internal audit as a self-declaration of its conformance. In other words, Pavewell will confirm its own conformance and then present the documented system and the result of the internal audit as evidence of conforming. Such a presentation will typically be made to customers.

Therefore, the company must assure that the internal audit is carried out with all of the formalities of a full registration audit. The same amount of time a registrar would spend on the audit must be duplicated for the internal audit. A formal plan of auditing, including a schedule, must be submitted to management from the internal audit team.

An opening meeting and a closing meeting—in which the internal auditors meet with management—must also be included. Like a registration audit, the opening meeting includes the internal auditors describing the scope and schedule of the audit. However, unlike a registration audit, guides will not be needed because the internal auditors are already familiar with the company's operation. At the closing meeting, the auditors will report their findings.

Task 2: Prepare an Audit Report for Management Review

Within one week of the completion of the internal audit, a written audit report should be submitted to management. This report should outline the scope of the audit, the evidence collected, the people interviewed, and the findings of the auditors. The report would also list any noncompliances.

You should note that unlike an ISO 9000 audit, this type of self-declaration audit report can include a list of opportunities for improvements. For example, the auditors may note that one particular work area has discovered new ways to increase work flow. The auditors can suggest in their report that management investigate and possibly change the work instructions for that area to incorporate the more efficient method.

Task 3: Take Corrective Action If Needed

Like a registration audit, if nonconformances are discovered, the management team must form a plan of corrective action. And, as before, the plan must identify each problem area and assign a specific person to be responsible for assuring that corrective actions are taken.

Task 4: Confirm All Corrective Actions

These should be confirmed as they are completed. A good corrective action process also involves a thorough search for the root cause of the nonconformance. When the root cause is discovered and permanently removed, the corrective action is usually considered completed. This would include any changes to your procedures or processes required as a preventive action. The internal audit team should be informed of each corrective action completion. When all corrective actions have been taken, the internal audit team can elect to reexamine the affected portions of the environmental management system.

Task 5: Inform All Employees, Customers, and Suppliers of the New Environmental Management System

Pavewell had a unique way of keeping employees informed about the new environmental management system. As the environmental management system was developed, those employees who were affected were kept up to date. For example, as new procedures were adopted, the employees in that department would meet for a training session known as "procedure of the month." Here the new procedure was introduced and reviewed with the employees, then the employees tried to use the new procedure. Every few days, a steering committee member would go out on the floor and talk with the employees about the success of the new procedure. This system of testing and feedback allowed document writers to better design their procedures while also training their employees in the new methods. At the same time, the employees felt that they were part of the system.

As mentioned before in this example, the self-declaration is primarily intended to benefit Pavewell in its relationships with customers. You should note that the task of seeking maximum benefit from registration is not presented in this example. Instead, the company will benefit from self-declaration by presenting evidence of its environmental management system to customers. Because none of its customers requires registration, the company benefits by achieving conformance without the expense of registration. At the same time, Pavewell can declare its environmental friendliness to many government agencies that purchase hot-mix asphalt.

The suppliers too are informed of the new environmental management system. They are notified that new environmental concerns will be seen on purchase orders and product specifications. At the same time, Pavewell will want to encourage participation by suppliers in their environmental management plans, so the steering committee will make a series of presentations to suppliers about Pavewell's environmental management system. They will point out the internal and marketing advantages of such a system. If key suppliers also want to adopt environmental management systems, then Pavewell can increase the depth and effectiveness of its own system.

THE BENEFITS OF THE APPROACH USED IN THIS SCENARIO

This approach to implementation demonstrates that several alternatives to the standard model of implementation are possible. For example, we saw that other ISO 14000 standards could be implemented concurrently. We also saw that registration is not the only outcome possible with implementation. In this example, the company deliberately avoided registration and performed a self-declaration of conformance. This made sense for the company's particular situation and it saved money.

Another benefit you can see from this scenario is the flexibility of the model of implementation I have presented. You are not locked into the order or the steps described in the previous chapter. As with any implementation project, you should spend some time examining your company's particular situation. Do you need registration? Is your system of documentation unique? Are you a small, large, or complex company? Is your company part of a larger entity? Do you have adequate resources for the implementation effort? Will outside consultants be necessary?

These are the types of questions you should ask before planning an implementation effort. Then the model I have presented should be consulted so that you have a starting point for discussing the actual way that you will implement ISO 14000. The idea is to design a scenario for your company that creates maximum benefits.

HOW DIFFERENT COMPANIES WOULD USE THIS APPROACH

Companies that do not need registration but still want an environmental management system can use an approach similar to the one described here. For example, a service-based company without customer pressure for environmental friendliness may consider self-declaration a path to more efficient internal operations. This would include the goal of making employees feel that they are making environmental contributions at their place of work.

SUMMARY

As we have seen in our three examples, different companies may require different approaches to implementation. The first example demonstrated that a common manufacturing company can use this model of implementation almost in its original form. The second example was to demonstrate that the model can be altered, in this case by combining steps to fit your particular situation. The third example showed how a unique company can add entirely new steps and greatly modify other steps to achieve implementation.

The lesson to learn from this chapter is that implementation does not have to be intimidating if you break the process of implementation down into identifiable steps and tasks. Then, by assigning each task to a particular person with a specific time line for completion, you will find that your implementation process will proceed fairly smoothly. However, it still takes management commitment and a strong implementation leader to assure successful implementation.

Chapter 8

HOW TO AUDIT INTERNALLY FOR ISO 14000 COMPLIANCE[1]

At several points in the implementation process, you need to look over your entire ISO 14000 system and make sure that it is working effectively. This is why you need the internal audits required in ISO 14000. By auditing, you examine the conformance and effectiveness of your ISO 14000-based management system and then report your findings back to management. The key word to remember is "effective." The audit will not be restricted to a conformance audit. Instead, your auditors will also look at how well the system is working and whether it can be improved. In ISO 14000 this is seen as part of the process of management review.

It is never too early in your implementation process to begin conducting internal audits. To conduct these audits, you will need policies, procedures, and work instructions in place. In addition, you must select and train your auditors with great care to obtain the maximum benefits. By efficiently training an internal audit group, you can save thousands of dollars in consultants' fees and begin accumulating evidence of conformance to this requirement.

THE GUIDE TO AUDITING LIES IN ISO 14010, ISO 14011, AND ISO 14012

Also moving quickly toward acceptance as international standards are the three guideline standards for environmental auditing—namely, ISO 14010, 14011, and 14012. Taken together, these guideline standards create a solid model for how to set up and operate your internal audit team.

---

[1] Portions of this chapter are drawn from the *Quality Manager's Complete Guide to ISO 9000*, Prentice Hall, 1993.

ISO 14010–THE GENERAL PRINCIPLES OF ENVIRONMENTAL AUDITING

This standard recognizes the universal need for guidelines for environmental auditing. Therefore, it provide the general principles for environmental auditing, as well as defining common terms. ISO 14010 emphasizes several key points:

1. An audit should clearly define its focus and scope.
2. The possible existence of a client commissioning the audit is recognized. A client is seen as either the auditee or possibly a regulatory body.
3. Findings can be both positive and negative.

Of interest to our discussion is the emphasis on clearly defining the scope of the audit. This standard was written with flexibility in mind. Different countries around the world treat environmental issues differently. Therefore, the scope of the audit is critical to the nature of the audit. For example, if a company's main concern is regulatory compliance, then the scope of the audit would concentrate on existing applicable laws and how the environmental management system accounted for the requirements. The general principles of environmental auditing are broken down into the following category by ISO 14010:

- Objectives and scope of the audit
- Objectivity, independence, and competence of the audit team
- The due use of professional care
- The use of systematic procedures
- The examination of audit criteria by the gathering of evidence to create findings
- Assurance of the reliability of the findings and conclusions
- Reporting to management and possibly the client

If you are already familiar with the process of conducting management audits, you will recognize these principles.

ISO 14011–HOW TO CONDUCT AN AUDIT OF AN ENVIRONMENTAL MANAGEMENT SYSTEM

The next standard in this series, ISO 14011, translates the general principles laid out in ISO 14010 into an established system of conducting an environmental audit. This standard makes it clear that you should begin with a clear set of objectives for conducting an environmental audit.

We have already discussed the two primary reasons for conducting an environmental audit. First, you can use an internal environmental audit as a gap analysis of your environmental management system during implementation of ISO 14001. Second, an internal audit can confirm your compliance to ISO 14001 for the purpose of self-declaring your conformance or to confirm your readiness for a registration audit. Later, you will use internal audits to maintain and monitor your environmental management system.

ISO 14011 also lays out the roles, responsibilities, and activities for all involved parties. This includes the work activities and responsibilities of the lead auditor:

- Working with the client to establish the audit scope
- Directing the activities of the internal audit team
- Gathering resources and previous information to prepare the team for the audit
- The actual formation of the audit team
- Preparing the audit plan
- Communicating audit results to all interested parties
- Resolving problems during the audit
- Determining whether an audit objective is obtainable
- Serving as liaison among the team, the client, and the auditee
- Reporting audit results in writing
- If called for, recommending improvement in the environmental management system

Due care should be taken to select both an experienced person for this job and a person possessing strong leadership capabilities. Knowledge of environmental issues can be key to the success of the auditor. Generally, when you have a strong lead auditor, you will have a successful audit team.

Also discussed in ISO 14011 is the role of the client. It can quickly be seen that the role of the registrar is being described. This includes the selection of the audit team, definition of the audit scope, approval of the audit plan, and the determination of audit criteria. This same section of the standard could apply to the management team's responsibilities when authorizing an internal environmental audit.

Finally, ISO 14011 discusses the activities that occur during the audit cycle. I will discuss the audit cycle and its related activities later in this chapter.

ISO 14012–WHO CAN BE AN AUDITOR?

Eventually, you will have to select members for your audit team. ISO 14012 provides extensive guidelines for this selection process. It begins with the qualifications for an auditor based on education and work experience. A qualified auditor will have as a minimum:

- A secondary education
- Five years of work experience or a college degree and four years of work experience
- Additional formal training in environmental science, environmental aspects of your company's operation, familiarity with related regulations, the standards involved in your environmental management system, and how to use existing audit procedures and techniques
- On-the-job training involving participation in environmental audits equaling 20 work days and a minimum of 4 audits

A good auditor will have strong personal skills and professional attributes. ISO 14012 outlines some of the ways to determine these characteristics. You should look for:

- Strong oral and written communication skills using simple words and a fluent style
- A sense of diplomacy seen through tactful responses to problems and a strong ability to listen
- A demonstrated ability to remain independent and objective
- Good personal organization
- Ability to make good judgments based on objective evidence

Naturally, the lead auditor would need additional leadership skills. This would include additional experience with audits. Both audit team members and the lead auditor must maintain their competency. This involves regular training in new topics, existing standards, and environmental management techniques. They should also maintain constant surveillance of environmental regulations that apply to your company.

Qualified auditors will also exercise due professional care at all times. In addition, the auditors should use the appropriate language for the situation. For example, in cases in which a foreign language is commonly used by some of the employees, a member of the audit team should be familiar with this language. It is possible to secure a guide or supervisor who understands the language to provide translation. Other possibilities might include an illiterate work force, the hearing impaired, or the visually impaired. Any of these types of situations must be accounted for in the scope of the audit.

Annex A in ISO 14012 provides some ideas for how you can evaluate a person's qualifications to be an internal auditor. This includes methods such as interviews, tests, review of past work history, peer review, and the like.

A QUESTION OF LIABILITY

Although ISO 14012 calls for education or experience with environmental matters for the auditors, there remains a controversy regarding this requirement. Specifically, some people think that a simple, basic understanding of the environmental issues involved is sufficient; however, I disagree. Instead, I highly recommend that people formally educated in the environmental sciences should be given priority; for example, people with education, training, or experience in chemistry, biology, or other physical sciences.

The reason for this recommendation comes from the issue of liability. If an internal auditor looks at an environmental management system and approves of its structure, he or she may be inadvertently approving a violation of environmental law. For example, an auditor may be aware that emissions to the air have to be kept below certain levels. However, the auditor may not be familiar with the various ways such emissions can be sampled and measured. He or she may accept the current method, not knowing that a more efficient method exists or that the current samples are being taken in a manner that creates a systematic error.

What might happen is that your company self-declares its compliance with ISO 14001 or may even receive a registration certificate only to be found out of compliance with a well-known regulation during a regulatory audit. Your internal audit findings may show that your internal management system was deficient and that your company is liable for the damage created. Therefore, common sense dictates that you err on the side of caution.

THE INFLUENCE OF ISO 10011

One of the most important supporting standards for ISO 9000 is ISO 10011—the international standard for auditing management systems. This three-part standard covers the general principles of auditing, the selection of auditors, and the way to conduct an audit. Therefore, you can see that ISO 14010, 14011, and 14012 were created with ISO 10011 in mind. When conducting an environmental audit, you must use the ISO 14000 standards on auditing. However, by knowing that these standards were modeled on ISO 10011, you will understand the intentions of a management audit. In addition, you can use both sets of standards for joint ISO 9000/ISO 14000 audits.

For example, ISO 10011 lays out a very rigid approach to management auditing. The same structure is repeated in the ISO 14000 standards for auditing. However, in ISO 14000, greater flexibility is given to the auditors and the scope of the audit. For environmental audits, if all parties agree, the auditors can point out opportunities for improvements. Also, the scope of the audit can be expanded or contracted to fit a particular situation. For the purpose of this book, this allows you to audit both ISO 9000 and ISO 14000 simultaneously.

HOW TO FORM, LEAD, AND USE THE INTERNAL AUDIT TEAM

Taking guidance from the three ISO 14000 standards previously discussed, you have the framework for creating an internal audit team. However, you should familiarize yourself with the practice of management audits before creating an internal audit system. Such knowledge can be obtained through experience or by attending seminars on how to conduct a management audit. There are also certification tests if you wish to become registered as a management auditor.

BEGIN WITH A WRITTEN AUDIT POLICY

When you write your policy for internal audits, you should be familiar with ISO 14010, ISO 14011, and ISO 14012. These are the standards on how to audit ISO 14001 or any other environmental management standard. The key words to remember during the writing of the Level I (policy) statement are "independence" and "management reporting."

Let's begin with the concept of independence. The auditors you use have to be independent of the functions under examination. In other words, if the quality manager is also the author of many of the ISO 14000 procedures, he or she is not a suitable auditor. The range of suitable auditors is wide for this particular situation. Purchasing agents with a history of auditing suppliers for environmental concerns, engineers, former environmental regulatory personnel, outside consultants, and departmental managers all could be excellent choices for auditors.

At the same time, you cannot lose sight of the fact that the information gathered from an audit has to be reported to management. In turn, management has to take documented actions to correct or improve the affected parts of your ISO 14000 system. It is this communication between the auditors and management that will be closely examined during a registration assessment.

WRITE THE PROCEDURES

A good internal audit system depends upon a well-written procedure for auditing. By basing your procedures on ISO 14011, you will give both structure and conformity to your system. The key elements of the audit activity to keep in mind include:

1. Management's creation of the mandate to audit (as the client)
2. Preparation of an audit plan
3. Assignment of people to the audit team
4. Creation of audit documents and check sheets
5. Opening meeting to explain scope and nature of the audit
6. Collection of observable evidence of compliance and effectiveness

7. Closing meeting and summary of findings
8. Submission of a written report to management
9. Corrective actions

If you need further guidance, refer also to ISO 14010 and 14012. By combining these pieces of information, with some training in auditing, you can create a simple yet comprehensive system of internal audits. For maximum efficiency, this audit system can be used for other audit needs. Financial, supplier, quality, and process audits can all use this same system.

Next, you should have set up an audit schedule. You must stick to this schedule. Examine every element of the ISO 14001 standard at least once every year. Critical elements of your system should be checked more often. If you have not performed a scheduled audit on time, chances are the registrar will cite you for nonconformance.

WRITE THE WORK INSTRUCTIONS

Although there are potentially many work instructions for auditing, the most important will be the instructions for the creation of an audit report and the documentation and tracking of corrective actions. Remember, the purpose of an audit is to open an opportunity for your company to improve through constant management review. Therefore, a formal written report is required to document these opportunities and to demand action. This report should contain the following:

1. The scope of the audit being conducted, including the applicable standards
2. Review of the audit plan and description of the audit period
3. List of auditors and the people interviewed during the audit
4. Identification of the audited organization and the client involved
5. List of nonconformances with supporting evidence
6. Summary of observations to highlight the strengths and weaknesses of the quality system
7. The agreed-upon criteria used in the audit
8. Distribution list
9. Statement of confidentiality

Also possible with the agreement of the client:

10. Summary of the audit process including obstacles encountered
11. Conclusions of the conformance of the environmental management system against agreed-upon criteria

12. Effectiveness of the operation and maintenance of the environmental management system
13. Determination of whether the internal review process ensures the suitability and continuous improvement of the management system

When the audit report is submitted, it is up to the management of your company to create a corrective action plan that names specific managers as responsible for each suggested action. The lead auditor should be given a copy of this plan. Using it, the lead auditor will create a log to track the completion of each corrective action. The audit file cannot be signed and closed out until all corrective actions have been taken. Failure to do so will most likely count as a noncompliance under the management review requirements of ISO 14001 (see Exhibit 8-1).

In addition to an audit plan, auditors also work with checklists, sampling plans, mandates with specific instructions, and a defined scope of their responsibilities. All of these can be seen as work instructions for the auditor; therefore, these should be written documents that are considered "controlled" under your document control system.

Work instructions that include forms to fill out will generate environmental records as evidence of conformance to internal audit requirements; however, it will not demonstrate full conformance. Only responses to and from management can complete the demonstration of conformance. Therefore, all work instructions for internal auditors should include instructions on who receives the output being generated. In most cases, a clear path toward upper management must be defined. In turn, management must generate written responses that are acted upon and recorded.

The call for an audit, the audit report, handwritten notes, minutes of management meetings, corrective action plans, and confirmation of corrective actions should be filed together in a case file. Each audit is treated as a separate project. The person named in your policy statement as responsible for the whole audit system should keep and track these files. If many audits occur during the year, project tracking software is highly recommended. The trick is not to lose track of the progress of an audit. If the purchasing manager was supposed to report on a corrective action on the fifteenth of the month, a memo asking for the results should be sent out on the fourteenth.

Only when the audit coordinator keeps careful and complete control over the process will your internal audit system meet the requirements of ISO 14001 and ISO 14011. When your policy, procedures, and work instructions are in place, you are ready to select and train your auditing team.

Exhibit 8-1: Example of Internal Audit Work Instruction

Work Instruction #QA-24 **Internal Audit Paperwork** (See also Procedure QA-3 and ENG-5)

1.0 General

Existing policies (CP 4.17) and procedures (QA-3 and CP-2) require annual internal audits of the quality system against ISO 9002 and the environmental management system against ISO 14001. Such audits will have as deliverable items audit reports and corrective action notices.

2.0 Audit Report

2.1 It is the responsibility of the audit team leader to gather all audit findings and report them in a written summary to management.

2.2 Form # 223-D, Report Form, will be used for the purpose of reporting audit results.

2.3 The audit team leader fills in the names of the audit team, the people who were interviewed, the scope of the audit, the date, and the distribution list for the final report.

2.4 In the space provided for comments, the audit team leader will write out a list of nonconformances and concerns discovered during the audit. These will be supported with a summary of the evidence obtained to make these conclusions. Both strengths and weaknesses of the system should be reported. After each finding, the audit team leader should estimate the company's ability to correct the situation.

2.5 The report will be signed by the audit team leader and submitted to the Quality Assurance and Engineering managers for approval of content and accuracy.

2.6 The Quality Assurance and Engineering managers and audit team leader will present the final report to the management steering committee no later than ten days after the conclusion of an audit. The steering committee will then take corrective actions as needed.

3.0 Corrective Actions

3.1 When nonconformances are noted on a final report, the audit team leader will complete Form #323-C, Corrective Action Report (CAR), for each nonconformance. These will accompany the final report to the management steering committee.

3.2 The management steering committee will then assign specific department managers the role of taking the corrective actions they feel are necessary. CARs can be rejected by the steering committee, but the reason has to be noted in the meeting minutes.

3.3 The audit team leader will note the CARs and the names of the managers responsible for taking actions in the corrective action logbook. The audit team leader will also note the projected date of completion.

3.4 Each specific department manager will respond in writing as to whether the corrective action was completed successfully. The audit team leader will note this by closing out entries in the corrective action log. Date of completion should be noted.

02/07/95 Revision 2.1.1 Approved by:

(**Exhibit 8-1** continued)

Form 223-D Report Form for the XYZ Company		
Date: Facility: Filed by:	Team Members:	Guests/Interviewees:
Scope:		
General Comments: (use additional sheets as needed)		
Detailed Report: (use additional sheets as needed)		
Distribution List: Report Approved by: ________________ Date: ________		
Revision 1.5.0	11/19/95 "c:\wp\report.frm"	Approved by:

(**Exhibit 8-1** continued)

Form 23/B	**Internal Audit Corrective Action Log**			
Date reported:	Person responsible:	Corrective action suggested:	To be completed by:	Date completed:
02/07/96	J. Hooper	CAR #23 - write work instruction for presses	04/01/96	03/15/96
03/11/96	D. Facto	CAR #24 - implement control of blueprints	05/01/96	
03/11/96	I. Mercedes	CAR#25 -inadequate training for emergency response	07/01/96	

HOW TO SELECT AN AUDITOR

ISO 14012 lists the specific characteristics a person must possess to be an auditor. Remember, a fully qualified auditor should have no power. The role of an auditor is to examine a system and report back to management. A person perceived to have the power to discipline people will inhibit the accurate collection of information that is vital for management to make competent decisions.

The next attribute of a good auditor is training in the formal approach to management audits. This includes training in methods of interviewing, observing, documenting, and reporting. The auditor must be able to plan, coordinate, communicate, and potentially lead a team of auditors. In addition, good training should make the participant well informed on the interpretation of ISO 14001. Obviously, people who have passed a course for certified lead assessors or internal auditing for ISO 14000 would probably qualify. Also possible would be people already holding certification as an ISO 9000 auditor with experience in environmental sciences.

The level of education should be post-secondary school. In other words, auditors tend to be drawn from the college educated or from people eligible for college education. The level of experience is more critical. ISO 14012 spells out that ISO auditors should have at least four years of experience in the business they are auditing. The standard also recommends that the auditor candidate observe and participate in at least four audits. It is assumed that such a person would be under supervision of an experienced auditor.

These, of course, are guidelines for auditors seeking registration. They can be used to establish your own qualifications for internal auditors. We strongly recommend that you use common sense in establishing your own qualifications for an internal auditor. For example, if you are a regulated industry, familiarity with ISO 14000 and the applicable regulations should be part of your own requirements.

At the same time, you must never lose sight of the matching of personalities. One of the key characteristics to look for in an auditor is personality. For example, a dominant person might not fit in well with passive management teams. In contrast, a good-humored, sensitive individual can put interviewees quickly at ease and increase the efficiency of an audit.

Experienced auditors can testify to the importance of the characteristics defined by ISO 14012. An average auditor will be subjected to noncooperative people, lack of sleep, wide ranges of personalities, countless distractions, managers who try to direct him or her away from weak areas of the system, and unexpected situations (e.g., observed safety violations). Through it all, the auditor must keep a cool head and collect the needed information. Diplomacy, imagination, and tenacity are critical characteristics.

Finally, a good auditor will be fluent in the language or languages in use within a company. The existence of bilingual work forces around the world make this a point of growing importance. You may not think that this is important if all your workers speak the same language as management. But experience has shown that an auditor who can speak the slang of the shop floor will win quick respect of the workers. Likewise, as an American auditor working in Quebec, speaking French will help to promote understanding and cooperation.

To select a good auditor, it is highly recommended that you form a small evaluation panel. Such a panel should be made up of the ISO 14000 coordinator, a management representative, and at least one experienced auditor—preferably, the designated lead auditor. It is best when the lead auditor can have a strong say in picking the team members.

Naturally, you would have established levels of education, training, and experience. This would sort out some good choices for candidates or identify potential candidates who may need additional training and/or experience. The panel should examine the résumés and personnel records of this pool of candidates with an eye to the management capabilities of the individuals under examination—that is, the panel should look at the person's ability to carry out audits on managers and conduct other management audit activities.

Face-to-face interviews with finalists will help identify those who work well under pressure and determine how well they adapt to rapidly changing situations. This is not to imply that the finalists should be interrogated for hours. Instead, a simple set of prepared questions with a few sample situations should be adequate. For example, you could say to each candidate, "You are starting an interview with a purchasing manager when he informs you that he doesn't have time for 'this auditing nonsense.' How would you respond?" Answers to such a question should quickly identify the people who will work well as an auditor. To maintain the competency of your selected auditors, take the following steps:

1. Ensure that the auditors are kept up to date with current interpretations of the standard. Various newsletters and other publications provide this information.
2. Require regular training in new audit methods. Usually, every year you should determine whether additional training of the auditors is required. The recent revision of the ISO 9000 standard would be an example of such an event.
3. Perform an evaluation review of each auditor at least once every three years. The record of performance, comments from the lead auditor, and a review by a panel similar to the one just described is recommended.

TRAIN THE AUDITORS

There are several schools of thought on how to train people to become auditors for ISO 14000. One group suggests that a two- to three-day internal auditor's course is adequate to bring people up to speed. Another group thinks that auditors should attend the week-long lead assessor training. In both cases, these auditors should take additional training in the environmental sciences.

As usual, no single approach is entirely correct for every company. The best first step is to look at your situation. What are your internal needs? How important is the ISO 14000 system? How much experience do potential auditors already have? Do you have a corporate image or level of professionalism to maintain? How much auditing must you do? How large is your company, and does it have multiple sites?

Begin by looking at the size of your organization. If you are a 50-person job shop, perhaps only one person needs to be trained as an auditor. If you are a corporation with many sites, perhaps a trained audit team is necessary. In comparison, a medium-sized manufacturing firm usually uses between two and five auditors.

Next, you have to consider the experience of the people nominated to be auditors and the level of professionalism you wish to project. A nationally known corporation may want all auditors certified after attending the week-long lead assessor course. At the same time, a small manufacturing firm may feel that a two-day course on internal auditing for ISO 14000 given to experienced quality system auditors is adequate.

A strongly recommended step is that the level of experience and training required for a qualified auditor be documented as part of your audit procedure. You can add to this your test of independence. In this way, you will have clearly demonstrated that your auditors are appropriate for the job. This could include a description of the communication and leadership skills an auditor must possess to be effective.

THE AUDIT CYCLE

The process of auditing follows a well-established structure. In general, the following steps are taken during every audit, whether internal or external:

1. Receipt of a mandate
2. Preparation
3. Notification/negotiation
4. Opening meeting
5. Collection of evidence of conformance/effectiveness
6. Closing meeting
7. Written report
8. Corrective actions
9. Follow-up until closure

The external audits performed by a registrar will add surveillance to the end of this list. An internal audit is performed for the whole system at least annually, so surveillance is usually not required. Areas of special attention are audited more frequently by the internal team.

RECEIPT OF A MANDATE

An official act by management is required to initiate an internal audit. It can be as simple as issuing a memo from the ISO steering committee that an audit take place. Thus, your management has taken the role of the client under the definitions provided by ISO 14000. Such a mandate has to identify the person responsible for coordinating and leading the audit. It should also state the scope and purpose of the audit. The scope of an audit will describe the areas to be checked and the standards to be applied.

ISO 14011 places emphasis on the creation of the audit scope. The scope is determined by negotiation between the client and the lead auditor. The auditee is sometimes part of the scope development process. The scope covers the standard to be used, physical locations involved, organization activities to be assessed, and the manner of reporting the results. Resources dedicated to the audit should match the scope.

PREPARATION

In general, the person receiving this mandate will be the lead auditor. The lead auditor bears the brunt of the work assignment for an internal audit. The lead auditor must begin by further defining the audit plan. The audit plan includes many details—areas to be checked have to be matched up with a timetable, determine which people will be interviewed, determine the standards to be checked, and determine the evidence that needs to be gathered. This requires that the lead auditor review organizational charts, policies, procedures, environmental criteria, and other information to determine how much auditing will be required to find the level of conformance and effectiveness in an environmental management system. If the management system seems inadequate at this point, the lead auditor has to report back to management that the audit is not possible until a working system is in place.

Let's look at a specific example. Assume that the lead auditor has been told to audit the document control system at his or her company. The objective of the preparation phase is to create an audit plan. The lead auditor would read through the requirements for document control, look for an official company policy on this subject, and review the procedures related to document control. If satisfied that a system seemed to be in place, he or she would then look at the people responsible for control and which documents should be under control. From this information, he or she would form an audit plan that would describe who will be doing what at which time and at what location.

Specifically, he or she would detail the audit scope and objectives, identify the significant people in the process, list requirements from the standard, list the audit team members, lay out a schedule for the audit, identify the areas to be checked, assure confidentiality, and state the distribution list for the final report. All of these items taken together constitute the audit plan. The audit plan for the document control system might look like this:

> *The scope and purpose of this audit is to assure that the document control process at XYZ Corporation conforms to the requirements of ISO 14001, element 4.3.5. Therefore, we propose the following actions for the audit to assure conformance and evaluate the effectiveness of document control:*
>
> 1. *The managers of Engineering have the responsibility of the document control system. The respective administrative assistants are responsible for the distribution of documents under this system.*

2. All documents and computer records related to design, purchasing, production, inspection, environmental planning, and the environmental management system will be sampled and audited for conformance to the document control procedure. Areas to be checked will include all management offices, workstations, purchasing, quality assurance labs, engineering specification storage, and environmental sampling stations.

3. The lead auditor will be Ralph Megs, assisted by Amy Sweeny. The opening meeting will be held at 8:00 A.M. on Monday, November 8, in Conference Room B. The closing meeting will be at the same location at 4:00 P.M. on the same day.

4. The following schedule is proposed:

8:15–9:00	*Interview key managers of document control system*
9:00–10:30	*Examine records in engineering, management, and purchasing*
10:30–11:30	*Examine environmental records*
11:30–12:30	*Lunch*
12:30–2:30	*Examine production areas*
2:30–3:30	*Examine sampling areas*
3:30–4:00	*Prepare findings*

5. All information gathered will be held in strictest confidence. The final written report will be distributed to members of the ISO 14000 steering committee and the manager of Engineering.

Such an audit plan would be submitted to those being audited for approval. Time schedules must be coordinated so that meetings with key people do take place and that an effective audit is conducted.

Finally, the lead auditor selects the audit team members. Typically, a small company has an audit team of one or two. Large corporations have been known to use as many as five or more people for an audit team. Either way, you should use the minimal number of people for an effective audit.

This selected team meets to go over the audit plan and to draw up their working documents. If there have been previous audits, the team would review the past reports as a guide to weak areas that need more attention. Particular members of the audit team are assigned specific areas to examine and tasks to perform by the lead auditor.

The individual members of the audit team draw up checklists for their assignments. These will be used later to gather evidence of conformance. The lead auditor reviews these checklists and other supporting documents to make sure the team is ready for the audit.

NOTIFICATION/NEGOTIATION

When the client (management in an internal audit) and the lead auditor have agreed to the proposed audit plan and the audit team has made its preparations, notification takes place. For an internal audit, a simple memo can serve as the notification. It would be sent to all people and departments targeted by the audit. It would tell them who is coming to audit, the purpose of the audit, and the time period for their part of the audit. In other words, it is a short summary of the formal audit plan. Once notified, usually at least a week in advance, it is up to anyone who has a scheduling or other conflict to call the audit team to negotiate changes to the audit plan.

OPENING MEETING

The actual audit begins with a short opening meeting. At this meeting, the lead auditor explains the purpose and scope of the audit, as well as the proposed schedule. Top managers from the areas affected should be at this meeting. This is the time to quickly summarize the purpose of the audit again to assure that all involved managers are fully informed. It also allows the audit team to learn of any last-minute problems to clear them up before the audit begins. If your company has a written procedure about the authority of auditors and the priorities of the audit, this would be a good time to remind all participants. The audit team would announce the time and place of the closing meeting. For internal environmental audits it is also a good idea to review safety and emergency procedures for all people involved.

COLLECTION OF EVIDENCE

The bulk of any audit is the collection of objective evidence and interview data. Objective evidence is gathered by examining and copying documents, observing activities, and testing system components. Coupled with this is the interviewing of managers and participants in the system under examination. Usually, the items to be examined are part of a checklist.

Let's look at one possibility for a checklist item for document control:

> *Request the master list of environmental regulations that apply to this company. Obtain a copy of this list and check against previous reports on applicable regulations submitted by external consultants. Report results.*

It is sometimes necessary, however, for an auditor to follow a "hunch." In other words, to assure a conformance, the auditor has to push beyond what is on a checklist. If an auditor was examining customer specifications for revision dates and noticed handwritten notes on some of the contracts, he or she might question whether the notes are controlled and approved. Thus, the auditor expands the investigation to follow this lead. That is why the education of an internal auditor is so important. It is very difficult to stick to the objectives of an audit and follow such leads. A good auditor has to know how far to check without becoming vindictive and, thus, no longer an independent, unbiased party.

While the evidence is being collected, the auditors will document all that they see, hear, smell, and feel about a particular system. These are recorded on the checklists and other related documents. These observations are reported to the lead auditor. It is the lead auditor, working with the team, who creates findings for each element of a system under examination. A finding in a registration audit is stated as conformance, nonconformance, or concern. In an internal audit, these same labels can be used, but the audit team has the freedom to describe strengths and weaknesses in detail. The objective is to provide enough information so that an effective action plan can flow from the final written report. All findings must be fully supported by documented observations.

At any time during an audit, the lead auditor can make changes in assignments and tasks as conditions warrant. Therefore, it is critical that the lead auditor stay in touch with the progress of all audit team members. Lunch breaks are especially good times to review the progress of an audit.

As a final note, safety and health violations should merit special attention during an audit. If a safety or health violation is spotted during an audit, the audit should be stopped and the appropriate managers notified. When the violation is corrected, the audit may proceed. If you don't follow this procedure, your audit team will be observing a safety and health problem and endorsing it by not taking corrective action. If health and safety are in the scope of the audit, such violations would be reported as nonconformances.

When evidence is collected, typically the auditors will have prepared checklists. Such checklists ensure that the auditors will sample the right records, ask the right questions, and examine each of the requirements of the standard. Exhibit 8-2 shows one possible checklist for ISO 14001.

CLOSING MEETING

At the end of an audit, the lead auditor meets with team members to collate the evidence and reach specific findings. A quick summary of the results are prepared for oral presentation during the closing meeting. The closing meeting should include the key managers from the targeted areas and any other interested parties. At least one member of senior management should be present. The lead auditor provides a quick review of the purpose of the audit and the overall findings, then specific nonconformances, concerns, and strengths are highlighted. The lead auditor promises to prepare a written report and asks for questions. Minutes should be taken at this meeting. Most closing meetings take less than one hour.

Exhibit 8-2: One Possible Checklist for ISO 14001 Compliance

Audit Checklist (Environmental Management System)	
ISO 14000 Item	Checklist Questions
4.1 Policy	Is a written environmental policy in existence?
	Was the policy produced and distributed by top management?
	Is the environmental policy appropriate to the nature, scale, and environmental impacts of the company?
	Does the policy contain commitments to the prevention of pollution and does it support continuous improvement?
	Does the policy support a commitment to comply with environmental regulations and customer requirements related to the environment?
	Is there a framework for setting environmental objectives and targets?
	Is there a framework for monitoring environmental objectives and targets?
	Has the policy been implemented, maintained, and communicated to all employees?
	Is the policy available to the public?
4.2 Planning	Does the company have a procedure for identifying the environmental aspects of its activities and products?
	Examine the company's list of environmental aspects.
	Do the environmental objectives of the company match the level of risks related to the list of environmental aspects?
	Is the list of environmental aspects and objectives up to date?
	Is there a procedure to identify and access the legal environmental considerations related to the company's activities and products?
	Does each significant level of the company have environmental objectives and targets at appropriate locations?
	Are all environmental objectives and targets consistent with the environmental policy?
	Are specific responsibilities documented at every level in the organization for each objective and target? Does this include the means and time frame for completion?
	Are new products or processes and their development included in the environmental management system?
4.3 Operation and Implementation	Does an organizational chart exist showing roles, responsibilities, and authorities of the environmental management system?
	Are there adequate resources to support the environmental management system?
	Has a management representative been appointed?
	Is there written evidence that the management representative is able to assure the establishment, implementation, and maintenance of requirements related to the environmental system?
	Does the management representative regularly report on the performance of the environmental management system to top management?
	Are training needs identified?
	Are personnel having a job with environmental impacts required to attend appropriate training? Is there a written record of such training? Is there a training schedule?
	Does training emphasize the importance of compliance with the environmental policy and procedures? Are employees aware of the environmental impact of their job function? Are employees aware that their personal performance can have positive environmental benefits?
	Is emergency preparedness and response part of the required training? Are employees aware of the consequences of departures from environmental procedures?
	Are there job descriptions outlining the education, training, and experience required for performing tasks that can cause significant environmental impacts?
	Is there a procedure for internal communications between various levels and functions?
	Is there a written procedure for receiving, documenting, and responding to relevant communications from external parties regarding environmental matters?
	Does the company have a procedure for transmitting communications to external parties concerning environmental matters?
	Does the company have a Level I environmental management manual? Does a Level II manual exist?
	Is there a written procedure for the control of key documents within the environmental management system?

(**Exhibit 8-2** continued)

	Does this procedure for document control include a list of where controlled documents can be located, that the documents are periodically reviewed for adequacy, that the current version of a document is in the appropriate location, that obsolete documents are quickly removed from the system, and that some obsolete documents be retained for legal or reference purposes?
	Looking at a sample of controlled documents, are they legible, correctly dated, readily identifiable, maintained in an orderly manner, and retained for a designated period of time?
	Are the procedures and responsibilities for the establishment and maintenance of new or revised documents established?
	Is there a documented list of operations and activities directly related to the environmental impacts identified by the company? Do these operations and activities fall within the scope of the company's environmental policy, objectives, and targets?
	Are these operations and activities planned and maintained with procedures and work instructions to ensure that there are no deviations from the environmental policies, objectives, and targets? Are there stipulated operating criteria in the written procedures and work instructions for operations?
	Has the company established a written procedure to identify the significant environmental aspects of the goods and services used by the organization (i.e., life cycle assessment)? Are these environmental aspects also communicated to suppliers and contractors?
	Has the company identified situations where there is a potential for accidents or emergency situations that have significant environmental impacts? Are there written procedures for emergency preparedness and response?
	Does the company review its emergency preparedness and response procedures regularly? After an accident or emergency, does the company perform a review of the emergency preparedness and response procedure? Is this procedure ever tested?
4.4 Checking and Corrective Actions	Does the company have a written procedure for monitoring and measuring key characteristics that have significant impacts on the environment? Are the measurements recorded and compared to objectives and targets?
	Is the monitoring equipment maintained and calibrated? Are records kept for equipment maintenance and calibration?
	Is there a procedure for evaluating compliance with relevant environmental regulations?
	Is there a procedure for investigating nonconformance and taking action to mitigate the environmental impacts that could result? Has a single job title been identified as the ultimate authority for this procedure?
	Are corrective and preventive actions taken appropriate to the size of the problem and the level of risk involved? Are there written records of the corrective and preventive actions?
	Does the company change its procedures and processes based on corrective and preventive recommendations? Are these changes documented?
	Is there a written procedure for the identification, maintenance, and disposal of environmental records? Are the environmental records legible, identifiable, and traceable to their related activity, product, or service? Are the environmental records stored to prevent deterioration or loss? Is there an established retention time?
	Is there a written procedure to establish and maintain a system of internal auditing of the environmental management system? Does the procedure establish an internal auditing system to assure that the environmental management system conforms to planned activities, has been properly implemented, is properly maintained, and are these findings reported to management?
	Is there a written audit schedule to which the company conforms completely?
	Does the internal audit procedure document the method for establishing the audit scope, audit frequency, methodologies to use, how to report results, and responsibilities of the audit team?
4.5 Management Review	Does the company's management regularly review the entire environmental management system? Is the environmental management system checked for its suitability, adequacy, and effectiveness?
	Is the management review documented? Did previous management reviews consider changes in policies or objectives based on the audit results, changing circumstances, or the need for continuous improvement?

WRITTEN REPORT

The lead auditor prepares a written report that states the findings of the audit team and the supporting evidence. This report must be signed and dated by the lead auditor and distributed to all parties on the company's previously agreed to distribution list. The report should contain the elements discussed earlier in this chapter. The report is submitted as soon as possible. At least one member of senior management should be on the distribution list, especially if senior management created the original mandate for the audit.

CORRECTIVE ACTIONS

Although not specifically required by ISO 14011, corrective action after each internal audit must be part of your system of management review under ISO 14001. This gives you the ability to modify your audit scope so that the internal audit team can conduct special audits (e.g., gap analysis).

Management should react to an audit report with a specific plan of corrective action broken into two parts. The first part should be the assignment of specific tasks to particular managers. These managers should respond in writing as the corrective actions are completed.

The second part is the job of management looking at their overall system and exploring the possibility of updating or changing existing procedures to increase the effectiveness of the system. I recommend that, in addition, the cost efficiency of procedures be examined as well.

The timetable for corrective actions should be compiled by management and submitted back to the lead auditor for follow-up tracking and closure of the audit.

When planning and taking corrective actions, the following five steps should be accounted for:

1. *Search for the root cause.* Many times a superficial reason can be found for a problem. The temptation is to correct the superficial error and not look for a root cause. It is vitally important that root causes be found and eliminated if continuous improvement is to be achieved. Management should outline the steps to be taken in the search for the root cause of each nonconformance.

2. *Take remedial corrective action.* Until the root cause is found, take some sort of corrective action to stop the nonconformance. Remedial action should be taken until a root cause is found and eliminated.

3. *Look at the effect over time.* The discovery of a nonconformance implies that it was in place before the audit. Management must investigate how long the nonconformance has been in place and apply corrective actions to the affected materials. For example, if an air quality monitoring gauge was found out of calibration, you should attempt to establish the amount of airborne discharges by another method since the date of the last calibration.

4. *Eliminate the root cause.* Once found, the root cause should be eliminated.

5. *Prevent recurrence.* The elimination of a root cause does not always assure it will stay away. If necessary, procedures and work instructions should be modified or changed to prevent a recurrence of the problem.

The completed corrective action plan is reviewed by management and submitted to the lead auditor. The lead auditor puts the corrective action plan in the audit file and schedules follow up for each action item.

FOLLOW UP UNTIL CLOSURE

All corrective actions taken must be documented. A simple memo reporting a successful corrective action or a directive issued to change a procedure are adequate evidence of management involvement. These documents will only help you during a registration audit.

The report of the completion of a corrective action step is sent to the lead auditor, who, in turn, marks on the corrective action plan that the step has been completed. Each action item should have an expected date of completion. As the dates pass, the auditor notifies the responsible manager in writing and requests a response. Every item on the corrective action plan must be completed before the lead auditor is allowed to sign and close the audit file. All items must be completed well ahead of the next scheduled audit for these elements of the system.

It is up to the discretion of the lead auditor as to whether to confirm the effectiveness of a corrective action with an audit of the particular area involved. The lead auditor should not sign off a corrective action step until he or she is satisfied that the action taken was completely effective. If a corrective action is not completed and requests for completion are ignored, the lead auditor should report this to top management and request a reaudit.

SUMMARY

The end results of an internal audit should be a better environmental management system. When you look at the function of the internal environmental audit, you can see that it is the final and confirming step in your environmental management system. It feeds needed information back to your management. Then your management can use this information to begin the upward spiral of continuous improvement through corrective and preventive actions. This is why ISO 14001 emphasizes management review as a key component of your environmental management system.

Keep in mind that a well-run audit team can be used for other internal evaluations, such as quality management conformance and health/safety issues. As I have emphasized in this book, ISO 9000 and ISO 14000 can coexist. In fact, because ISO 10011 and the ISO 14000 standards on auditing are so similar, you can conduct internal audits on both your quality and environmental management systems. This would include situations such as a company already registered to ISO 9000 conducting an internal audit to confirm its management system for quality assurance while simultaneously evaluating its possible conformance to ISO 14001.

Chapter 9

HOW TO PREPARE DOCUMENTATION FOR AN ISO 14000-BASED ENVIRONMENTAL MANAGEMENT SYSTEM

Throughout this book, I have pointed out that to show others that you have an environmental management system, you must be able to demonstrate the existence of your system. The best method for demonstrating the existence of any management system is documentation. Therefore, documentation represents the most critical component of your environmental management system.

In this chapter, we will look at two ways to create written procedures and work instructions. In previous chapters, we have seen how policies are developed and documented. In practice, you will find that creating policies is a relatively simple procedure. You use the language of ISO 14001 as a guideline and base your policy statements on the company-wide policy and your listed objectives and targets.

THE THREE LEVELS OF DOCUMENTATION

As a quick review, we will again examine the three levels of documentation required for an environmental management system according to ISO 14000.

Level I documents are policy statements for each element of Section 4 in ISO 14001. These policy statements explain why a company conforms to the particular element. Each policy statement should name a particular job title responsible for the implementation of the policy. A policy statement for a typical company should be one page or less in length. All policy statements, the company-wide environmental policy, and an organization chart should be assembled into an environmental policy management manual.

Level II documents are the written standard operating procedures that are used within a company. The Level II documents related to the environmental management standard are assembled into the environmental procedures manual. In some cases, these same procedures can be part of a larger company procedure manual. Standard operating procedures describe a particular process, usually carried out by a number of different people. It will describe the how, when, who, where, and with which equipment for the completion of a process comprised of related tasks.

Level III documents are the written work instructions used by an individual to complete one of the tasks listed in a standard operating procedure. The task is broken down into identifiable steps. In other words, a work instruction tells a person exactly what to do. A good working instruction uses a minimum of words to convey a maximum amount of information. Illustrations, diagrams, reference tables, and other job aids are strongly encouraged to support work instructions.

The environmental records created through the implementation of policies and the use of operating procedures and work instructions create what is sometimes called the fourth level of documentation. In this chapter, we will examine structured and systematic ways to create standard operating procedures and work instructions. The examples will help you in the creation of your own documentation. By using these methods, you should be able to create documents that show conformance to either ISO 9000, ISO 14000, or both.

HOW TO USE FLOWCHARTS TO WRITE YOUR DOCUMENTATION

Several times in previous chapters I have noted that you can use flowcharts to assist you in the creation of documentation. I would like to take a moment to discuss how this is done in detail. It begins with an understanding of how to flowchart a process. A process is any business activity that has a definite beginning with inputs and a definable ending with outputs. Typically, a process is a particular set of activities directed at achieving a specific end. For example, the process of environmental planning has the objective of creating an environmental management system.

Each process can be broken down into fundamental stages. Continuing with our environmental planning example, one stage is to study the environmental aspects of your company. Another stage is to review the legal and other related environmental requirements of your company.

In turn, each stage can be broken down into identifiable tasks that must be accomplished. Each task can then be broken down into the steps required to complete the task. A flowchart can be used to identify the fundamental stages of the process or to show the flow of tasks required to complete one stage of a process. Our first flowchart will be used to create standard operating procedures. Our second will be used to create written work instructions.

AN EXAMPLE OF WRITING A PROCEDURE: EMERGENCY RESPONSE

Let's take the example of the process of an emergency response to a chemical spill. This response represents a process. When a chemical spill occurs, the first stage of the process is to assess the situation. The people at the scene have to determine whether an immediate danger has been created for personnel. If so, the next stage of the process is to evacuate personnel from the area and to notify management immediately.

The next stage is to control the spill and to attempt to minimize the damage to the environment. If necessary, outside authorities should be notified and requests made for additional help. Otherwise, the next stage is to clean up the spill. At the same time, reports are filed with management and, possibly, local officials. Later assessments will be made to find the root cause of the spill and to attempt to prevent future occurrences.

Although the written description of the example gives you an idea of how the process works, a flowchart would provide even more information. Exhibit 9-1 shows this same process as a flowchart. The rectangle represents a stage of the process. Diamond-shaped boxes are decision points in the process. Other symbols can be used to represent activities such as connections to other processes or documentation being produced by the process.

TOWARD A BETTER FLOWCHART

Although flowcharts are great visual aids and conveyors of information, the basic flowchart can be modified to fit the specific need of creating a standard operating procedure. By breaking down each stage into the specific tasks involved, we begin to obtain the information necessary to write the procedure. For each identified task, we add information on who does what, when it is done, which equipment is used, what outputs are expected, and how it is done.

In Exhibit 9-2, we have created a form to accomplish this task. Using this form, we can draw out a normal flowchart and then add the information we need to create a written procedure.

Using the flowchart created for the emergency response process, we can fill out this form to help us write the emergency response procedure. This is accomplished by first drawing the flowchart in the first column. The flowchart should be created using a cross-functional team. Representatives from the departments involved in emergency responses would be represented. The team would look at the various ways in which emergencies are handled. For the sake of this discussion, let's assume that they are focusing specifically on chemical spills.

The team examines the way in which the company now responds to chemical spills. This would be laid out as a rough flowchart. Then the team would discuss the regulatory obligations involved in chemical spills. Next, they would discuss whether the existing process of reaction is the most sensible. This discussion would be followed by the creation of a new flowchart that represents the new and improved process of reacting to chemical spills.

This new flowchart would be drawn in the first column of the blank flowchart form (see Exhibit 9-3). The team would then change their discussion to focus on each particular stage of the process. For each stage, they would describe the tasks

Exhibit 9-1: Emergency Response Procedure for Chemical Spills

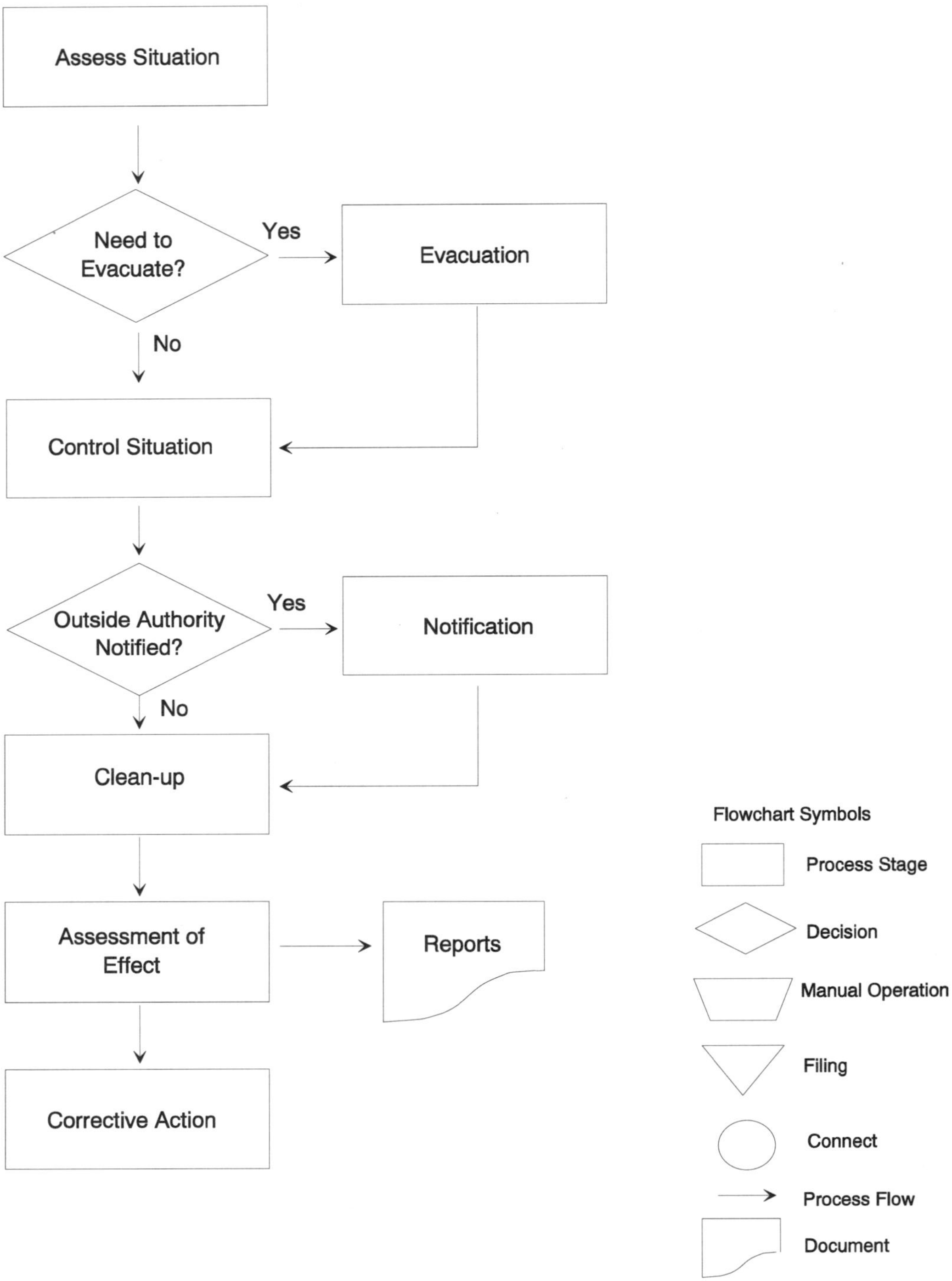

Exhibit 9-2: Blank Flowchart Form Designed for Assisting in the Writing of Standard Operation Procedures

Process Flow	Tasks	Who	When	Where	Equipment	Related Work Instructions

that have to be accomplished. These would be listed on the blank flowchart form in the second column. The tasks would be listed in the order in which they are carried out.

For each task, the team would determine who would be responsible for the completion of the task, when they would carry out the task, where these activities would take place, and what equipment would be used. If there are existing work instructions for completing this task, they are noted along with the previous information on our blank flowchart form. If the team decides that a work instruction must be created to support a particular task, the proposed work instruction is noted on the flowchart form (see Exhibit 9-3). The resulting filled-out form will give us all the information needed to create the standard operating procedure.

Taking one stage from the flowchart form, we can see how it is used to create a written operating procedure. But first, let's take a moment to describe a correctly formatted operating procedure.

THE PROPER DESIGN AND USE OF OPERATING PROCEDURES

There is no single design for operating procedures or work instructions specified by either ISO 9000 or ISO 14000. Opinions vary on the proper format for these documents. However, several items should be included in any documentation. These

Exhibit 9-3: Example of a Filled-in Flowchart Form (only part of the chemical spill reaction procedure)

Process Flow	Tasks	Who	When	Where	Equipment	Related Work Instructions
Stage 1: Assess Situation	Determine if immediate hazard exists	Senior person on scene	Immediately	From position of safety	Breathing, face and body protection	Safety equipment usage
	Attempt to stop spill	Person picked	When situation is controlled	From position of safety	Breathing, face and body protection	Safety equipment usage
	Consult hazardous chemical symbol	Senior person	As soon as possible	From position of safety	As needed	
	Notify area supervisor	Person picked	Immediately	Control area	None	
Stage 2: Decide Whether to Evacuate	Yes=go to Stage 3 No=go to Stage 4					
Stage 3: Evacuation	Sound alarm	Senior person	Immediately	From position of safety	None	Alarm activation
	Seal off area	Senior person	As soon as possible	From position of safety	None	
	Call management	Senior person	As soon as possible	From position of safety	Emergency phone	
Stage 4: Control Situation	Stop spill	Emergency team	As soon as possible	At spill site	Complete protective gear	Spill containment
	Prevent runoff	Emergency team	As soon as possible	At spill site	Complete protective gear	Spill containment
	Contain effects	Emergency team	As soon as possible	At spill site	Complete protective gear	Spill containment
(and so on)						

include the title of the document, its number, a signature indicating that the document has been authorized, the revision level, company name, and a page-numbering scheme.

A good format for operating procedures and work instructions is to number the paragraphs according to their level of description. For example, the topic of "Purpose" might be numbered 1.0. The general description of this topic might be numbered 1.1.0. The major topics to be covered in a standard operating procedure could include the following:

- Purpose
- Scope and objectives
- Responsibilities
- Procedures
- Definitions
- Related documents
- Audit questions

Naturally, you would use the topics that are appropriate to the type of documentation you are trying to create and their relevance to the process being described.

The Purpose section of the procedure should review the environmental policy statement (Level I document), which calls for this procedure. This is typically only one paragraph in length. The Scope and Objective section explains what a company is trying to achieve using this procedure. The Responsibility section names the job title of the person ultimately responsible for assuring that this procedure is implemented and maintained. A job title is used instead of the person's actual name so that if a new person steps into this position the procedure does not have to be updated.

The Procedure section is a breakdown of the stages of the process being described. Using the flowchart sheet from the previous discussion, you can write this section of your document easily. First, all identified stages receive a numbering sequence. Then each task is described for each stage. The information you recorded about who does what, when, and using which equipment is now used to complete the description of activities during each stage of the procedure. Exhibit 9-4 shows what a finished operating procedure looks like.

The Related Documents section is where you list the work instructions and policy statements related to this procedure. This would allow a user of the procedure to quickly identify where further information can be found. It also allows auditors to quickly understand how your documentation interrelates. This speeds the audit process.

Exhibit 9-4: Finished Standard Operating Procedure for Emergency Reaction to Chemical Spills

ENG-16: **Emergency Response to Chemical Spills** (issued 3/14/96)

16.0 General

This operating procedure is to be activated whenever a chemical spill occurs.

16.1 Purpose

By having a planned response to chemical spills, the XYZ Corporation is better able to meet its strategic goals of the prevention of pollution and the reduction of negative impacts on the environment.

16.2 Scope and Objectives

This procedure applies to the spilling of any identified hazardous material. Its primary objective is to prevent accidental discharge into the environment while protecting the health of our workers.

16.3 Responsibilities

The Engineering Manager is ultimately responsible for the implementation and maintenance of this procedure.

16.4 Procedure

16.4.1 Assessment of the Situation. Whenever a chemical spill occurs, an immediate assessment should be made of the situation.

16.4.1.1 The senior person on the scene of the spill should immediately determine from a position of safety whether the spill is creating a serious hazard to the people at the scene. At all times the senior person should be wearing proper safety equipment and, if necessary, breathing apparatus. If a hazard was created, then evacuation should commence.

16.4.1.2 If an immediate hazard does not exist, then an initial attempt should be made to stop the spill. This should be done by people selected by the senior person on the scene and only by people wearing proper protective gear.

16.4.1.3 The hazardous chemical identified on the container should be examined and the related hazardous reference sheets consulted. This should be done from a position of safety.

16.4.1.4 The supervisor of the area involved should be notified as soon as possible by a person selected by the senior person on the scene.

16.4.2 Evacuation. If the spill is creating an immediate hazard, then evacuation procedures should be activated. Otherwise, move on to item 16.4.3. Evacuation procedure ENG-17 should be consulted. The quick and safe evacuation of personnel is a priority.

16.4.2.1 The evacuation alarm should be sounded.

16.4.2.2 The area affected by the spill should be sealed off under the direction of the area's supervisor.

16.4.2.3 Company management should be notified as soon as possible of the situation.

16.4.3 Control Situation.

(and so on) . . .

16.5 Definitions

Emergency = situation requiring immediate response.
Spill = any accidental release of a liquid substance with hazardous effects.

16.6 Related Documents

OP-2: Safety equipment usage
OP-7: Alarm activation
ENV-3: Spill containment
ENV-1: Community alert process

16.7 Audit Questions

1. Are emergency procedures and instructions present in all areas known to store or handle hazardous chemicals?
2. Have all spills been documented with root cause identified?

Revision: B	Authorized by: RBC	XYZ Corporation	page 1 of 3

An optional section in your procedure can include the Audit Questions or an audit checklist to be used internally for confirming the effective usage of this procedure. If you choose to include this type of section in your procedure, then you should meet with your internal auditors to request their help in designing the best set of questions.

THE STYLE OF WRITING USED FOR PROCEDURES AND WORK INSTRUCTIONS

When writing your standard operating procedures, keep a few things in mind. For one, the procedure should be written in clear, concise, and simple language. Gear your narrative to the level of intelligence present at your company. In other words, write procedures that will be understood by any employee.

Procedures and work instructions must be typed or printed in a typeface that is at least 12 points in size and easy to read. Your selected format should make liberal use of white space on the page and have an attractive appearance. The idea is to make your manual of procedures easy to use so that people are encouraged to follow the written instructions. A procedures manual should not create a barrier to operations.

In addition to the written procedures, your procedures manual should be organized along the following lines. First, the manual should be constructed using a three-ring binder. This will allow easy updating of existing procedures. Next, the cover should clearly indicate that this is your environmental procedures manual. Feel free to use a company logo and put a control number on each manual as part of your document control system.

The first page of the manual should be a copy of your company-wide environmental quality policy. This should be followed by a table of contents that lists the enclosed procedures and their current revision levels. By listing revision levels, it will be easy for your internal audit team to confirm that your manual is up to date. A preface that describes the general purpose of your environmental procedures manual should follow the table of contents. This, in turn, is followed by a copy of the organizational chart.

Optional material to include in your environmental procedures manual include items such as a description of your company, a list of products affected by this manual, a summary of the environmental objectives and targets of your company, and cross-references to other standards and environmental regulations. Although you can technically add anything you want, the objective is to include the minimal amount of information that will support the procedures and explain why the use of environmental procedures is so important to the company.

When you have completed the writing of your standard operating procedures, these should be submitted to the identified authority for approval. The approval body or person will sign the new or revised operating procedures before they are placed in circulation.

When a new or revised procedure is created and issued, you should consider what type (if any) of training will be required to implement the new document. For example, we looked at the case of a company creating an emergency response procedure. This was the first time such a procedure was placed in writing. Therefore, the decision was made to educate all personnel who handled hazardous chemicals on the new procedure.

WRITING THE DOCUMENTATION–HOW TO CREATE A FINAL OPERATING PROCEDURE

Returning to our example of creating a standard operating procedure for handling chemical spills, we can use the filled-in flowchart to write the documentation. Starting with the first stage in the process of reacting to chemical spills, "assessing the situation," we translate the flowchart information into a written procedure. For example, we would use a standard format for any procedure that would include an area for the procedure title, revision date, revision level, signature of authorization, procedure number, and number of pages. To this we would add the purpose, scope, and responsibility sections (see Exhibit 9-4).

Note how Purpose is the first numbered section (1.0); Scope, the second (2.0); Responsibility, the third (3.0). The description of the procedure is then numbered as 4.0. Each stage of the process will receive a consecutive number starting with 4. something (4.x). For each stage, we will break the activity down into its identifiable tasks.

As an illustration, let's take the first stage of the chemical spill reaction procedure and identify the tasks involved with this stage of the process. As part of the assessment of the situation, the following tasks must be completed:

- If possible, the area's supervisor should be notified.
- The area supervisor or team leader on site of the spill should immediately look for signs of immediate danger, such as breathing problems, obvious fumes, and so on.
- The hazardous chemical label for the source of the spill should be consulted if possible.
- An additional attempt to stop the spill is encouraged only when doing so is considered nonhazardous.
- The senior person on site when the spill occurs takes control of the situation.

These tasks should be placed into a logical or chronological order in the procedure. For example, the first task is for someone to take control of the situation so that an initial assessment can be made. At the same time, the person taking control should send someone to seek out the supervisor for the area. The danger presented by the spill should be evaluated. If danger is present, the person taking control should move to the next stage of the process, which is to evacuate personnel. Otherwise, the next move is to attempt to stop the spill, if this has not already happened.

Because we identified the people responsible for each task in this stage of the process, we can easily flesh out the written description of this part of the procedure. We can see from our flowchart that the person taking control has to act quickly and have emergency breathing equipment nearby. It is also noted that depending upon the chemicals present in the area, there are work instructions on what type of protective gear everyone should already be wearing. Thus, we can continue to write the procedure (see Exhibit 9-4).

You would repeat this for each stage of the process. Then the team would discuss any definitions that should be included in the procedure and any other documentation that would relate to this procedure; for example, other procedures, policies, or work instructions. It could also list relevant regulations and standards. One example of this might be a reference to OSHA regulations involving chemical spills.

The completed draft of the operating procedure is then reviewed by the team to see whether it represents the most efficient and effective way to handle chemical spills. Then the draft procedure is tested by giving it to some of the people who would have to use such a procedure. Their comments and questions about the procedure would be noted so that, if necessary, the draft procedure could be modified. When the team is satisfied with the draft, it is submitted to the steering committee for approval.

THE PROPER DESIGN AND USE OF WORK INSTRUCTIONS

Unlike standard operating procedures, which tend to be collected into a single manual, written work instructions tend to be highly decentralized. For example, inspection instructions could exist at dozens of sites throughout the company.

Work instructions are also different from operating procedures in intention and presentation. First, the intention of a work instruction is to inform an individual on how to complete a single task. Instead of breaking down each stage of a process into tasks, we now take a single task and break it down into identifiable steps. The amount of detail needed within a work instruction will vary by several factors, such as:

- The complexity of the task
- The level of knowledge present in the work force
- The possibility of the tasks being completed by a temporary employee
- The language being spoken by employees
- The need for illustrations or samples

Second, a work instruction has a different presentation format. Like a procedure, there is an opening block with the name of the instruction, revision date, revision level, signature of authority, instruction number, and number of pages. Then the instruction begins by describing the task to be completed, including a description of the scope of application—in other words, where this instruction is to be used. This is followed by a list of equipment and other resources needed to complete the task. Then you begin the process of describing how the task is to be completed. After that, you can add additional information, such as defect checklists, criteria of workmanship, safety precautions, whom to contact if you have questions, and the like (see Exhibit 9-5).

Your intention is to write a work instruction that could be followed by a person responsible for the activity—even though that person may have limited knowledge of your company, product, and operations. Therefore, your instructions should include information on where to obtain the necessary equipment, precautions to follow, and the outcome to be achieved. At the same time, you want to use the fewest words needed to communicate the information, but enough instruction to match the needs of the particular situation.

AN EXAMPLE OF WRITING A WORK INSTRUCTION

Let's take the example of a company that is writing a number of work instructions so that they can conform to ISO 14000. In particular, we will examine the writing of the work instruction for how to receive external communications concerning environmental matters.

The administrative assistant is responsible for receiving the mail, faxes, e-mail, and phone calls related to management issues; therefore, she is responsible for receiving any external communication concerning environmental matters. She is the first person in the company to receive such communications, even when the intended recipient is a company manager or department head.

Because the reception of external communications is a critical function under ISO 14001, the steering committee feels that a work instruction should be written for this particular task. They have already developed a standard operating procedure for internal and external communications related to environmental issues. It is this procedure that the administrative assistant will refer to when drafting her own work instruction.

The process of receiving external communications is fairly straightforward for environmental matters. First, the communication can either be a complaint against the company, a new customer requirement, the updating of a relevant regulation, recognition of the company's environmental system, or a comment related to an environmental issue. When any of these types of communications are received, the administrative assistant will begin by logging in the date of receipt and the nature of the communication.

Exhibit 9-5: Example of Format for a Work Instruction

<table>
<tr><td colspan="3">Work Instruction</td><td>Date</td></tr>
<tr><td colspan="4">1.0 Task to Be Completed

2.0 Scope of Application

3.0 Equipment to Be Used

4.0 Steps to Complete the Task

5.0 Criteria of Workmanship

6.0 Safety Precautions (and potential environmental effects)

7.0 Source of Further Information</td></tr>
<tr><td>Revision:</td><td>Authorized by:</td><td>Company Name</td><td>page x of xx</td></tr>
</table>

Next, she will determine the intent of the communication and how it should be routed. For example, complaints are sent straight to the management corrective action committee. New regulations, updated regulations, and communications on customer requirements for environmental issues are routed to several key people according to a predetermined distribution list. A copy is also sent to the environmental management system coordinator for further actions. Compliments and comments are routed to the environmental management system coordinator to be noted in the monthly report that suggests opportunities for improvement and notes recent environmental successes. In all cases, the original communication is filed by the administrative assistant.

By using a flowchart, the administrative assistant can see more clearly the steps needed to complete the task. The flowchart will also help her to communicate the nature of the task to the steering committee. In this example, the flowchart will be used as a critical tool for developing work instructions (see Exhibit 9-6).

Exhibit 9-6: Flowchart for Work Instruction

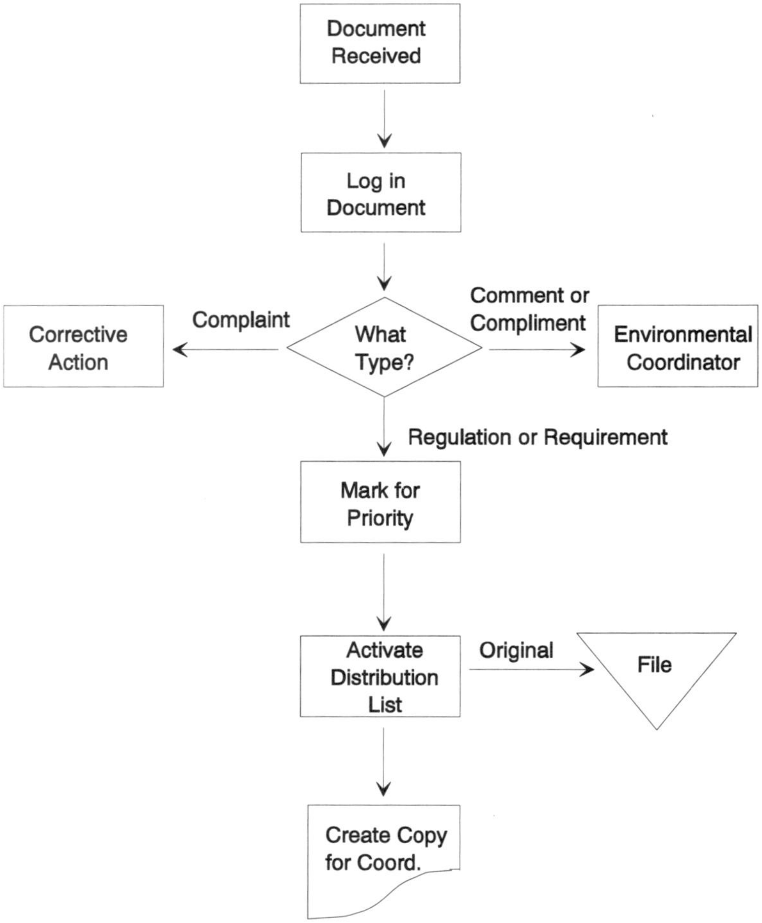

When the flowchart is completed, the administrative assistant should work with someone also familiar with the requirements of the task. The flow of the steps should be examined to see whether there is a way to promote greater efficiency in the completion of this task. For example, they may discover that the internal e-mail system is more efficient at distributing such communications. By using scanners, the written or faxed communications can be placed into the e-mail system. This way several people can be notified simultaneously and they can discuss its implications quickly using e-mail and conferencing capabilities within their company's computer system.

The people writing a work instruction should also take into account any actions to be taken when problems arise. Take the possibility of two messages coming from the same source but providing conflicting information. For example, a regulatory agency may state that you must use the standard amount of discharge to the air for your dust reduction system, but the auditor from the same agency sends a letter at the same time stating that an increased level of conformance applies to the same system. The team writing the work instruction has to consider problems such as this one and write out a brief reaction plan. In this case, they may state that the two communications must first be submitted to the environmental management system coordinator for action and resolution before distribution is allowed.

Other considerations, such as safety precautions (if applicable), equipment to be used, and the person to contact if you need further information should be listed on your flowchart. Exhibit 9-7 shows what such a form may look like.

By drawing out the flowchart from the external communication reception task, we can see the steps involved. We can also note the information needed to completely describe what each step involves. By including reaction plans within our work instruction, we make the document more effective. Our goal is to make the work instruction indispensable to the person performing the task (see Exhibit 9-8).

When the work instruction flowchart is completed, the document can be created by following the steps listed. In this example, we bring together all the information collected on this task and draft it as a work instruction. Once drafted, we would try to reduce the wording and where possible increase the use of illustrations to use the minimum amount of words to effectively describe the task. Then we would test the draft with a person unfamiliar with the task. Such a person should be able to efficiently complete the task using only the work instruction. When this is achieved, the draft work instruction is completed and ready for approval by the steering committee.

A well-written work instruction will achieve several benefits. First, it will allow you to quickly train a new hire or a temporary employee. Second, it will make employees more efficient by giving them specific written instructions to follow to complete a task. This would include a description of the successful outcome of the task. Thus, they would know the quality effect of carrying out an environmental activity. Third, it would relieve some of the firefighting that supervisors experience. Because reaction plans are incorporated into the work instructions, an employee doesn't have to seek out the advice of a supervisor for every problem that occurs.

Exhibit 9-7: Example of Work Instruction Creation Form

Task Flow	Actions	When	Who	Equipment	Reaction Plan
Step 1: Receive incoming communication	Open mail, print faxes, receive phone calls, e-mail	During business hours	Admin. Assistant		Misdirected mail is to be forwarded to the Admin. Assistant
	Date stamp all communications	ASAP	Admin. Assistant	Date stamp	
Step 2: Log in the communication	Note each communication before routing	ASAP	Admin. Assistant	Logbook	
	Forward e-mail to addressee	As time permits	Admin. Assistant	Network terminal	In case of network breakdown, print copies and distribute
Step 3: Determine type of communication	Complaints are sent to Environ. Manager for action	Right away	Admin. Assistant		If Environ. Manager is unavailable, Engineering Manager is notified
	Comments or complaints related to environmental issues go to Environ. Coord.	Same day	Admin. Assistant		
	Environmental regulations or customer requirements are sent to members on distribution list	Same day	Admin. Assistant	Distribution list on network or physical mailing list	
Step 4: File original communications	Physical copies are filed in Environ. Communications file	Within two days	Admin. Assistant or other office personnel	File cabinet	
	Electronic copies are backed up to disk	Each day	Admin. Assistant	Zip drive	Backup procedure OP-25 should be used
Step 5: Report to Environmental Coordinator	Environ. Coord. receives copy of all environ. communications	Each week	Admin. Assistant		

Exhibit 9-8: Completed Work Instruction

Work Instruction OP-34WI Environmental Communications (external)	12/21/95

1.0 Tasks to Be Completed

Receiving and handling incoming communications related to environmental issues. Distribution of such communications to affected parties in a timely manner.

2.0 Scope of Application

Any mail, e-mail, fax, phone call, or other form of communication related to an environmental issue.

3.0 Equipment to Be Used

Network terminal, fax machines, communication log book, date stamp, and copy machine.

4.0 Steps to Completing the Task

4.1 Receiving incoming communication. The Administrative Assistant dedicates a good portion of the day opening mail, taking calls, routing outside e-mail, and other related duties. Any communications related to environmental issues should be date stamped (if a date of receipt is not present).

4.2 Log in the communication. Each communication should be noted in the communications log book.

4.3 Determine type of communication. Complaints are to be immediately sent to the Environmental Manager for corrective action. Comment or compliments are routed to the Environmental Coordinator the same day. Regulations or customer requirements are distributed using the Environmental Communication Distribution List. Electronic communications can be forwarded using the network mail system.

4.4 File original communications. One copy of the original communication is placed in the Environmental Communication file cabinet. Electronic communications are backed-up to disk using the zip drive. This should be done daily with a note about the disk's contents also placed in the Environmental Communication file cabinet.

4.5 Environmental Coordinator should receive a weekly set of copies of all environmental communications.

5.0 Criteria of Workmanship

100% accuracy in receiving, routing, and copying environmental communications.

6.0 Safety Precautions (and Potential Environmental Effects)

None

7.0 For Further Information

Consult the Environmental Communication Distribution List or contact the Engineering Manager.

Revision: A	Authorized by: RBC	XYZ Corporation	page 1 of 2

HOW TO WRITE PROCEDURES, WORK INSTRUCTIONS, JOB DESCRIPTIONS, AND TRAINING MATERIALS AT THE SAME TIME[1]

To show conformance to ISO 9000 and ISO 14000, you must be able to demonstrate the existence and effectiveness of your management system of quality assurance. To demonstrate your system, you need documentation. As mentioned, most of this documentation will be written procedures and work instructions. What we did not mention is that in most cases, you will also need job descriptions, quality records, environmental records, training plans, and a host of other documents.

In this half of the chapter, we will explore how many of these documents can be developed concurrently to save time and money while also creating more effective documentation. Specifically, we will look at the process of job and task analysis in the creation of procedures, work instructions, job descriptions, skills lists, and training materials.

These documents, in turn, are used to conform to elements of ISO 9000, such as 4.1, "Management Responsibility," and Section 4.3.2 in ISO 14001. Part of Element 4.1 in ISO 9001 states that management will "provide adequate resources and assign trained personnel." Job descriptions and skills lists can help with this requirement. Likewise, Element 4.2, "Quality System," states that you must identify the skills required to meet your targeted levels of quality through a system of procedures and work instructions. Element 4.18, "Training," states that knowledge, skill, and experience for each job shall be identified. Section 4.3.2 in ISO 14001 repeats many of these requirements and includes other items, such as that employees must know the impact of departing from established policies and procedures.

WHAT IS JOB AND TASK ANALYSIS?

The creation of a product or the primary activity of a company is seen as a series of related processes. For each process, you need a written procedure. Within each process will be a series of tasks to perform. Tasks performed by an individual can be grouped together as a work instruction. To give structure to the process of creating procedures, work instructions, and other documents, we will use the techniques of job and task analysis.

Job analysis and task analysis are two separate techniques that share many similar traits. Job analysis looks at the components of a specific job. Task analysis looks at a particular process and its component tasks. We will consider them as one activity in this discussion. Whether job or task analysis is conducted, they both break down the process being examined into its smallest components so that they

---

[1] Some of this material originally appeared in the *Quality Manager's Complete Guide to ISO 9000*. The material has been updated and modified to better suit the requirements of ISO 14000.

can be classified, organized, and clarified. We shall see how this is done in the following examples.

A process will usually involve many people and require a written procedure. We will examine the process and identify the steps necessary to complete the process. Likewise, we will look at an individual's job and identify the steps needed to complete the task at hand. Then we will supplement this information with data about how the steps are to be completed, what to do when the step cannot be completed successfully, health and safety considerations, environmental considerations, the skills required, and other similar information. The result will be a database of information about the job or process under study. By using this database, we will be able to create many of the documents ISO 9000 and ISO 14000 require.

There are many approaches advocated for job and task analysis. In fact, there are many different schools of thought on how to perform job or task analysis. It is beyond the scope of this book to explore each of them. Instead, I will use a general approach that combines some of the methods. This approach will be adequate for creating the documentation needed for ISO 9000 and/or ISO 14000 conformance. However, if you wish to explore these techniques in greater depth, I recommend that you consult the literature for job and task analysis and seek the advice of an outside authority on this topic.

Exhibit 9-9 shows how job and task analysis can create a database of information that can be used to create a wide variety of documents. We will follow two tracks of document development. The first will be the creation of procedures and work instructions from the created database. The second track will use the same database to create job descriptions, skills requirements, competency checks, and training materials to help conform to Element 4.18 in ISO 9001 and Section 4.3.2 in ISO 14001.

HOW TO PERFORM A JOB AND TASK ANALYSIS

Earlier I advocated a method of writing procedures that involved the creation of a flowchart. The flowchart was a map of the process under study. From this map, a procedure was created. For creating procedures and work instructions under a deadline, this approach works just fine. However, if you have the time or if you wish to write several documents concurrently, then job and task analysis is recommended.

We will begin by looking at a single process using both methods. The comparison will show that each method has its particular advantages. Flowcharting is faster, but job and task analysis is more effective. At the same time, the two methods can easily be combined so that the flowchart helps a job and task analysis team better understand the process involved.

Let's look at the process of drilling into metal. Specifically, let's look at the daily job of the drill press operator in a pneumatic valve company. The valves are manufactured out of a block of aluminum about three inches square. The first production stages cut and smooth each face of the block. Then milling machines form the outer

Exhibit 9-9: Flowchart of Documents from Job and Task Analysis

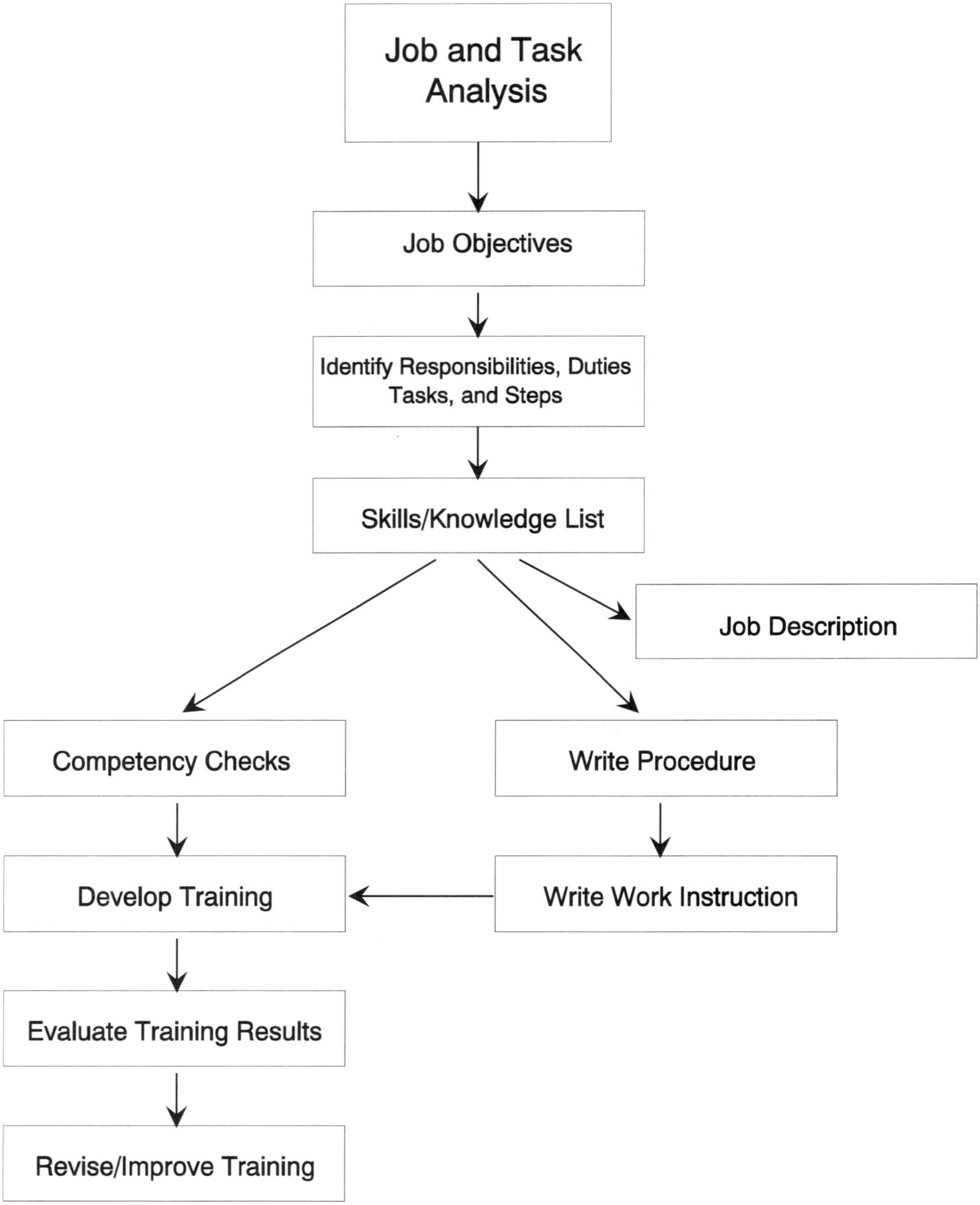

edges and the inner chambers of the block. The drill press operator bores a few holes in the valve block for air passages. Later operations polish and finish the surfaces. Then the assembly area inserts the moving components of the valve. After that, the assembled valve is tested and marked for identification.

Environmental impacts include the use and disposal of cutting oil, the noise and smoke created by the process, the disposition of scrap and cuttings, and the safety issues involved whenever heavy machinery is used. Our drill press operator represents just one person in the chain of production. Exhibit 9-10 shows a portion of the flowchart for the drilling operation.

Essentially, a partially finished valve block is given to the drill press operator. He ensures that this is the correct material, mounts a drilling tool, produces the proper holes, signs off on the operation, and sends the parts to the next operation. If we needed to create a work instruction for this operator, we could do so right from the flowchart. For each step on the flowchart, we would write a short instruction. We could gain knowledge from observing the drill press operator and discussing the responsibilities of his job. In addition, we might consult the quality plan for the valve and the environmental plan for this part of manufacturing operations.

We may find that the quality plan says that these holes have to be checked to assure that the right amount of airflow can pass through. To do this, the drill press operator uses an airflow gauge to randomly test the holes. You may decide that a control chart is needed for this check, specifically, an attribute chart, because the airflow gauge being used is essentially a Go/No Go gauge. This information is added to your work instruction.

The environmental plan may note that cutting oil is to be recycled, scrap and cuttings are to be collected and reprocessed, and that a list of safety precautions are to be followed by the operator. This information is also added to your work instruction. Talking to the operator reveals that a few other checks must be performed and some considerations made during drilling. For example, the operator is equipped with a can of cutting oil that he can apply if conditions warrant. Therefore, you make a note that the work instructions should explain when cutting oil is required.

The resulting work instruction may look like the example on page 229. Major steps in the process get paragraph numbers. Tasks within the steps get a lower sequence of numbers.

Exhibit 9-10: Example of Flowchart for the Drilling Process

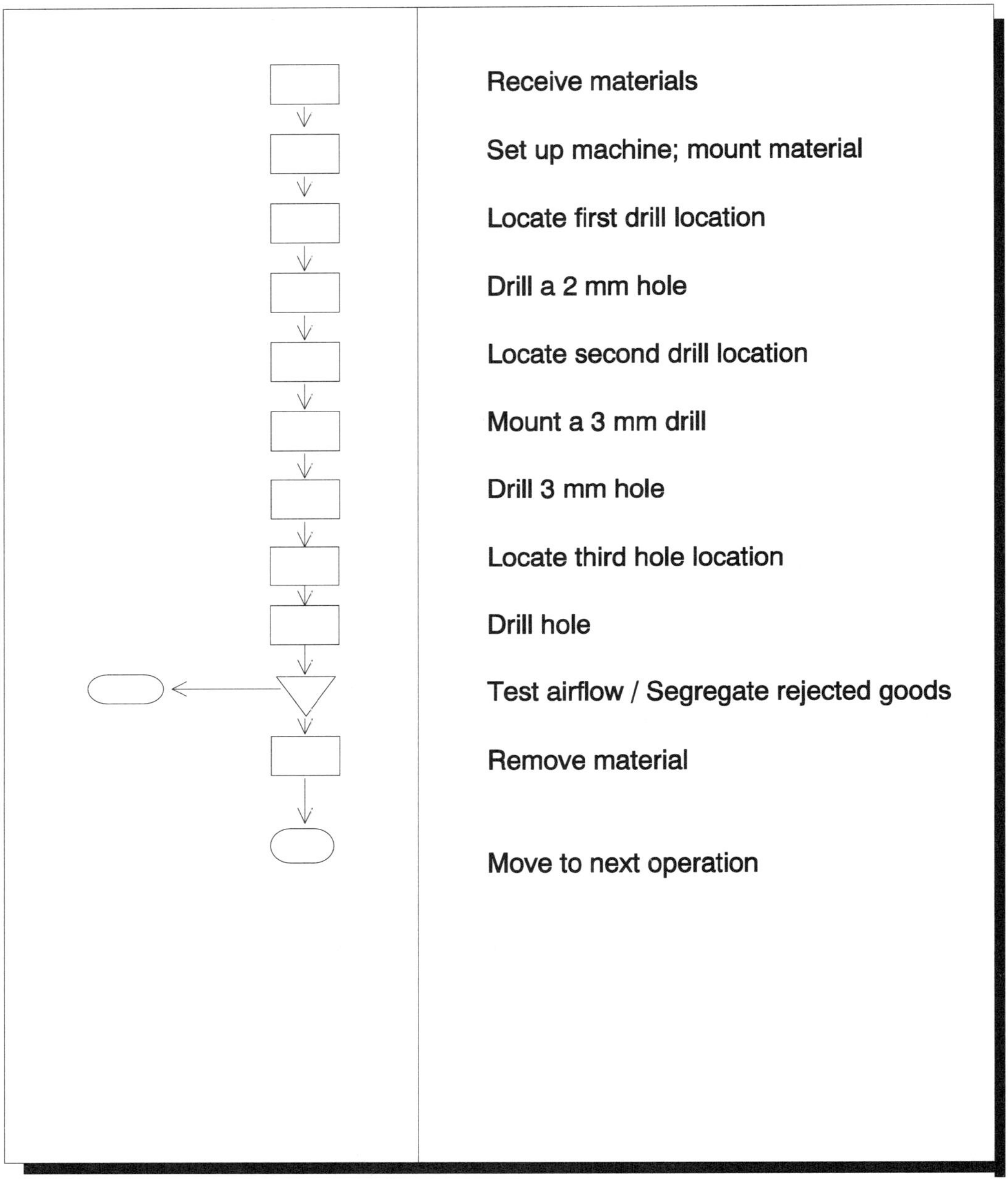

Work Instruction—Drill Press Operation
Parts Involved—Pneumatic Valve Blocks (all sizes)

1.0 Receiving Materials

1.1 Operator receives blocks ready for drilling

1.2 Operator ensures that these are the correct blocks by comparing the material identification tags with the blueprint specifications (Example: ADX-23 valves should use a #34 block)

1.3 Operator moves blocks into drilling area

2.0 Preparation and Drilling

2.1 A drilling tool is taken from the tool crib and mounted into the press. The tool should match the size of the holes to be drilled.

2.2 The jig for holding blocks in place is loosened and a block installed.

2.3 The jig is tightened and the first hole is drilled. If burring or smoking should occur, apply cutting oil. Ventilation should always be active. The operator should avoid inhaling the smoke.

2.4 The jig is loosened and the block rotated to the next position for drilling. The block is tightened and the hole drilled. This is repeated until all required holes are produced.

3.0 Inspection

3.1 Five drilled blocks are selected at random each half hour and placed on the airflow gauge for testing. All five should pass.

3.2 The results of this test are recorded on the control chart.

3.3 If any block fails the airflow test, the operator must contact his supervisor, segregate the affected lot of parts, and document the incident on the control chart.

3.4 A quality auditor will inspect the affected lot and make a disposition. The operator and his or her supervisor should examine the drilling tool and other factors to determine whether corrective action is needed.

4.0 Completion

4.1 When a tub of blocks has been drilled, the operator should sign off on the shop floor traveler that this stage of the process has been completed.

4.2 Each completed tub should be moved by hand cart to the next operation.

4.3 After each lot is completed, the scrap pieces and cuttings should be placed into a red tub for reprocessing.

4.4 After ten hours of cutting, the cutting oil should be changed, with the used oil placed into specially marked yellow bottles for recycling.

We have created a basic work instruction with criteria of workmanship included to satisfy the requirements of ISO 9001 and have incorporated environmental activities to comply with ISO 14001. This work instruction should be signed and dated as a controlled document to meet the requirements of ISO 9000/14000. However, our work instruction so far only looks at the production process. Surely, the drill press operator has other duties. And we still must create a job description that includes the skills, knowledge, and experience needed for drilling. Eventually, we will also need some sort of training materials to help a new person learn to be a drill press operator.

To do this effectively, we must form a good database of information about the job of drill press operator. If we use this information to help us intelligently combine documents, the day-to-day operation of the company will become easier and more efficient.

HOW TO GAIN KNOWLEDGE THROUGH JOB AND TASK ANALYSIS

Job and task analysis is a more structured approach to examining situations such as the drilling area. This is accomplished by systematically breaking down a situation into its components. The following four levels of descending complexity are used:

1. Job objective
2. Responsibilities
3. Duties
4. Tasks (with the steps taken to accomplish the task)

A job objective is the overall, general description of the job or process. In our example, it might look something like this:

Job Title: Drill Press Operator
Job objective: The drill press operator is responsible for the setup, operation, and routine maintenance of the drill press. In addition, the drill press operator is expected to meet customer and internal requirements for production pieces and to do so in an effective and efficient way that conforms to the level of environmental responsibility present in the company's overall environmental policy group.

A job responsibility is a broad description of related job duties. Job duties are a common collection of tasks the operator must perform. Tasks are the most basic units of work. Tasks are a collection of steps with a tangible output. Typically, a task is independent from other steps in the process; therefore, we could break down the drill press example into these respective categories. Let's begin with the job responsibilities of a drill press operator:

JOB RESPONSIBILITIES

1.0 Preparation
2.0 Processing Materials
3.0 Inspection
4.0 Maintenance

5.0 Paperwork

6.0 Housekeeping

Now let's take these responsibilities and list out the duties for each one:

1.0 Preparation
- **1.1** Receive materials
- **1.2** Prepare drill
- **1.3** Check instructions

2.0 Processing Materials
- **2.1** Process materials
- **2.2** Monitor process

3.0 Inspection
- **3.1** Watch for defects in material
- **3.2** Test for airflow
- **3.3** Take corrective actions when needed

4.0 Maintenance
- **4.1** Monitor the press
- **4.2** Check tools
- **4.3** Keep inventory
- **4.4** Repair when needed

5.0 Paperwork
- **5.1** Production forms
- **5.2** Timecard
- **5.3** Reaction logs
- **5.4** Corrective action reports (when needed)
- **5.5** Emergency environmental response report (when needed)

6.0 Housekeeping
- **6.1** Keep area clean
- **6.2** Check fire extinguisher
- **6.3** Properly store equipment and oils
- **6.4** Recycle cutting oil
- **6.5** Reduce noise
- **6.6** Prevent smoke

This type of information is obtained by direct observation of the process; talking to experts; examination of the quality, environmental, and production plans; consulting the existing procedures and policies; interviewing the operator and supervisor; reading the operating manual for the press; and time/motion studies. Some human resource people go so far as to use survey test instruments given to all operators in an area to establish norms.

I recommend that at a minimum, you observe the process, talk to the operators, and study the existing documentation. In addition, you may want to hold a meeting with the people responsible for planning and carrying out the drilling process. In this example, this might include the operators, the process engineer, the process supervisor, and a quality control representative familiar with the requirements for this process. Your findings can be presented to employees for evaluation of completeness and accuracy. The feedback from this group can be used to refine your list of responsibilities and duties.

While you have your team assembled, break each of the duties down into its constituent tasks. I recommend the use of index cards passed out to the assembled team. Each team member can jot down the tasks for each duty he or she is most familiar with. These can be posted under each duty on a bulletin board. Flipcharts, computer software, and other methods are also acceptable.

The team can freely arrange the tasks cards and discuss the addition or subtraction of tasks. Remember, a task should be stated as the minimal component of a duty and it should be independent. When describing the tasks, try to use a noun/verb format. To see how this looks, let's examine the tasks listed for one duty—the inspection of the process.

Responsibility: Inspection

Duty: Watch for defects in material

Task: Monitor hole locations

Task: Monitor material condition upon receipt

Task: Monitor processed material

Task statements should be brief and to the point. However, the tasks statements should not be so simple as to be obvious, such as "get material." You should state only what the operator must do to complete the duty. These should be observable behaviors of the operator. As we shall see later, this information on tasks will be key to creating the array of documents.

When the first list of tasks is developed, you should discuss the results in detail to obtain a final and complete list. Typically, you will find that you want to break down the tasks into their constituent steps. A step is a single action that leads toward completion of a task. For example, the task of drilling holes can be broken down into the steps of mounting a block, locating a drilling site, actually drilling, and the repositioning of the block.

By breaking tasks down into the specific steps taken by an operator, you can open up your discussion of a task—that is, by breaking down each task into the following considerations:

1. Materials, tools, or equipment needed
2. Criteria of workmanship
3. Special conditions (such as environmental concerns)
4. Safety considerations (health and safety issues)
5. Reaction plan (including emergency responses)

The criteria of workmanship is a description of the successful completion of the standards for a task—in other words, how the press operator knows that his or her task is successfully completed. Special conditions are a description of any particular circumstances that affect how the task is performed. Typically, these are environmental or process-based conditions. A reaction plan includes the steps an operator should take if something other than success occurs during the task. As always, safety during the task should be discussed and noted.

These five considerations will give you greater insight into how a task is performed. At the same time, you can define the skills and knowledge needed to perform the tasks. This is highly recommended for critical tasks or for situations in which temporary employees may be used or there is a high turnover in operators. The list of skills and knowledge will give you the ability to quickly locate a qualified operator, and the detailed list of steps to take will make training faster and easier.

While you are discussing the tasks, you may find that you need to add or combine duties or responsibilities for greater clarity. Feel free to do this so that you compile a list of responsibilities, duties, and tasks that are well organized and make sense for the job or process involved.

Your final list of tasks is used to create the database of information on this particular job. In this example, we looked at a drill press operator. Let's assume that we have examined one duty of the job, processing materials, task by task. Using the list of tasks for drilling holes, let's look at how each task would be broken down into these categories (see Exhibit 9-11).

As you can see, you are building up a considerable amount of information about this one job. You can also begin to see how information on the skills and level of knowledge for this job is being discovered. In our example, it is quickly becoming obvious that the ability to accurately read blueprints is a critical skill for this job. This should be noted at the bottom of the form used in Exhibit 9-11.

When you have completed your list of tasks and the conditions under which they are performed, be sure to show them to people familiar with the job. You want to confirm the accuracy and completeness of your work. In most cases, these people will want to make changes and you will want the final documents to accurately reflect the realities of the job.

Exhibit 9-11: Example of Job and Task Analysis Form for the Drill Press Operator

Job Title: Drill Press Operator		Date: 1/14/94	Dept.: Drilling	Authorized by:
Tasks (with steps)	**Materials, Tools, Equipment**	**Criteria of Workmanship**	**Safety/Special Conditions**	**Reaction Plan**
Task 2.1.1 Mount and Position Material Step 1: Loosen jig Step 2: Mount block Step 3: Align block	Hex wrench, chock key, pliers, screwdriver, positioning micrometer	Material and drilling tool fit tightly without wiggle Position should be within tolerance	For all tasks the following applies: Short hair or hairnet Wear safety glasses at all times	If proper tightening cannot be achieved, notify supervisor and preventive maintenance If improper positioning is observed, correct before drilling
Task 2.1.2 Drill Hole Step 1: Set speed / feed Step 2: Lower press to drill Step 3: Check completion of hole Step 4: Loosen jib and remove block	Cutting oil Hex wrench, chock key, pliers, screwdriver, positioning micrometer	Holes should be complete Speed and feed should be correct for material Hole size and position should match those on print Position should be within print tolerance	Wear gloves when handling material Keep hands clear of moving equipment and tools	If hole is incomplete, redrill
Task 2.2.1 Inspect Materials Step 1: Visually check holes Step 2: Test on airflow gauge Step 3: Record results	Airflow gauge, control chart for attributes	Holes should be complete and burr free Airflow should be within limits		If defect is observed or airflow test fails, mark part with red grease pencil and call for an audit of the affected lot; fill out CAR for the lot

Knowledge/Experience Requirements	**Skills Required**
Two years as a journeyman or certificate of journeyman training or be apprentice level III High school diploma or equivalent Completion of plant safety course Completion of 16-hour course on Statistical Process Control	Ability to read blueprints Knows how to set speeds and feeds of drill press Ability to work with small hand tools Ability to work with fractions Communicates verbally and in writing with effectiveness Ability to lift 40 pounds Ability to fill out control chart

HOW TO WRITE PROCEDURES OR WORK INSTRUCTIONS BASED ON THE DATA FROM JOB AND TASK ANALYSIS

Now that you have collected all this information, it is time to put it to work. The first job will be to create your needed procedure or work instruction. In the example of the drill press operator, you now have more than enough information to create your work instruction. In fact, you could even take the work instruction created using just a flowchart and add in your additional information to make a detailed document.

For each step in the process, you use the specific tasks you have identified. The information on safety, conditions, criteria of workmanship, reaction plans, and equipment needed are now noted.

A Work Instruction Example Created From Job/Task Analysis
Work Instruction—Drill Press Operation
Parts Involved—Pneumatic Valve Blocks (all sizes)

General Safety Considerations: The use of a hairnet or short hair is required for this job. Loose clothing is discouraged. Use safety glasses in the drill press area. Use gloves when handling the materials. Operator should be familiar with the firefighting equipment in this area. Cutting oils used should be handled and stored with caution. Exposure of skin to any machine oil should be minimized. Eyes need immediate treatment if splashed with oil, as per Safety Procedure 2.30.

1.0 Obtain Materials

1.1 Sign out materials for processing

Standard: These blocks should originate from the milling areas. The shop floor schedule should list points of origin for each job. Each lot is identified by tub. Each tub should have a shop floor traveler that identifies the lot code and the type of blocks. If any of this information is missing, notify your supervisor.

1.2 Match block to shop floor instructions

Standard: Operator ensures that these are the correct blocks by comparing the material identification tags with the blueprint specifications. The block identification is on the shop floor traveler in each tub. The needed block number is on the lower right side of the print in the area marked "specifications." Incorrectly labeled or delivered blocks should be returned to the point of origin and the operator notified of the problem.

2.0 Prepare Work Area

2.1 Sign out drilling tools from the tool crib

2.2 Mount the first drilling tool

2.3 Assure all proper paperwork is in place

Standard: For drilling, the operator should have a blueprint for the block, a shop floor traveler, the shop floor schedule of the day, a list of common defects to watch for, a control chart, a reaction plan, and a process log.

3.0 Drill Holes

3.1 Mount material to be processed

3.2 Set machine speed and feed

Standard: The speed and feed chart is located behind the machine. The speed and feed should match the tool being used and the material being drilled.

3.3 Position the material

Standard: The positioning micrometer on the table should be zeroed before positioning the block.

3.4 Drill the hole

Standard: Position should be within 0.010 inches in either X or Y axis.

Condition: If burring or smoking should occur, apply cutting oil.

3.5 Reposition the material

Condition: If the final hole is drilled, proceed to next step.

Reaction Plan: Any defects spotted on the block at this time should be marked with a red grease pencil and the block moved to the scrap box.

Inspection: When the drill is backed out of the hole, the operator should check to see whether the hole is completely through the material. If not, a second attempt should be made without moving the table. If that does not succeed, mark the part for repair using the blue grease pencil and take corrective actions.

The rest of the work instruction is expanded into the following responsibilities and duties. As you can see, the act of drilling has been divided into its own grouping. The standards, reaction plans, and special conditions have been added to the work instruction. The end of the work instruction might include the following information.

Further Duties:

4.0 Inspection

4.1 Five drilled blocks are selected at random each half hour and placed on the airflow gauge for testing. All five should pass.

4.2 The results of this test are recorded on the control chart.

4.3 If any block fails the airflow test, the operator should contact the supervisor, segregate the affected lot of parts, and document the incident on the control chart.

4.4 A quality auditor will inspect the affected lot and make a disposition. The operator and supervisor should examine the drilling tool and other factors to determine whether corrective action is needed.

5.0 Completion and Paperwork

5.1 When a tub of blocks has been drilled, the operator should sign off on the shop floor traveler that this stage of the process has been completed.

5.2 Each completed tub should be moved by hand cart to the next operation.

5.3 Control charts and logs should be kept up to date with accurate information.

5.4 Daily timecard must be kept up to date and turned in once a week.

5.5 Corrective actions should be reported (when needed).

5.6 Emergency environmental responses should be reported (when needed).

6.0 Maintenance

6.1 The drill press should be monitored continually for any unusual signs of wear or breakdown. Simple repairs and regular cleaning of the equipment can be performed by the operator. Preventive maintenance will handle more serious situations.

6.2 The sharpness of tools should be monitored, with questionable tools tagged for sharpening.

6.3 Inventory of all tools, materials, and supplies in the drill press area should be conducted weekly. Missing materials should be reported and replaced.

7.0 Housekeeping

7.1 The work area should always be kept swept and clear of obstacles by the operator.

7.2 The fire extinguisher for a drill press should be visually examined each week to assure that it has the proper charge.

7.3 Loose equipment and oils not in use should be placed in the storage cabinet.

7.4 Recycle cutting oil by storing used oil in the yellow bottles marked for recycling.

7.5 Noise reduction is to be constantly maintained through the proper use of cutting oils and placement of baffle boards.

7.6 Smoke prevention is to be achieved through the proper use of cutting oil, cutting machine RPMs, and proper feed rates.

Although this document is much larger than usually necessary, it is just as easy to use and it contains much useful information. This creates several advantages.

The first advantage is that an inexperienced operator can read through this work instruction and obtain much information on what to do and when to do it. This helps in the training of replacements or with the use of temporary employees. Second, an experienced operator needs only to scan the tasks as a checklist to ensure that the process is proceeding as planned. Reference to the step level is needed only when an unusual circumstance occurs or when learning a new job.

These first two advantages also create the third advantage—the relief of supervisors. Most supervisors will tell you that the majority of their day is spent "firefighting" on the shop floor—that is, telling people what to do and solving problems as they arise. The use of detailed work instructions will mean that the employees can take more responsibility for initially correcting problems and for making process decisions. This frees up the supervisors' time for more important activities, such as organizing continuous improvement.

However, if you would prefer to use short work instructions, this too can be accomplished using our original database. Every job will have common elements.

For example, most factory jobs will have safety rules, control charts, process logs, reaction plans, environmental control plans, and the like. These can be separated from the work instruction and posted as job aids at the work site. Exhibit 9-12 shows what one possible arrangement might look like.

Exhibit 9-12: Example of Job Aids in Position With Shorter Work Instruction

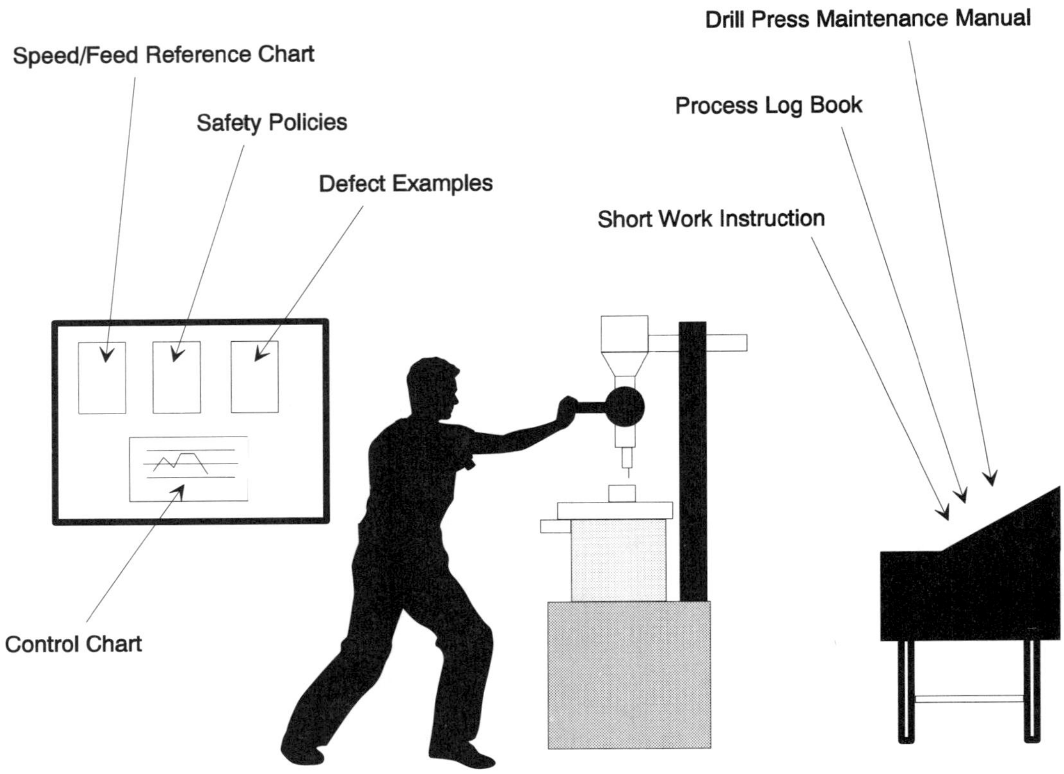

The tasks and steps unique to a particular location would then be summarized into a much shorter work instruction. Exhibit 9-13 shows what such a document might look like based on the longer document just presented.

Exhibit 9-13: Example of Shorter Work Instruction for the Drill Press Operator

Job Title: Drill Press Operator		Date: 1/9/94	Dept.: Drilling	Authorized by:
Tasks (with steps)	**Materials, Tools, Equipment**	**Criteria of Workmanship**	**Safety/Special Conditions**	**Reaction Plan**
1. Obtain materials; match lot I.D. to traveler			For all tasks the following applies:	
2. Preparation - Mount drilling tool - Confirm all paperwork is present on checklist - Set speed and feed	Hex wrench, chock key, pliers, screwdriver, positioning micrometer	Material and drilling tool fit tightly without wiggle Speed and feed should be correct for material	Short hair or hairnet Wear safety glasses at all times Wear gloves when handling material	If proper tightening cannot be achieved, notify supervisor and preventive maintenance
3. Drill Holes - Mount and position block - Drill hole - Check completeness of hole - Reposition and drill	Cutting oil	Position should be within tolerance; holes should be complete; hole size and position should match those on print; position should be within print tolerance	Keep hands clear of moving equipment and tools Use a handcart to move goods	If improper positioning is observed, correct before drilling
4. Inspect - Check flow on air gauge - Segregate nonconforming lots	Airflow gauge, control chart	Airflow should be at least 60 cubic inches per minute		If hole is producing less airflow than required, continue to redrill using progressively larger bits; increase bit size by 0.5mm until desired level of airflow is achieved
5. Completion/Paperwork - Fill out shop floor traveler - Move parts to next area		Accuracy and completeness		
Authorized by:			Revision 3.1	11/19/93 c:\group\form37

The important point to remember is to create a documentation system that is easy to use, appropriate for your industrial situation, and conforms to ISO 9000/14000. There are actually many ways to meet all your documentation needs, including electronic systems. Spend some time and imagination planning your system and estimating the lowest cost solution for your needs. The information gained from job and task analysis will enable you to create documents beyond the work instruction.

HOW TO CREATE A JOB DESCRIPTION, LIST OF SKILLS, COMPETENCY CHECKS, AND TRAINING PROGRAM

Let's begin with a job description. Element 4.18 of ISO 9001, 9002, and 9003 states that you must document the skills, knowledge, and experience for each job that affects quality. Section 4.3.2 of ISO 14001 also states that you must document these same items for any job that can have a significant environmental impact. Our job and task analysis produced just such information. A job description is a good way to organize this information.

According to Element 4.18 and Section 4.3.2, you must document the knowledge, skill, and education mix for each job within your plant. This is the core information reported within a job description, which will also include an outline of job responsibilities, pay range, levels of competency, and other relevant information. Naturally, many people may work under a single job description, so you should not have to create many job descriptions.

The data for completing a job description may be drawn from many sources, but the information generated in our previous job and task analysis will give you much of the data you need. Let's return to the drill press operator example and see how this is possible.

If we wish to write a job description for a drill press operator, we would begin by listing the responsibilities of the job. These can be fleshed out using the information gathered for the job and task analysis. Notice how the following job description flows from our earlier lists of job objectives and responsibilities.

Title: Drill Press Operator (Level I)

Job objective: The drill press operator is responsible for the setup, operation, and routine maintenance of the drill press. In addition, the drill press operator is expected to meet customer and internal requirements for production pieces and to do so in an effective and efficient way.

JOB RESPONSIBILITIES

1.0 Preparation of drill area for production work

2.0 Production of drilled holes

3.0 Inspection of parts for conformance to specifications

4.0 Maintenance of equipment

5.0 Paperwork related to process, including control charts

6.0 Housekeeping

To this we can add a list of skills, knowledge, and education required for the job. Knowledge is a person's awareness of how to perform a task or the way in which something works. Education can serve as a partial or full replacement for some knowledge requirements. A skill is something the person can demonstrate. Therefore, your next step in creating a job description is to incorporate the skills and knowledge required for the job we have already listed.

We should pause a moment to discuss further how skills and knowledge are described. Let's begin by taking a small section of our task list just created and discuss whether a skill or knowledge is required. For each numbered item, determine whether a skill or knowledge is required. We will begin with Task 2.1.1, "Mount and position material." The operator must assure that the right position is achieved to drill the proper hole. This assumes that he has knowledge of how to read a blueprint and the positioning micrometer. So we add the skills and knowledge required for these tasks to our list. Be sure to use index cards, flipcharts, chalkboards, or computer software to note your findings, because many will be duplicated. It will also help you to later organize your results.

The operator has to have the ability to mount a tool into the press. This is a skill—something that can be demonstrated. You will want to include this description along with other manual skills for the job under one statement. For example, on your skills list you may say, "Candidate must have demonstrated ability to work with simple hand tools used with a drill press."

Now look at Task 2.2.1, "Inspect materials." Part of the task will be the ability to use a control chart. So the candidate should have received some sort of training in the use of statistical process control. Continuing this process, you create the two lists illustrated at the bottom of Exhibit 9-11.

Now you have to make a series of decisions to complete this part of the job description. You must decide what levels of education will count as partial or full substitution for each item in the skills and knowledge list. For example, does a high school diploma demonstrate that a person can read and write effectively? Does it mean that they can work with fractions? It should; therefore, you will modify your knowledge and skills items to reflect these alternative ways to qualify for the job. The resulting statements may look like the following:

Candidate must have demonstrated ability to work with simple hand tools used with a drill press. Also must have the ability to correctly set machine feeds and speed. Or must hold a valid and current apprentice level III or journeyman's card.

Thus, being an advanced apprentice student or having completed journeyman training would substitute for the need to demonstrate many of the manual skills. What you are trying to achieve is the shortest possible list that covers all the skills, knowledge, or education needed to qualify for a particular job. It looks like a difficult process with many decisions, but you will find that having detailed tasks lists and a few job experts available will make the process easier.

When you add this mixture of skills, knowledge, and education to any other relevant information, you end up with a full job description.

Title: Drill Press Operator (Level I)

Job objective: The drill press operator is responsible for the setup, operation, and routine maintenance of the drill press. In addition, the drill press operator is expected to meet customer and internal requirements for production pieces and to do so in an effective and efficient way.

JOB RESPONSIBILITIES

1.0 Preparation of drill area for production work

2.0 Production of drilled holes

3.0 Inspection of parts for conformance to specifications

4.0 Maintenance of equipment

5.0 Paperwork related to process, including control charts

6.0 Housekeeping

SKILLS, KNOWLEDGE, AND EDUCATION REQUIRED

1. Candidate must have demonstrated ability to work with simple hand tools used with a drill press. Also must have the ability to correctly read machine feeds and speed. Or must hold a valid and current apprentice level III or journeyman's card.
2. Candidate must have graduated from high school or be able to show competency at reading blueprints, working with fractions, filling in forms, and communicating effectively.
3. Candidate must have at least one year of experience working with micrometers or have completed a training course in Basic Usage of Measurement Equipment (16 hours).
4. Candidate must have a certificate of completion for the plant safety course received within the past two years.
5. Candidate must be able to lift 40 pounds of materials.
6. Candidate requires a certificate of completion for the 16-hour course on statistical process control or be able to demonstrate the ability to correctly use

and understand control charts or must be transferring from a job in which control chart usage was a regular duty.

7. Candidate must attend four hours of training in emergency response procedures for environmental accidents.

As always, your final job description should be examined by someone familiar with the job to assure completeness and accuracy. If you are a quality manager, engineering manager, or otherwise work outside the Human Resources Department, share your description with them. They should be able to spot violations of regulations affecting job descriptions, such as the need to add right-to-know items to your lists.

To conform with Element 4.18 of ISO 9001 and Section 4.3.2 of ISO 14001, one of the operations you must document is that job descriptions are being used to assure the competency of the people assigned jobs related to quality or having possible environmental impacts. Obviously, the drill press operator in our example has some direct responsibilities for assuring the quality of this process. In addition, this drill operator could create negative environmental impacts. Therefore, during an assessment, the auditor could request the job description for a drill press operator and ask for the personnel records for all people holding this job. The needed certificates, competency checks, or other evidence of conformance to job requirements would be matched against the job description. If a person has not conformed to the job requirements, the auditor will look to see if training is being arranged to bring the person into conformance.

You may have noted that competency checks were listed in the job description example. You can use the information we have already created to form the competency checks to confirm that a person has the ability to perform the tasks assigned.

HOW TO DEVELOP COMPETENCY CHECKLISTS

To develop competency checks, you must identify the performance objectives for the job. Let's take item 1 from the list of skills, knowledge, and education requirements just developed.

> *1. Candidate must have demonstrated ability to work with simple hand tools used with a drill press. Also must have the ability to correctly set machine feeds and speed. Or must hold a valid and current apprentice level III or journeyman's card.*

To qualify, the operator must demonstrate his or her ability to work with simple hand tools. Going back to our list of tasks, we can identify these tools: a hex wrench, chock key, pliers, and screwdriver. Also using our tasks list, we can prepare a performance objective—a written description of the tasks to be completed, the conditions under which they are demonstrated, and how to judge the successful completion of the tasks.

For a skill requirement, a checklist could be used as the candidate demonstrates ability to work with the tools and the drill press. Other possibilities include the use of case studies, role-playing, simulations, form filling, and other such methods. Knowledge requirements can be checked using essays, multiple-choice tests, case studies, completion tests, or oral examinations.

Let's see how you might write and then test the performance objective for using small tools.

> *Given a hex wrench, chock key, pliers, and screwdriver, the candidate must mount a tool, mount and position a block of material, dismount the block, and dismount the tool within three minutes. The drilling tool and the block of material must be fully secured and in the correct position when mounted.*

From this statement you would develop a test for a candidate who doesn't have the necessary certificates to be exempt from this requirement. Perhaps a supervisor takes the candidate to the drill press, hands him or her the needed tools and materials, and then asks him or her to perform the listed tasks. While the candidate performs the various test tasks, the supervisor uses a checklist to notify the candidate which task to perform and to note how well the person performed the task. This is then scored, signed, and dated. It is filed with the personnel record for the candidate as evidence of competency to meet this requirement.

For a knowledge-based requirement, such as the ability to read blueprints, you could purchase a standard blueprint-reading test. On this test is a series of blueprint symbols and notes. The candidate answers questions about the symbols presented. For illustration sake, let's say that a person getting more than 74 percent of the questions right would qualify. Again, this evidence would be put in the personnel record.

Assign a specific level of competency for each qualification. These levels should accurately reflect the level of skill or knowledge needed for each job. For example, the demonstrated ability to fill in an environmental emergency report should have, let's say, 95 percent accuracy. Thus, from our initial job and task analysis, we have been able to create work instructions, job descriptions, lists of skills and knowledge, and competency checks.

HOW TRAINING MATERIALS CAN BE QUICKLY DEVELOPED FROM JOB AND TASK ANALYSIS INFORMATION

Now we can use this extensive collection of information for one particular job to create training materials. For the drill press operator, we have identified and sequenced the critical tasks of the job and know the skills and knowledge required. In addition, we have a set of performance objectives that must be met. Taken together, this information provides a training manual for people who want to learn to be a drill press operator.

We can use the information we have gathered to develop an instructional outline. We need only to translate skill and knowledge requirements into a series of instructional modules. For example, the drill press operator must learn the following topics:

1. Basic blueprint reading
2. Small-tool usage
3. Machine feed and speed setting
4. Working with fractions
5. Business communications
6. Statistical process control
7. Safety procedures
8. Basic measurement gauge usage
9. Basic machine maintenance
10. Environmental emergency responses

There are many paths you can take from this point. I recommend that you look at the requirements for groups of jobs—for example, all the factory-related jobs. Look for common training needs across all these jobs. You might discover that the following are required in most factory jobs:

- Statistical Process Control
- Safety procedures
- Basic machine maintenance
- Simple math
- Reading and writing skills
- Environmental policy awareness

This could form a core curriculum for your factory staff. In other words, anyone entering a factory job would be required to take training in these subject areas or demonstrate competency in these areas. For a particular job, such as drill press operator, you may find that you are left with a specific set of training requirements—for example:

- Speed and feed settings
- How to use a measurement gauge
- Working with small tools
- Environmental emergency response methods

This would represent a job-specific set of training topics. From here it is recommended that you investigate the need for this type of training. By checking on the competency and effectiveness of current employees, you may discover that working with small tools does not require a training program. However, you may also discover that some people need training in using a measurement gauge. If this is the case, you have a task list that can be used to develop the learning objectives for such training—for example, each participant will learn:

1. How to correctly read the barrel of a micrometer for measurement purposes and for correctly locating parts for drilling.
2. How to use and read an airflow gauge using actual production pieces.
3. How to confirm the speed and feed rates of a manual drill press.

From such lists would flow the instruction plan for potential or existing drill press operators. For example, you may develop a course where you lightly review the theory of metrology (accuracy versus precision, for example) and then teach gauge reading using a hands-on approach. This might be followed with a test based on the competency checks developed earlier. The same method might be repeated for airflow gauge training and speed/feed instructions.

The main point here is that you are not training in the dark. You are now armed with tasks lists, skills/knowledge requirements, competency checks, and job objectives to develop training material to fit your needs. Your primary need is to assure that the right people with the right abilities are doing their assigned jobs, as per ISO 9000 and ISO 14000 requirements.

Secondary to this is your ability to conform to Element 4.18 of ISO 9001 and Section 4.3.2 of ISO 14001. Because you have lists of training needs for all jobs and a way to check current competency, you can create a training schedule for the next several years. People entering a job for the first time, or being transferred, will now have a list of training courses to attend and skills to demonstrate to be fully qualified. If they are deficient, they attend the courses that will bring them into conformance. At the same time, you will be able to better estimate what training needs you will need to continually assure the abilities of your employees.

WHEN TO USE A FLOWCHART WITH JOB AND TASK ANALYSIS

Flowcharts can be used at any time during job and task analysis to help define the process involved. However, they are particularly important when frequent decisions have to be made during the process. Let's take a specific example and see how to incorporate a flowchart into the documentation. Let's say that there is one special job that is run on the drilling line. This particular part is used in a high-performance jet fighter, and the need for proper airflow through the holes is critical. Therefore, the operator must test while drilling and make several decisions.

The way this works is that the first hole is drilled and tested for airflow. If the flow is less than the required 80 cubic inches per minute, the hole has to be redrilled to a larger size. For the second hole drilled, the operator tests the airflow from both holes. The same is done for the third hole. Thus, the total airflow for any one hole is dependent upon the size of the other holes. If the second and third holes are producing less than the needed airflow, then they must be resized. That means that the operator is literally handcrafting the quality of each part. The flowchart for this process now has several decision points (see Exhibit 9-14).

The flowchart is an excellent tool for showing the decision point and the steps to take in response to each test. If we incorporated this type of flowchart into our work instructions, we would produce clearer communications and an easier-to-use document.

To do this, follow the flowchart for creating the work instructions. When you reach a decision point—such as the first airflow test—you branch off the instructions to the appropriate response. For each step in the flowchart, create a step in the work instructions. The knowledge in the database created from job and task analysis is used to fill in details on conditions, tools required, safety considerations, reaction plans, and the criteria of workmanship (see Exhibit 9-15). Some companies even include the flowchart as an additional column on their work instructions. If you select this option, you must train your personnel in the interpretation and use of flowcharts.

CONCLUSION AND CAUTION

The reason we went through this much analysis for just one job was to make a point: to demonstrate that job and task analysis can help you create work instructions and procedures as well as a flow of documents to help you meet your needs for training, job descriptions, competency checks, management of personnel, and a host of other needs. It is not the only way to accomplish this, but it is one of the more efficient paths to a better quality or environmental management system.

We looked at just one type of job, drill press operator, to see the power and scope of information and documents that can be developed from job and task analysis. These same principles would apply to any job title—from president to receptionist. Therefore, if you desire to go beyond conformance to ISO 9000/14000 and wish to use the information gathered for meeting training requirements to benefit your company in other ways, the procedures we have outlined are recommended. Exhibit 9-16 is a blank job and task analysis form you can use for that purpose.

As a word of caution, keep the analysis up to date. In other words, as processes and jobs change, so too must the database information. It is recommended that the people working in the particular area be active participants in the original creation of your database. Then as the process or job changes, these same people can help update the database information. The result will be an active, useful, and up-to-date system of documentation, with employees feeling very involved with their jobs.

Avoid the urge to create lengthy and detailed documents, however. Work instructions in particular should be kept short and to the point. Whenever possible, job aids, such as defect charts, reference diagrams, and the like should be used to keep the instructions simple to read and easy to use for the operator.

To learn more about job and task analysis, seek the guidance of an expert or enroll in a seminar on this topic. I recommend both if you are going to implement this technology seriously.

I would like to thank Barbara Jordan of Jordan Training and Consulting in Grand Rapids, Michigan, (616) 241-0570, for her guidance and assistance in preparing this material. Ms. Jordan is a recognized leader in the teaching of job and task analysis to individuals, corporations, and professional societies in North America.

Exhibit 9-14: Flowchart for the Special Drilling Process

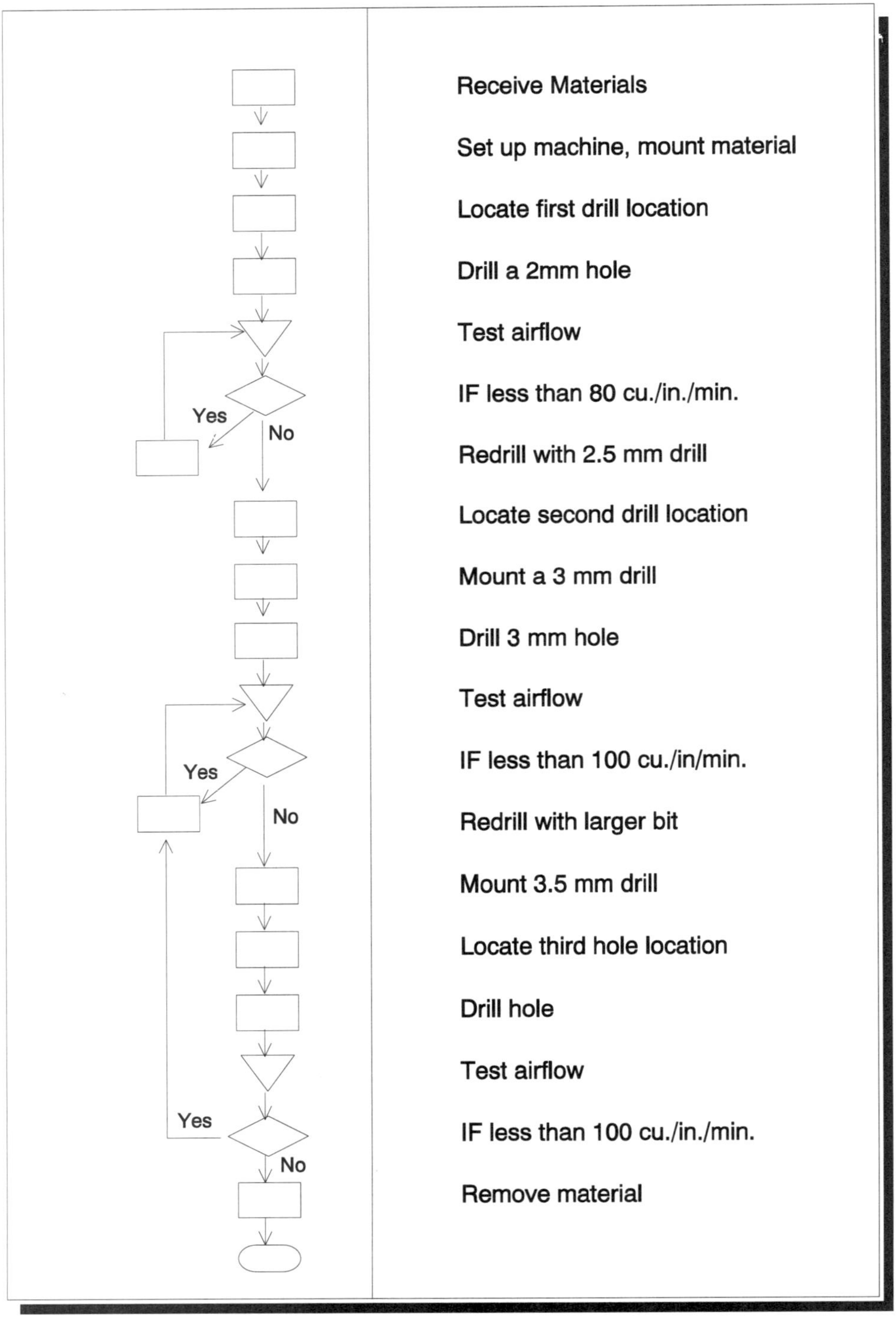

Exhibit 9-15: Job and Task Analysis-Based Work Instruction for Special Drilling Process

Job Title: Drill Press Operator		Date: 1/13/94	Dept.: Drilling	Authorized by:
Tasks (with steps)	**Materials, Tools, Equipment**	**Criteria of Workmanship**	**Safety/Special Conditions**	**Reaction Plan**
1. Receive Materials		Material and drilling tool fit tightly without wiggle	For all tasks the following applies:	If proper tightening cannot be achieved, notify supervisor and preventive maintenance
2. Set up machine, mount materials	Hex wrench, chock key, pliers, screwdriver, positioning micrometer	Position should be within tolerance	Short hair or hairnet	If improper positioning is observed, correct before drilling
3. Locate first hole position			Wear safety glasses at all times	
4. Drill 2mm hole	Cutting oil	Holes should be complete		
5. TEST: airflow If less than 80 cu/in./min. then redrill with 2.5mm drill	Airflow gauge	Speed and feed should be correct for material Hole size and position should match those on print	Wear gloves when handling material Keep hands clear of moving equipment and tools	If hole is producing less airflow than required, continue to redrill using progressively larger bits; increase bit size by 0.5mm until desired level of airflow is achieved
6. Locate second hole and mount 3mm drill bit	Hex wrench, chock key, pliers, screwdriver, positioning micrometer	Position should be within print tolerance		
7. Drill with 3mm drill bit	Cutting oil			
8. TEST: air flow If less than 100 cu./in./min. then redrill with 3.5mm bit				
9. Locate third hole, mount 4mm drill bit	Hex wrench, chock key, pliers, screwdriver, positioning micrometer			
. . . .				
Authorized by:			Revision 4.4 2/16/94 c:\wp\form23.cd	

Exhibit 9-16: Blank Job and Task Analysis Form

Job Title:		Date:	Dept.:	Authorized by:
Tasks (with steps)	**Materials, Tools, Equipment**	**Criteria of Workmanship**	**Safety/Special Conditions**	**Reaction Plan**

Knowledge/Experience Requirements	**Skills Required**

APPENDIX A: LIST OF COUNTRIES AND STANDARDS BODIES PARTICIPATING IN ISO 14000

The following listings are the first reference points for a particular country to get copies of ISO 14000, ISO 9000, and the contact information for registrars, support organizations, and the like. Each listing represents a member body of the International Organization for Standardization.

Albania

Drejtoria e Standardizimit dhe Cilesise Keshilli i Ministrave
Bulevardi Deshmoret e Kombit
Tirana

Telephone: 355 42 2 62 55
Fax: 355 42 2 62 55

Algeria

Institut algearien de normalisation et de propriete industrielle
5, rue Abou Hamou Moussa
B.P. 1021 - Centre de tri
Alger

Telephone: 213 2 63 51 80
Fax: 213 2 61 09 71
Telex: 6 64 09 inapi dz

Argentina

Instituto Argentino de Racionalizacion de Materiales
Chile 1192
1098 Buenos Aires

Telephone: 54 1 383 37 51
Fax: 54 1 383 84 63

Australia

Standards Australia
1 The Crescent
Homebush - N.S.W. 2140
Postal address:
P.O. Box 1055
Strathfield - N.S.W. 2135

Telephone: 61 2 746 47 00
Fax: 61 2 746 84 50
Internet: intsect@saa.sa.telememo.au

Austria

Osterreichisches Normungsinstitut
Heinestrasse 38
Postfach 130
A-1021 Wien

Telephone: 43 1 213 00
Fax: 43 1 21 30 06 50

Bangladesh (BSTI)

Bangladesh Standards and Testing Institution
116-A, Tejgaon Industrial Area
Dhaka 1208

Telephone: 880 2 88 14 62

Belarus (BELST)

Committee for Standardization, Metrology, and Certification
Starovilensky Trakt 93
Minsk 220053

Telephone: 375 172 37 52 13
Fax: 375 172 37 25 88
Telex: 25 21 70 shkala

Belgium (IBN)

Institut belge de normalisation
Av. de la Brabanconne 29
B-1040 Bruxelles

Telephone: 32 2 738 01 11
Fax: 32 2 733 42 64

Brazil

Associacao Brasileira de Normas Teacnicas
Av. 13 de Maio, no 13, 27o andar
Caixa Postal 1680
20003-900 - Rio de Janeiro-RJ

Telephone: 55 21 210 31 22
Fax: 55 21 532 21 43

Bulgaria (BDS)

Committee for Standardization and Metrology at the Council of Ministers
21, 6th September Str.
1000 Sofia

Telephone: 359 2 85 91
Fax: 359 2 80 14 02

Canada (SCC)

Standards Council of Canada
45 O'Connor Street, Suite 1200
Ottawa, Ontario K1P 6N7

Telephone: (613) 238 3222
Fax: (613) 995 4564

Chile (INN)

Instituto Nacional de Normalizacioan
Matias Cousino 64 - 6o piso
Casilla 995 - Correo Central
Santiago

Telephone: 56 2 696 81 44
Fax: 56 2 696 02 47

China (CSBTS)

China State Bureau of Technical Supervision
4, Zhi Chun Road
Haidian District
P.O. Box 8010
Beijing 100088

Telephone: 86 10 203 24 24
Fax: 86 10 203 10 10

Colombia (ICONTEC)

Instituto Colombiano de Normas Tecnicas
Carrera 37 No. 52-95
Edificio ICONTEC
P.O. Box 14237
Santafe de Bogota

Telephone: 57 1 315 03 77
Fax: 57 1 222 14 35

Costa Rica (INTECO)

Instituto de Normas Tecnicas de Costa Rica
Barrio Gonzalez Flores
Ciudad Cientiafica
San Pedro de Montes de Oca
San Jose
Postal address:
P.O. Box 6189-1000
San Jose

Telephone: 506 283 45 22
Fax: 506 283 45 22

Croatia (DZNM)

State Office for Standardization and Metrology
Avenija Vukovar 78
41000 Zagreb

Telephone: 385 41 53 99 34
Fax: 385 41 53 66 88

Cuba (NC)

Oficina Nacional de Normalizacion
Calle E No. 261 entre 11 y 13
Vedado, La Habana 10400

Telephone: 53 7 30 00 22
Fax: 53 7 33 80 48

Cyprus (CYS)

Cyprus Organization for Standards and Control of Quality
Ministry of Commerce, Industry, and Tourism
Nicosia 1421

Telephone: 357 2 30 34 41
Fax: 357 2 36 61 20

Czech Republic (COSMT)

Czech Office for Standards, Metrology, and Testing
Vaclavske namesti 19
113 47 Praha 1

Telephone: 42 2 24 22 47 34
Fax: 42 2 24 22 47 26

Denmark (DS)

Dansk Standard
Baunegaardsvej 73
DK-2900 Hellerup

Telephone: 45 39 77 01 01
Fax: 45 39 77 02 02

Ecuador (INEN)

Instituto Ecuatoriano de Normalizacion
Baquerizo Moreno 454 y
Av. 6 de Diciembre
Casilla 17-01-3999
Quito

Telephone: 593 2 56 56 26
Fax: 593 2 56 78 15
Internet: inen1@inen.gov.ec

Egypt (EOS)

Egyptian Organization for Standardization and Quality Control
2 Latin America Street
Garden City
Cairo

Telephone: 20 2 354 97 20
Fax: 20 2 355 78 41

Ethiopia (ESA)

Ethiopian Authority for Standardization
P.O. Box 2310
Addis Ababa

Telephone: 251 1 61 01 11
Fax: 251 1 65 01 90

Finland (SFS)

Finnish Standards Association SFS
P.O. Box 116
FIN-00241 Helsinki

Telephone: 358 0 149 93 31
Fax: 358 0 146 49 25

France (AFNOR)

Association francaise de normalisation
Tour Europe
F-92049 Paris La Defense Cedex

Telephone: 33 1 42 91 55 55
Fax: 33 1 42 91 56 56

Germany (DIN)

DIN Deutsches Institut fur Normung
Burggrafenstrasse 6
D-10787 Berlin
Postal address:
D-10772 Berlin

Telephone: 49 30 26 01-0
Fax: 49 30 26 01 12 31
Internet: postmaster@din.de

Greece (ELOT)

Hellenic Organization for Standardization
313, Acharnon Street
GR-111 45 Athens

Telephone: 30 1 201 50 25
Fax: 30 1 202 07 76

Hungary (MSZH)

Magyar Szabvanyugyi Hivatal
Ulloi ut 25
Pf. 24.
H-1450 Budapest 9

Telephone: 36 1 218 30 11
Fax: 36 1 218 51 25

Iceland (STRI)

Icelandic Council for Standardization
Keldnaholt
IS-112 Reykjavik

Telephone: 354 587 70 00
Fax: 354 587 74 09
Internet: stri@iti.is

India (BIS)

Bureau of Indian Standards
Manak Bhavan
9 Bahadur Shah Zafar Marg
New Delhi 110002

Telephone: 91 11 331 79 91
Fax: 91 11 331 40 62

Indonesia (DSN)

Dewan Standardisasi Nasional - DSN
(Standardization Council of Indonesia)
c/o Pusat Standardisasi - LIPI
Jalan Jend. Gatot Subroto 10
Jakarta 12710

Telephone: 62 21 522 16 86
Fax: 62 21 520 65 74

Iran, Islamic Republic of (ISIRI)

Institute of Standards and Industrial Research of Iran
P.O. Box 31585-163
Karaj

Telephone: 98 261 22 60 31
Fax: 98 261 22 50 15

Ireland (NSAI)

National Standards Authority of Ireland
Glasnevin
Dublin-9

Telephone: 353 1 837 01 01
Fax: 353 1 836 98 21

Israel (SII)

Standards Institution of Israel
42 Chaim Levanon Street
Tel Aviv 69977

Telephone: 972 3 646 51 54
Fax: 972 3 641 96 83

Italy (UNI)

Ente Nazionale Italiano di Unificazione
Via Battistotti Sassi 11/b
I-20133 Milano

Telephone: 39 2 70 02 41
Fax: 39 2 70 10 61 06

Jamaica (JBS)

Jamaica Bureau of Standards
6 Winchester Road
P.O. Box 113
Kingston 10

Telephone: 1 809 926 31 40-6
Fax: 1 809 929 47 36

Japan (JISC)

Japanese Industrial Standards Committee
c/o Standards Department
Ministry of International Trade and Industry
1-3-1, Kasumigaseki, Chiyoda-ku
Tokyo 100

Telephone: 81 3 35 01 92 95
Fax: 81 3 35 80 14 18

Kazakhstan (KAZMENST)

Committee for Standardization, Metrology, and Certification
pr. Altynsarina 83
480035 Almaty

Telephone: 7 327 2 21 08 08
Fax: 7 327 2 28 68 22

Kenya (KEBS)

Kenya Bureau of Standards
Off Mombasa Road
Behind Belle Vue Cinema
P.O. Box 54974
Nairobi

Telephone: 254 2 50 22 10/19
Fax: 254 2 50 32 93
Internet: kebs@arso.gn.apc.org

Korea, Dem. P. Rep. of (CSK)

Committee for Standardization of the Democratic People's Republic of Korea
Zung Gu Yok Seungli-Street
Pyongyang

Telephone: 85 02 57 15 76

Korea, Republic of (KIAA)

Industrial Advancement Administration (KIAA)
2, Chungang-dong, Kwachon-city
Kyonggi-do 427-010

Telephone: 82 2 503 79 38
Fax: 82 2 503 79 41

Libyan Arab Jamahiriya (LNCSM)

Libyan National Centre for Standardization and Metrology
Industrial Research
Centre Building
P.O. Box 5178
Tripoli

Telephone: 218 21 499 49
Fax: 218 21 69 00 28

Macedonia Yugoslav (ZSM)

Zavod za standardizacija i metrologija (ZSM)
Ministry of Economy
Samoilova 10
91000 Skopje

Telephone: 389 91 22 47 74
Fax: 389 91 23 19 02

Malaysia (SIRIM)

Standards and Industrial Research Institute of Malaysia
Persiaran Dato' Menteri, Section 2
P.O. Box 7035, 40911 Shah Alam
Selangor Darul Ehsan

Telephone: 60 3 559 26 01
Fax: 60 3 550 80 95

Mauritius (MSB)

Mauritius Standards Bureau
Reduit

Telephone: 230 454 19 33
Fax: 230 464 11 44

Mexico (DGN)

Direccion General de Normas
Calle Puente de Tecamachalco No 6
Lomas de Tecamachalco
Seccion Fuentes
Naucalpan de Juarez
53 950 Mexico

Telephone: 52 5 729 93 00
Fax: 52 5 729 94 84

Mongolia (MNISM)

Mongolian National Institute for Standardization and Metrology
Ulaanbaatar-51

Telephone: 976 1 35 83 49
Fax: 976 1 35 80 32

Morocco (SNIMA)

Service de normalisation industrielle marocaine
1, Place Sefrou (Tour Hassan)
Rabat

Telephone: 212 7 76 63 17
Fax: 212 7 76 62 96

Netherlands (NNI)

Nederlands Normalisatie-instituut
Kalfjeslaan 2
P.O. Box 5059
NL-2600 GB Delft

Telephone: 31 15 69 03 90
Fax: 31 15 69 01 90

New Zealand (SNZ)

Standards New Zealand
Standards House
155 The Terrace
Wellington 6001
Postal address:
Private Bag 2439
Wellington 6020

Telephone: 64 4 498 59 90
Fax: 64 4 498 59 94

Nigeria (SON)

Standards Organisation of Nigeria
Federal Secretariat
Phase 1, 9th Floor
Ikoyi
Lagos

Telephone: 234 1 68 26 15
Fax: 234 1 68 18 20

Norway (NSF)

Norges Standardiseringsforbund
Hegdehaugsveien 31
Postboks 7020 Homansbyen
N-0306 Oslo 3

Telephone: 47 22 46 60 94
Fax: 47 22 46 44 57

Pakistan (PSI)

Pakistan Standards Institution
39 Garden Road, Saddar
Karachi-74400

Telephone: 92 21 772 95 27
Fax: 92 21 772 81 24

Panama (COPANIT)

Comision Panamena de Normas Industriales y Tecnicas
Ministerio de Comercio e Industrias
Apartado Postal 9658
Panama, Zona 4

Telephone: 507 2 27 47 49
Fax: 507 2 25 78 53

Philippines (BPS)

Bureau of Product Standards
Department of Trade and Industry
361 Sen. Gil J. Puyat Avenue
Makati
Metro Manila 1200

Telephone: 63 2 890 51 29
Fax: 63 2 890 49 26

Poland (PKN)

Polish Committee for Standardization
ul. Elektoralna 2
P.O. Box 10
00-950 Warszawa

Telephone: 48 2 620 54 34
Fax: 48 2 620 07 41

Portugal (IPQ)

Instituto Portugues da Qualidade
Rua C a Avenida dos Tres Vales
P-2825 Monte da Caparica

Telephone: 351 1 294 81 00
Fax: 351 1 294 81 01

Romania (IRS)

Institutul Roman de Standardizare
Str. Jean-Louis Calderon Nr. 13
Cod 70201
Bucuresti 2

Telephone: 40 1 211 32 96
Fax: 40 1 210 08 33

Russian Federation (GOST R)

Committee of the Russian Federation for Standardization, Metrology, and Certification
Leninsky Prospekt 9
Moskva 117049

Telephone: 7 095 236 40 44
Fax: 7 095 237 60 32

Saudi Arabia (SASO)

Saudi Arabian Standards Organization
Imam Saud Bin Abdul Aziz Bin Mohammed Road (West End)
P.O. Box 3437
Riyadh 11471

Telephone: 966 1 452 00 00
Fax: 966 1 452 00 86

Singapore (SISIR)

Singapore Institute of Standards and Industrial Research
1 Science Park Drive
Singapore 0511

Telephone: 65 778 77 77
Fax: 65 778 00 86

Slovakia (UNMS)

Slovak Office of Standards, Metrology, and Testing
Stefanovicova 3
814 39 Bratislava

Telephone: 42 7 49 10 85
Fax: 42 7 49 10 50

Slovenia (SMIS)

Standards and Metrology Institute
Ministry of Science and Technology
Kotnikova 6
SI-61000 Ljubljana

Telephone: 386 61 131 23 22
Fax: 386 61 31 48 82
Internet: ic@usm.mzt.si

South Africa (SABS)

South African Bureau of Standards
1 Dr Lategan Rd, Groenkloof
Private Bag X191
Pretoria 0001

Telephone: 27 12 428 79 11
Fax: 27 12 344 15 68

Spain (AENOR)

Asociacion Espanola de Normalizacion y Certificacion
Fernandez de la Hoz, 52
E-28010 Madrid

Telephone: 34 1 432 60 00
Fax: 34 1 310 49 76

Sri Lanka (SLSI)

Sri Lanka Standards Institution
53 Dharmapala Mawatha
P.O. Box 17
Colombo 3

Telephone: 94 1 32 60 51
Fax: 94 1 44 60 18

Sweden (SIS)

SIS - Standardiseringen i Sverige
Tegnergatan 11
Box 3295
S-103 66 Stockholm

Telephone: 46 8 613 52 00
Fax: 46 8 411 70 35

Switzerland (SNV)

Swiss Association for Standardization
Muhlebachstrasse 54
CH-8008 Zurich

Telephone: 41 1 254 54 54
Fax: 41 1 254 54 74

Syrian Arab Republic (SASMO)

Syrian Arab Organization for Standardization and Metrology
P.O. Box 11836
Damascus

Telephone: 963 11 445 05 38
Fax: 963 11 441 39 13

Tanzania, United Rep. of (TBS)

Tanzania Bureau of Standards
Ubungo Area
Morogoro Road/Mpakani Road
Dar es Salaam
Postal address:
P.O. Box 9524
Dar es Salaam

Telephone: 255 51 4 32 98
Fax: 255 51 4 32 98

Thailand (TISI)

Thai Industrial Standards Institute
Ministry of Industry
Rama VI Street
Bangkok 10400

Telephone: 66 2 245 78 02
Fax: 66 2 247 87 41

Trinidad and Tobago (TTBS)

Trinidad and Tobago Bureau of Standards
#2 Century Drive
Trincity Industrial Estate
Tunapuna
Postal address:
P.O. Box 467
Port of Spain

Telephone: 1 809 662 88 27
Fax: 1 809 663 43 35

Tunisia (INNORPI)

Institut national de la normalisation et de la propriete industrielle
B.P. 23
1012 Tunis-Belvedere

Telephone: 216 1 78 59 22
Fax: 216 1 78 15 63

Turkey (TSE)

Turk Standardlari Enstitusu
Necatibey Cad. 112
Bakanliklar
06100 Ankara

Telephone: 90 312 417 83 30
Fax: 90 312 425 43 99
Internet: tse-d@servis.met.tr

Ukraine (DSTU)

State Committee of Ukraine for Standardization, Metrology, and Certification
174, Gorky Street
GSP
252650 Kiev-6

Telephone: 7 044 226 29 71
Fax: 7 044 226 29 70

United Kingdom (BSI)

British Standards Institution
389 Chiswick High Road
GB-London W4 4AL

Telephone: 44 181 996 90 00
Fax: 44 181 996 74 00

United States (ANSI)

American National Standards Institute
11 West 42nd Street
13th floor
New York, NY 10036

Telephone: 1 212 642 4900
Fax: 1 212 398 0023

Uruguay (UNIT)

Instituto Uruguayo de Normas Tecnicas
San Jose 1031 P.7
Galeria Elysee
Montevideo

Telephone: 598 2 91 20 48
Fax: 598 2 92 16 81

Uzbekistan (UZGOST)

Uzbek State Centre for Standardization, Metrology, and Certification
Ulitsa Farobi, 333-A
700049 Tachkent

Telephone: 7 371 2 46 17 10
Fax: 7 371 2 46 17 11

Venezuela (COVENIN)

Comision Venezolana de Normas Industriales
Avda. Andres Bello-Edf. Torre Fondo
Comun
Piso 12
Caracas 1050

Telephone: 58 2 575 22 98
Fax: 58 2 574 13 12

Viet Nam (TCVN)

Directorate for Standards and Quality
70, Tran Hung Dao Street
Hanoi

Telephone: 84 4 26 62 20
Fax: 84 4 26 74 18

Yugoslavia (SZS)

Savezni zavod za standardizaciju
Kneza Milosa 20
Post Pregr. 933
YU-11000 Beograd

Telephone: 381 11 64 35 57
Fax: 381 11 68 23 82

Zimbabwe (SAZ)

Standards Association of Zimbabwe
P.O. Box 2259
Harare

Telephone: 263 4 88 34 46
Fax: 263 4 88 20 20

APPENDIX B: LIST OF PROPOSED STANDARDS IN THE ISO 14000 FAMILY

ISO 14001—Environmental Management Systems—Specification With Guidance for Use

ISO 14004—Environmental Management Systems—General Guidelines on Principles, Systems, and Supporting Techniques

ISO 14010—Guidelines for Environmental Auditing—General Principles on Environmental Auditing

ISO 14011/1—Guidelines for Environmental Auditing—Audit Procedures—Auditing of Environmental Management Systems

ISO 14011/2—Guidelines for Environmental Auditing—Compliance Audits

ISO 14011/3—Guidelines for Environmental Auditing—Statement Audits

ISO 14012—Guidelines for Environmental Auditing—Qualification Criteria for Environmental Auditors

ISO 14013—Management of Environmental Audit Programs

ISO 14014—Initial Reviews

ISO 14015—Environmental Site Assessments

ISO 14020—Goals and Principles of All Environmental Labeling

ISO 14021—Environmental Labeling—Self-Declaration Environmental Claims—Terms and Definitions

ISO 14022—Environmental Labeling—Symbols

ISO 14023—Environmental Labeling—Testing and Verification Methodologies

ISO 14024—Environmental Labeling—Guiding Principles, Practices, and Criteria for Multiple Criteria-Based Practitioner Programs (Type I)

ISO 1402X—Type III Labeling

ISO 14031—Evaluation of Environmental Performance—General Methodology

ISO 14032—Evaluation of Environmental Performance—Industry-Specific Indicators

ISO 14040—Life Cycle Assessment—Principles and Guidelines

ISO 14041—Life Cycle Assessment—Life Cycle Inventory Analysis

ISO 14042—Life Cycle Assessment—Impact Assessment

ISO 14043—Life Cycle Assessment—Interpretation

ISO 14050—Terms and Definitions

ISO Guide 64—Guide for the Inclusion of Environmental Aspects in Product Specifications

APPENDIX C: SOURCES OF FURTHER INFORMATION

The major organizations: Use these contacts only when you need information from a key organization (e.g., applying to become a registered auditor) or when you need to know the status of a registrar.

International Organization for Standardization (ISO)
Case Postale 56, CH-1211
Geneve 20, Switzerland
Phone: 41 22 749 0111
Fax: 41 22 733 3430

United Kingdom Accreditation Service (formally the NACCB)
Audley House
13 Palace Street
London SW1E 5HS
Phone: 0171 233 7111
Fax: 0171 233 5115

RvA (Raad voor Accreditatie)
Radboudkwartier 223
Postbus 2768
3500 GT Utrecht
Netherlands
Phone: 31 30 239 4500
Fax: 31 30 239 4539

Standards Council of Canada (SCC)
45 O'Connor Street, Suite 1200
Ottawa, Ontario K1P 6N7
Canada
Phone: 1 (613) 238 3222
Fax: 1 (613) 995 4564

Registrar Accreditation Board (RAB)
611 East Wisconsin Avenue
P.O. Box 3005
Milwaukee, WI 53201-3005
USA
Phone: 1 (800) 248-1946—U.S. only
Phone: 1 (414) 272-8575
Fax: 1 (414) 765-8661

European Commission
Rue de la Loi 200
B-1049 Brussels
Belgium
Phone: 32 2 299 03 24
Fax: 32 2 295 56 84
Contact Mr. Mark Moys (DG XI-C-6) for information on the Eco-Labeling scheme in Europe and a list of competent bodies.

To obtain a copy of the ISO 14000 standards, contact your national standards body. Copies of the Standard can be obtained in the United States from the following:

American National Standards Institute (ANSI)
11 West 42nd Street, 13th Floor
New York, NY 10036
USA
Phone: 1 (212) 642-4900
Fax: 1 (212) 302-1286

ASTM Customer Service
100 Barr Harbor Drive
West Conshohocken, PA 19428
USA
Phone: 1 (610) 832-9500
Fax: 1 (610) 832-9666

Environmental Information Organizations

There are many organizations that can provide information and support on environmental matters. You should contact these organizations for their information packages and decide which can benefit you best.

U.S. Environmental Protection Agency
401 M Street SW
Washington, D.C. 20460
USA
Phone: 1 (202) 260-5636
Fax: 1 (202) 260-3923

National Center for Environmental Publications and Information
P.O. Box 42419
Cincinnati, OH 45242-2419
USA
Fax: 1 (513) 891-6685

Emergency Planning and Community Right-to-Know-Act
401 M Street SW (5101)
Washington, D.C. 20460
USA
Phone: 1 (800) 525-0202
Fax: 1 (202) 775-6680

Environmental Auditing Roundtable
Attn: Jean McCreary
3925 Embassy Parkway
Akron, OH 44313
USA
Phone: 1 (216) 374-3951
Fax: 1 (216) 374-2471

Environmental Auditors' Registration Association
Gregory Croft House
Fen Road East Kirby
Lincolnshire, PE23 4DB
United Kingdom
Phone: 441 790 763613
Fax: 411 790 763360

Enviro-Health (clearinghouse of the National Institute of Environmental Health Sciences)
100 Capitola Drive
Suite 108
Durham, NC 27713
USA
Phone: 1 (800) NIEHS-94
Fax: 1 (919) 361-9408

Environmental Law Institute
1616 P Street NW
Suite 200
Washington, D.C. 20036
USA
Phone: 1 (202) 328-5150
Fax: 1 (202) 328-5002

National Safety Council
P.O. Box 558
Itasca, IL 60143-0558
USA
Phone: 1 (800) 621-7619
Fax: 1 (708) 285-0797

Canadian Environmental Law Association
517 College Street
Room 401
Toronto, Ontario M6G 4A2
Canada
Phone: 1 (416) 960-2284
Fax: 1 (416) 960-9392

Environmental Legal Assistance Center
Apartado Postal 2741
Calle 2a Oeste 2-46
Cali, Colombia
Phone: 23 821723
Fax: 23 830797

International Council of Environmental Law
Adenauerallee 214
53113 Bonn, Germany
Phone: 228 269 2240

Japan Center for Human Environmental Problems
c/o Prof. Yoshihiro Nomura
Faculty of Law
Tokyo Metropolitan University
1-1 Minamiosawa
Hachioji
Tokyo 192-03, Japan

Pan American Center for Human Ecology and Health
Apartado Postal 37-473
06696 Mexico City, DF
Mexico

Publications

Various publications are available on environmental management. Those that deal specifically with ISO 14000 include:

International Environmental Systems Update
CEEM
10521 Braddock Road
Fairfax, VA 22032-2236
USA
Phone: 1 (800) 745-5565 or 1 (703) 250-5900
Fax: 1 (703) 250-5313

Continuous Improvements
National ISO 9000/14000 Support Group
9864 Cherry Valley
Suite C
Caledonia, MI 49316
USA
Voice/Fax 1 (616) 891-9114

A "must have" publication in the United States is:

EPA National Publication Catalog
Office of Administration and Resources Management
EPA200-B-94-001
This can be ordered from the EPA or any of its regional offices at no charge.

Environmental Publications

Journal of Environmental Engineering
(American Society of Civil Engineers)
United Engineering Center
345 East 47th Street
New York, NY 10017-2398
USA
Phone: 1 (212) 705-7496
Fax: 1 (212) 980-4681

Environment Today
1483 Chain Bridge Road
Suite 202
McLean, VA 22101-4599
USA
Phone: 1 (703) 448-0322

Noise Control Journal
P.O. Box 3206
Arlington Branch
Poughkeepsie, NY 12603
USA

Environmental Protection
P.O. Box 2573
Waco, TX 76702-9910
USA
Phone: 1 (817) 662-7037 or 1 (800) 207-3535

Total Quality and Environmental Management
Executive Enterprises Publication Company
22 West 21st Street
10th Floor
New York, NY 10010-6990
USA
Phone: 1 (212) 645-7880 ext. 208 or 1 (800) 332-8804

Chemical Health and Safety
American Chemical Society
1155 Sixteenth Street NW
Washington, D.C. 20077-5768
USA
Phone: 1 (800) 333-9511

Internet Resources

The Internet is a worldwide network of computer networks. The number and nature of resources on any topic change very rapidly. However, you should begin with the sources listed below to gain more information on ISO 14000 and to learn of new resources. Also, try the search engines on the World Wide Web to find new sources of information on environmental management.

Mailing Lists

Send an e-mail message to:

Listserv@vm1.nodak.edu

with the message SUBSCRIBE QUEST [your first name] [your last name]

Send a second message:

SUBSCRIBE ISO14000 [your first name] [your last name]

You can also subscribe to ISO 9000 to get on a mailing list discussing ISO 9000-related topics.

Also try the environmental engineering mail list at:

listserv@vm.temple.edu

World Wide Web Pages

National ISO 9000/14000 Support Group
http://www.cris.com/~isogroup

American National Standards Institute
http://www.ansi.org

American Society for Quality Control
http://www.asqc.org

Australian Environmental Resources Network
http://kaos.erin.gov.au/erin.html

Canadian Forest Service
http://www.nofc.forestry.ca/

EcoNet
http://www.igc.apc.org/igc/en.html

EnviroLink Network
http://envirolink.org/

Environmental Protection Agency (U.S.)
http://www.epa.gov

Environmental Resource Center
http://ftp.clearlake.ibm.com/ERC/HomePage.html

Global Recycling Network
http://client.fi/grn/

Green Manufacturing
http://euler.berkley.edu/green/cgdm.html

OSHA
http://www.osha-slc.gov

South African Environmental Information Gateway
http://www.iaccess.za/ecoserv/index.html

Technical Information Services (U.S. Dept. of Energy)
http://Dewey.tis.inel.gov

Telnet Resources

Air Pollution BBS
tnnbbs.rtpnc.epa.gov

Environmental Protection Agency
epaibm.rtpnc.epa.gov

Gopher Sites

Environmental Protection Agency
gopher.epa.gov

Chemical Substance Factsheets
ecosys.drdr.virginia.edu

Other Database Resources

Try contacting the following to get even more information on environmental management. These databases are all available through the DIALOG information service, 1 (800) 334-2564 in the USA, 1 (415) 254-7000 everywhere else. You can also Fax them at 1 (415) 254-7070.

CHEMTOX Online
Water Resources Abstracts
Registry of Toxic Effects of Chemical Substances
Energyline
Environmental Bibliography
Enviroline
Pollution Abstracts

Services that monitor regulations and other environmental information are invaluable within an ISO 14000 system. The following are examples of such services:

Counterpoint Publishing
84 Sherman Street
P.O. Box 928
Cambridge, MA 02140
USA
Phone: 1 (617) 547-4515
Fax: 1 (617) 547-9064

CPI Electronic Publishing
7505 East Main Street
Suite 400
Scottsdale, AZ 85251
USA
Phone: 1 (602) 994-4560
Fax: 1 (602) 994-4456

RegScan
1 Executive Plaza
Suite 300
330 Pine Street
Williamsport, PA 17701
Phone: 1 (717) 323-1010 or 1 (800) 747-0916
Fax: 1 (717) 323-8082

Stevens Publishing Corp.
3630 J. H. Kultgen Freeway
P.O. Box 2573
Waco, TX 76702-2573
USA
Phone: 1 (800) 727-7573

IHS Logistic Library
15 Inverness Way East
Inglewood, CO 80112
USA
Phone: 1 (800) 320-5660 or 1 (519) 659-1400
Fax: 1 (303) 486-1710 or 1 (519) 659-1426

Achieve Technology, Inc.
P.O. Box 668
Amherst, NH 03031-0668
USA
Phone: 1 (800) 446-3427
Fax: 1 (603) 595-0088

The Chemical Manufacturers Association in the United States has a database of material safety data sheets for thousands of chemicals. This can be accessed for a fee to rapidly obtain safety information for any chemical or compound you may be using at your company. For further information contact the CMA and ask about MSDS Central.

Chemical Manufacturers Association
2501 M Street NW
Washington, D.C. 20037
USA
Phone: 1 (800) 388-6737 or 1 (202) 887-1100
Fax: 1 (202) 887-1237

APPENDIX D: EXAMPLE OF DOCUMENTATION USED FOR ISO 14000 COMPLIANCE

The following examples show all three levels of documentation created for a fictitious company. These should be used for reference and illustration only. Your own company must design a system of documentation that accounts for your unique operations and processes.

The following also includes pages from an Environmental Policy Manual and the Standard Operating Procedures Manual.

Exhibit D1-1: Structure of the Environmental Management Policy Manual (Level I)

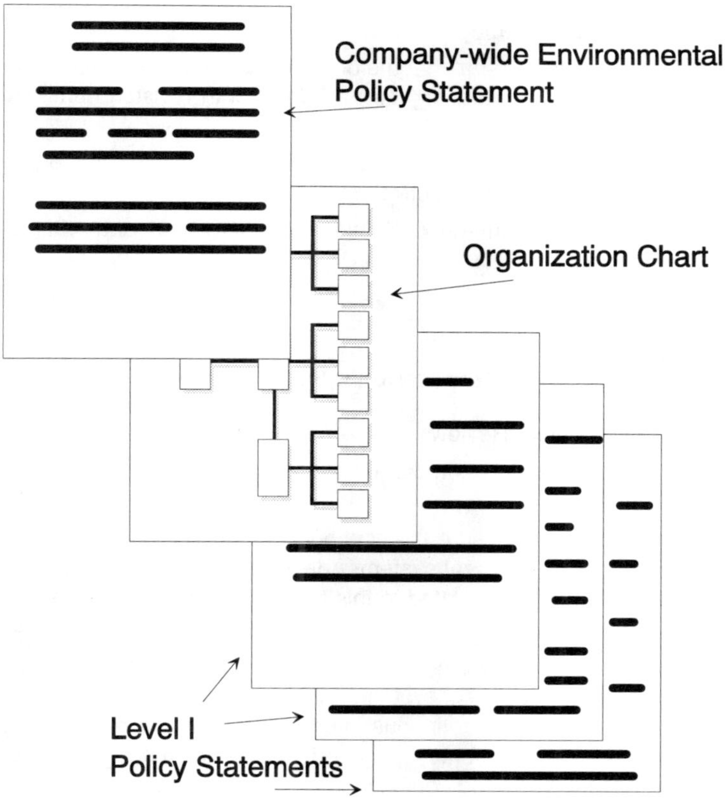

Example of Policy Statement and Procedure for Document Control

XYZ Corporation's Policy Statements:

Section 4.3.5—Document Control

4.3.5.1 All new or revised documents shall be approved by a central authority. This central authority will then track the status, revision number, and location of all documentation.

4.3.5.2 The central authority for each type of document is as follows:

QA Manual and documents related to testing and inspection—QA Manager

Engineering drawings, customer specifications, environmental control plans, and similar documents—Engineering Manager

Purchase orders, customer contact forms, and similar documents—Purchasing Manager

Sales-related documents, environmental marketing items—Sales Manager

Other documents—Office Manager

4.3.5.3 Each authority will assure that the documents under his or her responsibility are up to date, available where needed, signed and dated with revision numbers, and reissued when appropriate.

4.3.5.4 A master list of document locations and revisions will be created, maintained, and audited at least once a year for effectiveness.

This policy meets the requirements of Section 4.5 of ISO 9001 and 4.3.5 of ISO 14001

Rev. # 1.2 Date: July 19, 1995 Authority: BC Page 1 of 1

XYZ Corporation's Policy Statements:

Element 4.5—Management Review

4.5.1 The management of this corporation shall review the entire environmental management system annually.

4.5.2 The annual audit will assure the continuing suitability, adequacy, and effectiveness of the environmental management system. Adequate information will be gathered to make such assurances. All activities related to this evaluation will be documented.

4.5.3 Management will, as part of the review process, look for changes in circumstances or the external markets. Management shall also examine the results of the annual review of the environmental management system. This information will be compared to the objectives related to the policy for continuous improvement. Where necessary policies, objectives, targets, and other elements of the environmental management system may be changed to meet these changing conditions.

This policy meets the requirements of Section 4.5 of ISO 14001

Rev. # 1.2 Date: July 19, 1995 Authority: BC Page 1 of 1

Exhibit D1-2: Structure of the Procedures Manual (Level II)

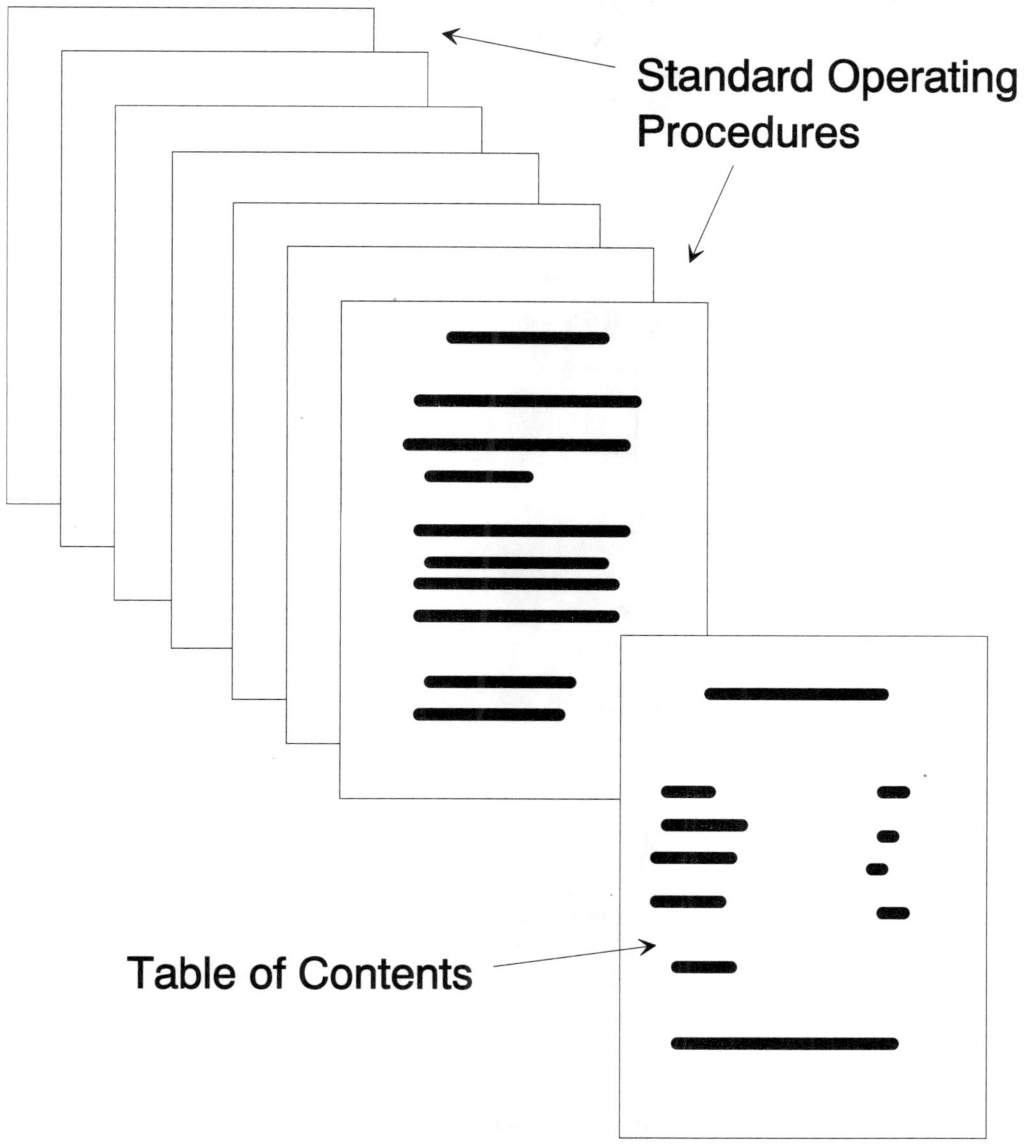

Example of a Corrective Action Procedure

ISO 9000/14000 Procedure
Corrective Action

Approved:

Title Name Date

Revision	Date	Responsible Person	Description of Change
A	7/14/95	R. Barrett	Initial Release

Change Record
Distribution List

- Quality Assurance
- Production
- Engineering
- Purchasing
- Warehouse
- Shipping
- Management Team

1.0 Purpose

- To establish and specify systematic steps for corrective action in the resolution of quality, health, safety, and environmental problems.
- To analyze and resolve these problems.
- To create a permanent solution that prevents recurrence of nonconformance or potential nonconformance.

2.0 Scope

This procedure applies to internal or external customers related to quality, reliability, safety, environmental impact, or performance of any product offered by XYZ Corporation.

Any written or oral expression of dissatisfaction by either internal or external customers related to the identity, quality, reliability, safety, environmental impact, or performance of any product or service offered by XYZ Corporation is subject to investigation for root cause and irreversible corrective action.

3.0 Responsibilities

Department management reviews problems for resolution.

Management implements permanent changes through the use of crossfunctional teams or local problem-solving teams.

4.0 Procedure

4.1 Request for Corrective Action

Corrective actions are required for supplier nonconformance, parts that cannot be reworked, quality audit findings, environmental audit findings, safety hazard reports, worker health reports, and other related information.

For product corrective actions, the Quality Manager initiates a corrective action request by completing the Corrective Action Request form. Quality Manager reviews the Corrective Action Request. Quality Manager assigns an employee to resolve the nonconformance within 30 days.

For supplier corrective actions, the Purchasing Manager initiates a Corrective Action Request. Quality Manager reviews the Corrective Action Request. Quality Manager assigns an employee to resolve the nonconformance within 10 days.

For corrective actions resulting from quality audit findings, Quality Manager initiates a Corrective Action Request by completing the Corrective Action Request form. Top management reviews the Corrective Action Request. Quality Manager assigns a team to resolve the nonconformance within 30 days.

For corrective actions related to health, safety, or the environment, the Corrective Action Request can be filled out by any employee or auditor. The Engineering Manager reviews the request and assigns appropriate people and resources. The nonconformance has to be corrected within 30 days.

4.2 Execute System

Quality Manager or the Engineering Manager analyzes reported items to eliminate potential causes of nonconformance.

Quality Manager can offer solutions to a corrective action by completing the Corrective Action Request; the same is true for the Engineering Manager.

If an extension is needed, a Corrective Action Request is submitted to the originator of the corrective action, stating the amount of additional time needed and the reason for the extension. The request is filed with the Quality Manager or Engineering Manager, as appropriate.

The Quality Manager or Engineering Manager reviews the resolution and indicates acceptance on the Corrective Action Request. If not acceptable, the appropriate manager may review and reassign the investigation. If the problem is not resolved, it is brought to the top management team. Upon approval, the appropriate manager ensures that the corrective action instructions are passed to appropriate personnel for implementation.

The Quality or Engineering Manager indicates the corrective action closure on the corrective action log.

4.3 Investigate Root Cause

To determine the root cause, Quality or Engineering Manager does the following:

- Implements remedial actions to minimize the problem
- Reexamines affected products produced since the believed beginning of the problem
- Investigates for the root cause of the problem, documenting all sources of the problem detected during the investigation
- When the root cause is found, corrects the problem
- Implements preventive actions or changes the system to prevent recurrence

Quality Manager or Engineering Manager completes a report of the investigation and recommends solutions to prevent recurrence on the corrective action review report. Each manager is responsible for ensuring that the Corrective Action Instructions are implemented.

4.4 Corrective Action Meetings

At the monthly management meetings, corrective actions are reviewed. The following are reviewed:

- Corrective Action Reports
- Internal audit results
- Customer complaints
- Environmental citations or communications

Vice President of Operations maintains records of the monthly management meeting. The meeting minutes are stored in the fireproof file in the administration offices for at least three years.

4.5 Initiate Preventive Actions

Solutions to corrective actions are maintained in the corrective action log.

If a change to a process or document is required, a Corrective Action Request is used to initiate the change.

Quality Manager handles disputes between the company and the vendor. Problematic vendors are removed from the approved vendor list.

Environmental improvements to the operations of the company are suggested to the Engineering Manager for his approval. Such approved changes are then forwarded to top management for final approval. The Engineering Manager oversees the implementation of such changes.

4.6 Verification of Effectiveness

Test data from the affected site are used to verify the effectiveness of the corrective action.

Statistical analysis is performed to determine the effectiveness of the corrective action using any of the approved statistical methods listed in QA procedure 23.

Each month, management examines the corrective action log to determine any trends in defects. If any trends exist, appropriate corrective actions are taken.

4.7 Related Documentation to Outside Agencies

A corrective action involving accidental discharge into the water or air requires the specific department manager to fill out an accidental discharge report to be submitted to management, our legal department, and the Michigan Department of Environmental Quality.

An accidental spill of a known hazardous material requires the filing of a spill notification report. Also, the manager of the appropriate department must immediately notify the local fire chief and apprise him or her of the seriousness of the situation. If necessary, during a serious spill, the fire chief will deploy special chemical cleanup personnel and take charge of the site.

Discovery of a safety-related problem will be recorded on the Corrective Action Report and also on an internal Safety Incident Report. Both reports will be forwarded to your department manager. If possible, immediate corrective action should be deployed.

Related Procedures and Work Instructions

SOP 13—Preventive Actions

SOP 11—Handling and Disposition of Nonconforming Goods

WI-Eng 04—How to Fill Out a Corrective Action Report

WI-Eng 05—How to Report the Spill of Hazardous Materials

WI-Eng 09—How to Report Accidental Discharges Into the Air or Water

WI-QA 223—Testing for the Presence of a Hazardous Chemical

WI-QA 204—Reaction Plan (General) for Nonconformances

WI-QA 209—Creating Minutes for a Corrective Action Report Review

WI-QA 211—Placing Material in Process on Hold

Standard Operating Procedures for XYZ Corporation

15.6 Quality Assurance Document Control

15.6.1 Authority and Responsibilities

The Quality Assurance Manager will be defined as the central authority for the control of quality assurance documents. The Engineering Manager will be responsible for environmental management system-related documents. This will include:

- twice-a-year audit of the effectiveness of the control system
- maintenance of a master list of documents
- approval of new or revised documents

15.6.2 Document Tracking

All documents created or revised by the corporation's personnel shall have as minimum identification a title, date of creation, date of revision, signature of the appropriate manager, page number, and file name. These characteristics will be on every page. The document must be neatly formatted and legible. Documents will be produced using the word-processing system. Handwritten or typewritten documents are not allowed.

15.6.3 Initiating a Document

To initiate a document, an individual must submit a Document Approval Form (DAF) to the QA or Engineering Manager. Attached to this form should be the proposed document. The QA or Engineering Manager will then check the proposed document to assure that it is in the proper format, does not duplicate existing documents, and that a list of people who should receive copies is completed. Approval shall be indicated by the manager's signature and appropriate distribution of the document. Once approved, the document is stored in the database of the corporation's Local Area Network (LAN). The distribution list is noted in the document description section of the software. The LAN Administrative Assistant is then charged with printing enough copies of the document for all destinations listed on the circulation sheet.

15.6.4 Changing an Existing Document

To change an existing document, a Change Request Form (CRF) is attached to a copy of the document in question. The CRF should specify what is being changed and why. This is then processed by the QA or Engineering Manager for approval. When distributed, a memo shall be attached explaining why the change was necessary. Following this, obsolete versions of the documents will be removed from the system.

15.6.5 Removal of Obsolete Documents

After no more than six revisions of a document, a new document should be issued under a new version number. If a document becomes obsolete or if time-sensitive documents expire, then the QA or Engineering Manager should be notified. The distribution list for the document is used to confirm the retrieval of the documents involved. A notification of successful retrieval is sent to the QA or Engineering Manager.

If a document cannot be retrieved, then the party to whom the document was assigned is responsible for accounting for its location or confirmation of its destruction. A Document Incident Report (DIR) is filed by the QA or Engineering Manager, describing the circumstances surrounding the inability to retrieve a document. Unauthorized copies of documents are also reported using this form.

Obsolete documents that are retained for legal or reference purposes will be clearly marked in red ink as "Obsolete—Do Not Use or Copy." These shall be kept in the Engineering file cabinet under lock and only distributed by signing out the document from the Engineering secretary.

Exhibit D1-3: Relationship Between Procedure and Work Instructions (Level III)

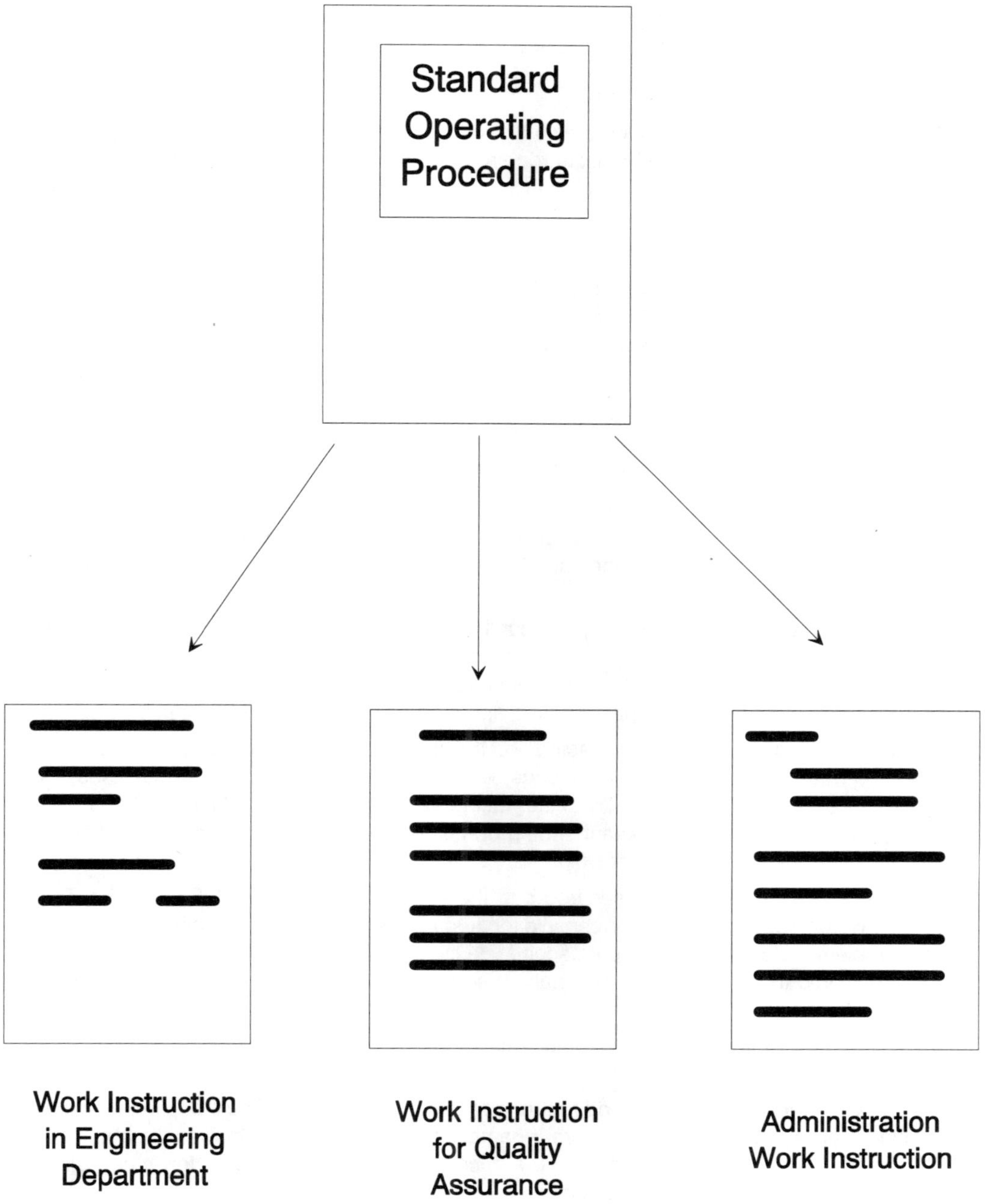

Example Work Instruction

Work Instruction for Water Discharge Sampling
Date 10/24/95

1.0 Task to Be Completed

As part of our stormwater pollution prevention plan a sample of plant water discharge must be taken twice a day. The water discharge sampling will look for total organic carbon present in the waste water. The amount found is reported to management and to the state EPA office.

2.0 Scope of Application

Water discharge sampling is to be restricted to the main discharge pipe accessible through service tunnel 4. Sampling is to occur once the daily discharge begins and once about an hour before the end of daily production.

3.0 Equipment to Be Used

Safety equipment to wear includes eye protection, rubber gloves, and adequate portable lighting. A sampling bucket is located in the facility maintenance office. Analysis is conducted using the TOC analyzer located in the same office.

4.0 Steps to Completing the Task

4.1 The maintenance supervisor will appoint each day the person to obtain the stormwater sample. That person will secure the sample bucket and needed safety equipment from the facility maintenance office.

4.2 The stormwater pipe is accessible about 100 feet down service tunnel 4. The tunnel is opened by unbolting the two security latches located on the left side of the entrance door. Once inside the tunnel the safety equipment should be worn and the portable light source activated. The access spigit is painted blue and marked "Stormwater sampling."

4.3 The sample bucket should be readied and the spigit turned to the left to open up a water flow. The water should flow for ten seconds before a sample is taken. The sample is taken by filling the bucket up to the red line. After taking the sample the bucket lid should be shut and the spigit turned off. A moment should be taken to assure that all stormwater flow is cut off from the spigit.

4.4 The tunnel door should be secured and the sample taken to the TOC analyzer. The sample water is transferred to a clean vile located on the right side of the analyzer. A control sample should be poured into a second vile clearly labeled for this purpose. Both viles are placed into the machine and the analysis sequence 1 is choosen. Results will be printed out automatically.

4.5 The control sample should have less than 10 parts per million of TOC. If not, then notify the facility manager immediately.

4.6 The viles should be cleaned and returned to their proper places. The sampling log book should be filled in with today's date, your name, time of sample, and the results obtained. The printed reports are placed into the facility manager's in-basket for processing. Equipment is returned to its proper place.

5.0 Criteria of Workmanship

A successful sampling will result in a control reading of less than 10 parts per million and no warning about an insufficient sample.

6.0 Safety Precautions (and Potential Environmental Effects)

Employees should avoid all contact with the stormwater. When working inside of the tunnel, caution should be taken to assure adequate lighting to avoid accidents. A second person should be notified that you are entering the tunnel. If you fail to emerge ten minutes after entering, a safety alert should be sounded. If the sampling spigot is not fully turned off potentially harmful waste water could bypass the discharge point.

7.0 Source of Further Information

Contact the environmental resource person to answer any questions you may have on this set of instructions.

APPENDIX E: REPRINT OF AN ENVIRONMENTAL AUDIT

Reprinted by permission of the *Detroit Free Press.* The following is a sample of the actual environmental audit report conducted on the operations of the *Detroit Free Press.* Please note the use of specific regulations and targets that can be converted into the environmental targets and objectives of the environmental management system. Also note that some of the regulations cited in the report are now changed or discontinued. This information is provided for illustrative purposes only.

BACKGROUND

The *Detroit Free Press* is a morning newspaper published daily with a weekday circulation of approximately 598,000. The *Detroit News* is an evening newspaper published daily with a weekday circulation of approximately 446,000. The *Detroit News* and *Detroit Free Press* publish a combined newspaper on Saturday and Sunday with a circulation of approximately 1,202,000. The *Detroit Free Press* and *Detroit News* have a Joint Operating Agreement to publish newspapers under the general management of the *Detroit Newspaper Agency.*

OBJECTIVES

The objective of the study was to conduct an environmental, safety, and health compliance audit of *Detroit Free Press*'s environmental, safety, and health programs. Federal, Michigan State, and local regulations were reviewed. Problems identified in this survey should be corrected in a timely fashion to avoid additional problems with federal, state, and local regulatory agencies.

The following programs were reviewed and evaluated during the study:

- Occupational Noise
- Hazard Communication
- Safety
- Air Pollution Control
- Waste Management
- Waste Water
- Emergency Response and Community Right to Know (SARA Title 111)
- Government Liaison
- Control of Hazardous Energy (Lockout/Blockout)
- Fleet Safety and Powered Industrial Trucks
- Underground Storage Tanks
- Stormwater Discharge

- Ergonomics
- Bloodborne Pathogens
- Recycling

METHODS

Prior to the study, management of *Detroit Free Press* was provided with a list of programs and records that NAA would review during the environmental audit. The environmental audit was conducted by reviewing and discussing these programs and records with the newspapers' management. Problem areas were identified during the discussions. Following the discussions, walk-through plant inspections were conducted and additional problem areas were identified. After the discussions and inspections were completed, debriefings were held to review the major problem areas encountered during the audit.

RESULTS AND RECOMMENDATIONS

The results and discussion of the environmental audit conducted for the *Detroit Free Press* on May 10–12, 1993, are presented by program. The following is an explanation of the language used in the "Recommendations" sections of this report:

- "Must" or "required": Refers to legal requirements of a local, state, or federal regulation.
- "Should": Used when there is an overriding reason, in the professional opinion of the industrial hygienist, to implement a particular recommendation.
- "Recommended": Refers to a good engineering practice that will enhance a particular environmental or health and safety program.

Occupational Noise

Regulations

The Michigan Hearing Conservation Regulations are the same as the Federal Regulations.

The major components of the OSHA Occupational Noise Standard [29 CFR (Code of Federal Regulations) 1910.951] are as follows:

- Occupational noise exposure
- Hearing conservation program
- Noise monitoring
- Employee notification
- Observation of monitoring
- Audiometric testing program
- Evaluations of audiograms
- Hearing protectors
- Record keeping
- Transfer of records
- Training program

The OSHA Occupational Noise Exposure Standard (29 CFR 1910.95) states that protection against the effects of noise exposure shall be provided when the sound levels exceed those shown in Table G-16 when measured on the A scale of a standard sound level meter at slow response. When employees are subjected to sound levels exceeding those listed in Table G-16, feasible administrative or engineering controls shall be utilized. If such controls fail to reduce sound levels within the levels, personal protective equipment shall be provided and used to reduce sound levels to meet permissible noise exposure levels.

TABLE G-16 Permissible Noise Exposures

Duration per day, hours	Sound level (dBA) slow response
8	90
6	92
4	95
3	97
2	100
1.5	102
1	105
0.5	110
0.25 or less	115

If an employee's noise exposure equals or exceeds an eight-hour time-weighted average (TWA) of 85 decibels on the A scale (50 percent dose), the employee must be included in a Hearing Conservation Program.

Employers must develop and implement a monitoring program whenever information indicates that an employee exposure may equal or exceed an eight-hour TWA of 85 decibels on the A scale. The sampling strategy must be designed to identify employees for inclusion in an effective Hearing Conservation Program and to enable the proper selection of hearing protectors. The monitoring must be repeated whenever a change in production, process, equipment, or controls increases noise exposures to the extent that additional employees may be exposed or the attenuation provided by the hearing protector may be inadequate. The employer must notify each employee exposed at or above an eight-hour TWA of 85 decibels of the results of the monitoring. The employer must provide affected employees or their representatives with an opportunity to observe any noise measurements conducted.

The noise standard requires employers to establish and maintain audiometric testing as part of the Hearing Conservation Program by making audiometric testing available to all employees whose exposure levels equal or exceed an eight-hour TWA of 85 dBA (action level). The audiometric testing shall be provided at no cost to the employee. Testing involves a baseline audiogram and annual audiograms thereafter. Baseline audiograms must be obtained within six months of an employee's first exposure at or above an eight-hour TWA of 85 dBA. Subsequent audiograms must be taken at least annually and compared against the baseline audiogram to determine if the audiogram is valid or if a standard threshold shift has occurred. A standard threshold shift is defined as a change in hearing threshold relative to the baseline audiogram of an average of ten dBA or more at 2000, 3000, and 4000 Hz in either ear. If the annual audiogram indicates that an employee has suffered a standard threshold shift, the employer may obtain a retest within 30 days and consider the results of the retest as the annual audiogram. If an employee experiences a standard threshold shift of an average of 25 dBA or more at 2000, 3000, or 4000 Hz, it must be recorded on the OSHA Form 200.

All audiograms must be reviewed by an audiologist, otolaryngologist, or physician to determine if there is a need for further evaluation. If a comparison of the annual audiogram to the baseline audiogram indicates a standard threshold shift has occurred, the employee must be informed in writing within 21 days of the determination.

Hearing protection must be provided to an employee who is exposed to an eight-hour TWA of 85 dBA (50 percent dose) and is required for employees exposed to 90 dBA or above. The OSHA Occupational Noise Standard requires that hearing protectors attenuate employee noise exposure to an eight-hour TWA of 90 dBA for all employees included in a Hearing Conservation Program. However, for employees who have experienced a standard threshold shift, the hearing protectors must attenuate employee noise exposure to an eight-hour TWA of 85 dBA or below. If the employee has experienced a threshold shift, hearing protection is required when exposed to an eight-hour TWA of 85 dBA (50 percent dose). Hearing protection devices must be evaluated for the specific noise environment in which they will be used.

An employer must maintain an accurate record of all employee noise exposure measurements for two years, all employee audiometric test records for the duration of the affected employee's employment, and all records of personnel attending noise training sessions. If the newspaper ceases to do business, it is required to transfer all noise records to the successor employer.

The OSHA Occupational Noise Standard requires that employees who are included in an annual Hearing Conservation Training Program be trained in the use of hearing protectors and be provided with information about hearing loss and audiometric testing. Training must be conducted annually.

The employer must make available to affected employees copies of the OSHA Occupational Noise Standard. In addition, a copy of the Standard must be posted in the workplace.

Observations

On February 19, 1993, a citation was issued to *The Detroit Free Press* by the State of Michigan, Department of Public Health, concerning violations of the Michigan Occupational Noise Standard and other regulations. Certain violations were upheld on appeal. The noise standard violations which were upheld include the following:

- The employer did not perform personal monitoring of workers in the reel room, press room, and loading dock.
- The employer did not inform workers in the reel room, press room, mail room, and loading dock of the company's noise monitoring that suggested that they were over the action level.
- The employer did not obtain an audiogram for all the workers in the reel room.
- The employer did not compare the 1992 audiograms against the baseline audiograms to determine if an STS had occurred. Specifically, the employer did not provide the company performing the 1992 annual audiograms with the baseline audiometric results.
- The employer did not follow the required follow-up procedure for employees with STS.

- The employer did not provide annual noise training for all workers in the reel room.
- The employer did not provide MIOSHA with the audiometric test results for 1991 and years prior in which such testing was performed, after the Division requested these test results.
- The employer did not post a copy of the noise standard in the reel room.

Subsequently, a new firm was hired to manage the Hearing Conservation Program. As of March 1, 1993, the Hearing Conservation Program for employees of the Detroit Newspaper Agency is managed by the following firm:

Corporate Health Dimensions
6200 Metropolitan Parkway
Sterling Heights, Michigan 48312

Corporate Health Dimensions is located at the Health Unit of the Sterling Heights Facility (North Plant), which is the production plant for the *Detroit News*. At the time of the audit, all equipment and records related to the Hearing Conservation Program for the *Detroit News* and the *Detroit Free Press* were located and maintained at the Health Unit in the North Plant. Personnel that work in the downtown buildings or at the Riverfront Plant must go to the Health Unit in the North Plant to receive hearing tests.

Corporate Health Dimensions has an in-house hearing test booth at the North Plant. New baseline and annual audiograms for all employees in the Hearing Conservation Program are being conducted. A new testing booth and the associated equipment has been purchased for installation at the Riverfront Plant. Annual hearing testing is required for employees who are in the Hearing Conservation Program. Employees refusing to take an audiogram or participate in the Hearing Conservation Program are not allowed to work. Corporate Health Dimensions maintains the calibration records for the hearing test equipment at the North Plant.

Corporate Health Dimensions uses an expanded survey form to evaluate employee audiograms. Employees are questioned about activities conducted on their own time which may compromise their hearing acuity, such as listening to loud rock music.

If the results of the audiometric tests of employees show a threshold shift, the employee is sent for retesting and confirmation of the threshold shift. Copies of the results of the audiometric tests are sent to the employees of Detroit Newspaper Agency.

The Detroit Newspaper Agency has a comprehensive written Hearing Conservation Program which is used by both the *Detroit News* and the *Detroit Free Press*. The most recent noise survey at the *Detroit Free Press* Riverfront Plant was conducted on January 3–4, 1993. The report indicated that noise levels exceeding the noise standard were measured in the press room, reel room, mail room, and loading dock.

Training for the Hearing Conservation Program is under development and will be conducted by Corporate Health Dimensions at the North Plant.

Engineering controls for reduction of noise include construction of quiet rooms at the Riverfront Plant and installation of folder enclosures. Noise Standards are posted in the workplace and "Hearing Protection Required" signs are posted on the entrance doors and walls of the production areas where there are high noise levels. The Detroit Newspaper Agency provides several different types of hearing protection for employee's use, including earmuffs and plugs.

Recommendations

The Detroit Newspaper Agency should review their Hearing Conservation Program to determine whether it addresses all the requirements of the Michigan Occupational Noise Standard and that all elements of the Hearing Conservation Program are implemented.

The Detroit Newspaper Agency should periodically conduct a comprehensive noise survey using dosimeters and sound level meters to determine which employees must be included in the Hearing Conservation Program. All full-time and part-time workers, including substitutes, who work in areas with noise levels exceeding the action level should be included in the Hearing Conservation Program.

Hazard Communication

Regulations

The Michigan Hazard Communication Standard is the same as the Federal Standard. The following outline lists the basic components required by the Hazard Communication Standard, 29 CFR 1910.1200:

I. Program Records
   A. Written Program
   B. Chemical Product List
   C. Material Safety Data Sheets
II. Employee Training and Educational Materials
   A. Preliminary Training
   B. MSDS Interpretation Guide
   C. Proper Work Practices
   D. Emergency Procedures
   E. Primary Training
III. Container Labeling and Other Provisions
   A. Container Labeling
   B. Nonroutine Work Practices
   C. Contractor Notification Procedures
   D. Waste-Handling Procedures

The Hazard Communication Standard requires that employers provide employees with information and training on hazardous chemicals in their work area at the time of their initial assignment or whenever there is a new hazard introduced into their work area. Any chemical used by an employee that has a material safety data sheet (MSDS) is covered by this regulation. Material safety data sheets must be maintained and made available to the employees. The employees must be trained on the Hazard Communication Program before they begin their assigned duties. The employer is required to maintain a written Hazard Communication Program outlining the following procedures: training, new and updated material safety data sheets, updating the chemical inventory list, container labeling, informing the employees of the hazards of nonroutine tasks, and contractor awareness. This written program must be available to all employees.

It is the employer's responsibility to obtain material safety data sheets for the chemicals used at the facility. Although the employer must obtain and maintain the material safety data sheets, it is the chemical manufacturer's responsibility that the information on the MSDS is correct.

A list of hazardous chemicals known to be present in the work area (chemical products list) must be part of the written Hazard Communication Program. It is recommended that the list contain the following information: chemical product name (as listed on corresponding MSDS), manufacturer's name, address, and phone number.

Employers are required to develop a training program conveying the physical and health hazards of chemicals in the workplace to all employees who use hazardous chemicals. The following items must be included in the overall training program:

- The requirements of the law
- Details of the newspaper's Hazard Communication Program
- The location and availability of the newspaper's written program, chemical product list, and material safety data sheets
- Hazards of the chemicals in the workplace
- Operations in which hazardous chemicals are used
- Ways in which employees can detect the presence of hazardous chemicals in the workplace

Training must be provided to all employees covered under the Standard prior to exposure to any hazardous chemicals. Training of new employees is required before they are assigned to work with hazardous chemicals and retraining of current employees is necessary prior to the introduction of new hazardous chemical products into the workplace. New or transferred employees must receive training at the time of their initial assignment.

It is required that product suppliers adequately label the products that are shipped to the purchaser. It is the employer's responsibility for labeling squeeze bottles, pails, and other temporary containers used by employees. Formal guidelines must be established for labeling alternate containers used for chemical products that are transferred for use or storage from a drum or bulk tank. The following rules apply to labeling of alternate containers:

- Temporary, short-term containers intended for immediate use do not require labels if they will only be used by the employee who fills the container.
- All other alternate containers must have labels.
- When labeling alternate containers, all important information from the label on the original container should be duplicated.
- The important information that must appear on the alternate container includes: product or chemical name (the same name as that found on the corresponding MSDS), hazardous chemical contents, and all physical and health hazard warnings—such as "flammable liquid" or "eye irritant."

Section (e)(2) of the Hazard Communication Standard covers "Multi-employer workplaces." This means that contractors must be informed about the potential hazards present. Employers must provide contractors with copies of the material safety data sheets or make them available at a central location in the workplace. In addition, emergency procedures must be outlined.

Observations

The Hazard Communication Program at the Detroit Newspaper Agency was first started in 1985. Subsequently, there was a gap in implementation of the program until 1990 when the present management took over the program. The written Hazard Communication Program is used by both the *Detroit News* and the *Detroit Free Press.*

The master hazard communication binders containing material safety data sheets for all chemicals in the building are located in the Building Manager's Office at each of the Detroit Newspaper Agency facilities. The individual departments in the buildings have hazard communication binders containing material safety data sheets for chemicals located in the department. Departmental hazard communication binders can be found in the press room, mail room, plate room, newsprint storage, engineering, machine shop, electrician's shop, and building maintenance. Signs are posted showing where the hazard communication binders are located.

The individual Department Managers are responsible for review and update of hazard communication binders. Outdated material safety data sheets are usually kept for three years. Some of the old material safety data sheets at the *Detroit Free Press* Fleet Garage may have been discarded when the binders were updated.

All employees using chemicals are trained annually concerning hazard communication. Training records are located in the *Detroit News* Main Building. The components of the training include:

- Purpose of training
- A slide presentation
- Review of correct labeling and procedures
- Instruction on how to read a material safety data sheet
- Review of the written program
- A video presentation
- Question and answer period followed by a quiz
- Distribution of Certificates of Training

The most recent hazard communication training was conducted in March 1993. At the time of the audit, at least one employee in the machine shop and a new photographer had not been trained concerning the hazards of the specific chemicals encountered on their job.

Hazardous Material Information System (HMIS) labels are used for container labeling in all buildings and production plants. Missing or improper labels are replaced or repaired during periodic safety inspections. Weekly inspections are conducted by building and department managers, and monthly inspections are conducted by the members of the safety committee to identify mislabeled products.

As part of the written Hazard Communication Program at the Detroit Newspaper Agency, all contractors are notified about the requirement to exchange hazard communication information about the chemicals encountered in the workplace. Typically, contractors are notified verbally. The person in charge of a project involving a contractor lets the contractor know where the hazard communication binders are located. Documentation of the exchange of information is not maintained.

Recommendations

The Detroit Newspaper Agency must keep all outdated material safety data sheets for a minimum of 30 years. The outdated sheets should be kept in a separate binder.

The Detroit Newspaper Agency must train all new employees concerning the chemical hazards encountered on their job prior to the employee starting the job.

The Detroit Newspaper Agency must require contractors, such as roofing contractors, to supply copies of the material safety data sheets for chemical products to be used at the facility. Contractors must be provided with the opportunity to review material safety data sheets for chemicals encountered when working at the facility. Records of the exchange must be kept.

Safety

During the environmental audit performed on May 10–12, 1993, the NAA Industrial Hygienist conducted walk-through safety inspections of several areas of the *Detroit Free Press* facilities. The potential safety problems noted during the inspection can be found in the Recommendations Checklist section of the report entitled "Walk-Through Plant Inspection."

Safety requirements for industry are generally spelled out in the federal OSHA regulations found in 29 CFR 1910, which are available in paperback version from the Government Printing Office. Annual updates to this publication are available after July 1 of each year.

Selected Safety Regulations

Employee Emergency Action Plans are addressed under 29 CFR 1910.38(a). The plans shall be in writing and cover those designated actions employers and employees must take to ensure employee safety from fire and other emergencies.

The following elements, at a minimum, shall be included in an Emergency Action Plan:

- Emergency escape procedures and emergency escape route assignments
- Procedures to be followed by employees who remain to operate critical plant operations before they evacuate
- Procedures to account for all employees after emergency evacuation has been completed
- Rescue and medical duties for those employees who are to perform them
- The preferred means of reporting fires and other emergencies
- Names or regular job titles of persons or departments who can be contacted for further information or explanation of duties under the plan

Before implementing an Emergency Action Plan, the employer shall designate and train a sufficient number of persons to assist in the site and orderly evacuation of employees. The employer shall establish an employee alarm system which complies with 29 CFR 1910.165.

Machine guarding (29 CFR 1910 Subpart 0) must be provided to protect the operator and other employees in the machine area from hazards such as those created by point of operation, in-going nip points, rotating parts, flying chips, and sparks. It is required that machine guards be in place when the equipment is in operation.

If fire extinguishers are provided for the use of employees in fighting fires, then training on the use and limitations of the fire extinguishers is required.

Good housekeeping is a vital part of an effective safety program. Besides providing an aesthetically pleasant environment that improves morale and productivity, good housekeeping is a cost-effective way to prevent accidents. Departments and functional areas kept neat and clean require fewer repairs and replacement of expensive items.

OSHA regulations require good housekeeping which is an essential part of a satisfactory disaster plan and fire safety plan. Dirty and cluttered aisles and floor space prevent employees from making their way to exits quickly and safely during emergencies. Clean working environments can also help prevent fires from starting and spreading.

Bulk quantities of flammable and combustible liquids must be kept in closed containers or safety cans stored in flammable material safety cabinets or a fire-rated room. No more than 25 gallons of class 1A flammable liquids are allowed in the building or in a fire-safety zone (designated by management and could include the entire facility).

Eyewash stations and/or safety showers must be located in areas where chemicals are used. The eyewash must be plumbed or contain enough liquid to maintain a steady flow of liquid for a minimum of 15 minutes. Eyewash stations and safety showers must be located within 100 feet of a chemical hazard and be accessible to employees. Eyewash stations and safety showers should be checked on a regular basis to assure that they are in working order.

Personal protective equipment (goggles and protective gloves, and so on) must be worn by employees when using solvents such as blanket wash if it is recommended on the material safety data sheet. Other personal protective equipment, such as occupational foot protection, must be provided and worn wherever it is necessary by reason of hazards of processes or environment, chemical hazards, radiological hazards, or mechanical hazards encountered on the job. Preventive maintenance is critical to safety. Poorly maintained machines or equipment can pose a number of dangers to employees.

Observations

The Detroit Newspaper Agency has a written Safety Policy Emergency Evacuation Plan and Disaster Plan. Emergency evacuation route diagrams are posted in the major corridors and hallways of all Detroit Newspaper Agency facilities.

The *Detroit Free Press's* fire detection and firefighting equipment include smoke detectors, heat detectors, a sprinkler system, and audible fire alarms that sound throughout the buildings. Portable hand-held fire extinguishers are located throughout the buildings.

The fire extinguishers were visually inspected on a monthly basis and the monthly inspection tags were signed. Hydrostatic tests are conducted every three years.

The Detroit Newspaper Agency sounds the fire alarm several times per year to conduct fire drills. However, due to the size of the organization, it is difficult to account for all employees.

Under the 1990 Clean Air Act Amendments, Halon, which is used in Halon fire-extinguishing systems found at Detroit Newspaper Agency, has been identified as a Class 1 Ozone-depleting chemical and will be phased out by year 2000. At the present time, there is no satisfactory alternative to Halon 1031.

Inspections at the Detroit Newspaper Agency are conducted by the Fire Department at least annually. If the Fire Department issues citations, immediate corrective actions are taken by the Facilities Maintenance Department. As an example, Strobe lights for the hearing impaired were installed on the fire alarms as a result of a directive from the Fire Department.

The *Detroit Free Press* has different safety committees for hourly workers and union workers, which originated prior to the Joint Operating Agreement. There are individual safety committees at The *Detroit Free Press* Main Building, the *Detroit News* Main Building, the Riverfront Building, and the North Plant. Minutes for most of the safety committee meetings have been maintained. Recommendations of the safety committees are submitted to top management of the Detroit Newspaper Agency. The responsibilities of the safety committee include building inspections which are done on a monthly basis. Safety checklists are used in the inspections.

Personal protective equipment such as goggles, glasses, aprons, and gloves were used at the facility. Eyewash stations and safety showers were recently installed in areas where chemicals are used. Management did not require employees to wear safety shoes in the production areas.

Safety guards were observed to be in place on the Goss Metro Presses in the Riverfront Plant.

Electrical grounding straps were not observed on metal drums and tanks containing flammable materials.

All electrical tools mounted on stands (such as grinders) were not fastened to the floor.

OSHA 200 logs are posted on the bulletin boards at each facility of the Detroit Newspaper Agency from February 1 to March 1 each year. Reminder notices are mailed to the facilities from the Knight Ridder Corporate Office in Miami.

Recommendations

The *Detroit Free Press* must develop a procedure which accounts for all employees after an emergency evacuation has been completed. Before implementing the emergency action plan, the newspaper must train a sufficient number of persons to assist in the safe and orderly emergency evacuation of employees. Documentation of all emergency evacuations should be maintained.

It is recommended that the *Detroit Free Press* adopt a policy of requiring employees to wear safety shoes in the press room, reel room, loading docks, and other areas where heavy objects might fall and injure the employee's feet.

Electrical grounding straps should be attached to metal drums and tanks containing flammable materials at the *Detroit Free Press.*

The *Detroit Free Press* should check all tools on stands, such as grinders and drill presses, to determine whether the stand is permanently fastened to the floor.

Air Pollution Control and Indoor Air Quality

Regulations Concerning Air Control

The 1990 Clean Air Act Amendments require state and local air pollution control agencies to pass regulations which restrict the emissions of volatile organic compounds (VOCs such as solvent-based blanket wash, fountain solution offset, and letterpress ink and photographic chemicals) from industrial plants located in specified ozone nonattainment areas. An ozone nonattainment area is defined as an area that does not meet the National Ambient Air Quality Standard (NAAQS) of 0.12 parts per million (ppm) of ozone.

The Detroit Newspaper Agency is located within the Detroit-Ann Arbor, Michigan CMSA (metropolitan statistical area), which is classified as a "moderate nonattainment area" for ozone. Stationary sources of air pollution within the nonattainment area are prohibited from emitting more than 100 tons per year volatile organic compounds (VOCs). Large stationary sources must have an operating permit, and the best available control technology must be installed to reduce source emissions.

Records of quantities of VOC chemicals used and their VOC content must be maintained, and a compliance schedule must be prepared if required by the operating permit. The Michigan State Agency uses Method 24 for determining VOC content of chemical mixtures.

The Environmental Protection Agency is developing Control Techniques Guidelines (CTG) which provide suggestions on air pollution control methods and equipment to use to attain the standard. More information will be available to the newspaper companies after EPA has completed the control techniques guidelines for offset lithography.

Observations

A recent emissions inventory was prepared for the *Detroit Free Press* by Knight Ridder Personnel but was not available at the time of the audit.

All *Detroit Free Press* buildings are heated either by steam from Detroit Edison or natural gas/hot water. The Fleet Garage is heated by natural gas. No significant quantities of volatile organic compounds (VOCS) are emitted to the atmosphere from the heating systems at *Detroit Free Press* buildings.

In order to reduce air pollutants emitted to the atmosphere, the *Detroit Free Press* is reducing the number of trucks in the fleet and is converting some of the remaining trucks to use diesel fuel rather than gasoline.

Monitors were installed on the receiving and loading docks at the Riverfront Building to measure the concentration of carbon monoxide on the docks resulting from idling trucks.

There have been complaints about indoor air quality at the photographic lab on the fourth floor, and at Customer Service on the second floor of the *Detroit Free Press* Main Building. The complainants were examined by a physician at Detroit Industrial Clinic in September 1992, but no specific cause of the complaints could be identified. The physician indicated that the problem could possibly be carbon monoxide poisoning. Liberty Mutual Insurance and staff from the Detroit Newspaper Agency conducted tests, but no problem was identified. At the time of the audit, there was no indication that OSHA permissible exposure limits

(PELS) had been exceeded in those areas. However, no air quality tests were made by NAA as part of the audit.

During the renovation of the *Detroit Free Press* Main Building, asbestos was removed from the building. Certified engineers were used to remove the asbestos, which was double bagged for disposal. All personnel wore respirators. Ten-day notice to the state agency was provided and agency representatives monitored air quality during the asbestos removal process.

Recommendations

The Detroit Newspaper Agency should identify and quantify all sources of air pollutant emissions from their facilities in Detroit including fueling stations, underground storage tanks, and mobile sources.

As an air pollution control strategy, the Detroit Newspaper Agency should substitute low VOC chemicals for those in use with high VOC content. In addition, work practices should be evaluated and revised to reduce emissions of VOCs to the workplace air. For example, covers should be closed on all chemical containers and rag bins when not in use to prevent escape of chemical vapors into the air.

It is recommended that the *Detroit Free Press* conduct an additional indoor air quality survey in the areas of the *Detroit Free Press* Main Building where indoor air quality complaints originated. Parameters to sample should include temperature, humidity, carbon monoxide, and carbon dioxide, as well as the concentrations of chemicals in use in the workplace. It may be useful to sample for asbestos in the areas where asbestos was removed. Material safety data sheets for the chemicals used in the photolab should be consulted to determine which chemicals may be present in the workplace air.

Waste Management

Although a significant number of complex federal rules and regulations apply to the management of hazardous waste, most states have been delegated authority to regulate hazardous waste disposal within each state's jurisdiction. The state regulatory agencies' rules and regulations must be equal to or more stringent than those of the federal agencies. Therefore, a newspaper generating hazardous waste should contact, and directly work with, the state regulatory agencies concerning most hazardous waste disposal matters.

Regulations

The most important federal waste disposal acts which affect the newspaper industry are as follows:

- Resource Conservation and Recovery Act (RCRA)
- Hazardous and Solid Waste Amendments of 1984 (HSWA)
- Hazardous Materials Transportation Act (HMTA)
- Comprehensive Environmental Response, Compensation and Liability Act (CERCLA), known as Superfund
- Superfund Amendment and Reauthorization Act (SARA)
- Clean Air Act (CAA)

- Toxic Substance Control Act (TSCA)
- Clean Water Act (CWA)

A detailed discussion of waste disposal procedures under the above acts can be found in the attached "ANPA Hazardous Waste Guide."

Whether or not a newspaper is a large-quantity or a small-quantity generator, training of employees is required under EPA/RCRA regulations. Under 40 CFR 265, training is required for persons involved in handling and disposing of hazardous waste as well as spill cleanup and emergency procedures involving hazardous waste.

The following outline provides the basis for an effective waste management program:

- Personnel
- Waste Manager
- Emergency Coordinator Role and Responsibilities
- Emergency Management
- Waste
- Recycling/Reclamation
- Training
- Commercial Waste Management Contractors
- Waste Management Audits
- Inspections from Regulatory Agencies
- Record keeping, Labeling, and Reporting
- EPA Generator Identification Number
- Permits
- Manifests (federal and state)
- Manifest Exception Reports
- Biennial Reports
- Written Procedures for Waste Management
- Hazardous Waste Labeling

Observations

The Detroit Newspaper Agency does not have a written waste management plan.

Waste ink and solvents generated in the production areas at the Riverfront Plant are pumped from the press room to an underground storage tank (UST), which is located outside the plant. Once each month, the waste is pumped out of the UST and transported by Detrex Company, a waste management firm, and is fuel blended in Cleveland, Ohio, at the Research Oil Company. The waste is tested every year to determine whether it is hazardous waste.

The Detroit Newspaper Agency submits biennial hazardous waste reports to the Michigan Department of Health by March 1 of each even-numbered year.

Recommendations

It is recommended that the Detroit Newspaper Agency develop a written Waste Management Program. Newspaper management is responsible for proper handling of waste from the time it is generated through disposal at an appropriate facility. The best way to ensure that all wastes are properly managed is to implement an effective Waste Management Program and routinely conduct audits to determine the program's effectiveness. Each newspaper is encouraged to establish a formal Waste Management Program administered by a designated coordinator to assure that all wastes generated are properly disposed. The administration of an effective Waste Management Program requires management support to ensure its success.

Waste Water

Some photographic processing wastes can be discharged legally to the sewer system, depending on the component substances in the photographic-processing waste and the industrial discharge regulations of the local sewer authority.

Regulations

Effluent from a photoprocessing unit usually contains significant quantities of silver, which are prohibited by most local sewer authorities. EPA categorizes waste water with more than 5.0 milligrams silver per liter as a hazardous waste, and some municipalities have stricter discharge limits. The discharge limit for silver in Detroit is 2.0 mg/liter.

Observation

The Detroit Newspaper Agency is in the Detroit City Sewer District, which has separate sanitary and storm water sewer systems.

The Detroit Newspaper Agency is an industrial user of the Detroit City Sewer System and has an industrial user's permit because the facilities discharge over 25,000 gallons of industrial process waste water per day. The sources of process waste water on company property are the cooling towers, plate processing, the Baldwin units, and the photoprocessors.

The Detroit Newspaper Agency has silver recovery systems with tailing units on all the photoprocessors. The waste water is discharged to the sanitary sewer system.

Samples of waste-water discharge from the Detroit Newspaper Agency are collected and analyzed on a quarterly basis by the City of Detroit and a consultant, Ernest Phillips, working with the analytical laboratory Engineers & Consultants, Inc. The samples are analyzed for heavy metals, biochemical oxygen demand, fats, oils and grease, total phosphorus, total suspended solids, and pH. The results indicate that the levels of pollutants in the waste-water discharge are within the limits set by the Detroit Sanitary Sewer District.

Tanks, drums, and containers of oil or hazardous chemicals at the Fleet Garage were observed to have no secondary containment. For example, a tank containing lubrication oil in the garage was observed without spill containment. If a container leaks or is punctured, there is potential for hazardous or flammable materials (chemicals) spilling into the environment.

Recommendations

The Detroit Newspaper Agency should have secondary containment (drip/spill containers) for all tanks, drums, and large containers of hazardous or flammable chemicals.

Emergency Planning and Community Right to Know (EPCRA)

Regulations

CERCLA (Comprehensive Environmental Response, Compensation and Liability Act) also known as Superfund was amended in 1986. These amendments were named SARA (Superfund Amendments and Reauthorization Act). SARA Title III is found in the Code of Federal Regulations under 40 CFR in three major parts: Emergency Planning and Emergency Release Notification (Part 355), Community Right-to-Know Reporting (Part 370), and Toxic Chemical Release Reporting—Emissions Inventory (Part 372). CERCLA defines an emergency release as a release or threat of release into the environment of a hazardous substance, pollutant, or contaminant.

Emergency Planning and Emergency Release Notification

The Emergency Planning and Emergency Release Notification regulations require newspaper companies to provide a representative to serve on the local planning committee if requested by the governor. It also requires newspaper companies to immediately notify the Local Emergency Planning Committee and the State Emergency Response Commission if there is a release of a listed hazardous substance that exceeds the reportable quantity for that substance. Substances subject to this requirement are found in Part 355 Appendices A and B of the regulations. Also cited in this section is the CERCLA list. This list is called the "Hazardous Substances and Their Reportable Quantities List" and is found in Section 302.4 of the Act (SARA Title 111). Reportable quantities differ from chemical to chemical and are based on the chemicals' characteristics of toxicity and radiation hazard potential. A notification to the National Response Center is required in the event of a reportable quantity release anywhere on site.

Community Right to Know

The Community Right-to-Know reporting regulations apply to any facility which must comply with the OSHA Hazard Communication Standard. The hazardous chemicals covered are the same as in Part 355. Employers are required to submit material safety data sheets on or before October 17, 1990 (or within three months after the facility first becomes subject to SARA Title III) reporting for all hazardous chemicals present in their plant at any one time in amounts equal to or greater than 10,000 pounds and for extremely hazardous substances present at the newspaper in an amount greater than or equal to 500 pounds or the threshold planning quantity, whichever is lower. Employers must submit either copies of material safety data sheets for the hazardous chemicals used in the facility according to the minimum threshold schedule (370.20) or a list of those chemicals and a hazardous chemical inventory form (Tier I or Tier II form) to:

The state emergency response commission

The local emergency planning committee

The local fire department

CHEMICAL INVENTORY

The Tier I and Tier II forms contain information on the hazardous chemicals stored or used on plant property. Employers must submit the Tier I (or Tier II) form on or before March 1, 1991 (or March 1 of the first year after the facility first becomes subject to this section), and annually thereafter. This form should cover all hazardous chemicals present at the newspaper at any one time during the preceding calendar year in amounts greater than or equal to 10,000 pounds or the threshold planning quantity, whichever is lower. Tier II forms must be submitted only upon request from the local emergency planning committee, state commission, and/or the local fire department.

TOXIC CHEMICAL RELEASE REPORTING AND EMISSIONS INVENTORY

The Toxic Chemical Release Reporting and Emissions Inventory regulations apply to companies which had spills in the past year exceeding the reportable quantity.

OBSERVATIONS

Black and colored inks, gasoline, and fuel oil are stored on site at the Detroit Newspaper Agency in quantities exceeding 10,000 pounds. Tier II forms are submitted for the above three substances to the Michigan Department of Public Health on an annual basis. Photochemicals such as developer and fixer are not stored in quantities exceeding 10,000 pounds even though 10,000 pounds might be used in a year. A Tier II form was previously filed for hydroquinone. This paperwork was discontinued because the threshold planning quantity for hydroquinone was not exceeded.

INDEX

J

L